EngageME

EngageME

Will Leaders Listen?

———— *by* ————

DR. JOHN VIZZUSO

authorHOUSE®

AuthorHouse™
1663 Liberty Drive
Bloomington, IN 47403
www.authorhouse.com
Phone: 1 (800) 839-8640

Published by AuthorHouse 05/06/2015

ISBN: 978-1-5049-0801-6 (sc)
ISBN: 978-1-5049-0802-3 (hc)
ISBN: 978-1-5049-0800-9 (e)

Print information available on the last page.

Dedication

This book is dedicated to my wife Jennifer, sharing 25 years of happiness, sadness, forgiveness, humility, empathy, love, laughter, and salvation.

Contents

List of Tables

Acknowledgments

I would like to acknowledge my family, past and present coworkers, fellow students, and faculty members for the support and encouragement in meeting my personal and professional goals.

Foreword

When John approached me to write the foreword for his book, I was flattered and excited about introducing such an important and timely account about a subject that he has devoted much of his career to understanding.

John and I have known each other for several years, both as friends and colleagues and have many interests and perspectives in common. Early on in our relationship, I was intrigued to learn that John was a successful wrestler, particularly as I had been a very poor one. I realized early on that I did not have the endurance, and tenacity to suffer through the incredible demands of the sport. Those very same characteristics that that I observed day in a day out in John, which made him a success as a competitive wrestler, have typified his personal and professional life and his approach and commitment to the study and understanding of the role of employee engagement in the success of medical organizations.

The intensely personal accounts, contained in *EngageME Will Leaders Listen?*, are typical of the openness and emotional commitment that he exhibits in dealing with subordinates, management, friends and family.

As someone who has witnessed innumerable strategies and people, come and go in health care administration over the last three decades, John stands out both as an individual of enormous character and credibility as well as by virtue of his commitment to improving the quality of care delivery and performance in the work environment through the enhancement of relationships between management and their employees. His early focus on these interactions, before their popularization, demonstrated a keen and prescient understanding of the importance of this issue in the workplace.

EngageME Will Leaders Listen? is a very personal account of his experience and journey through health care management over almost two decades. The review of key publications, detailing studies, which examine the critical issue of employee engagement, is interspersed with lively anecdotes and examples of the good and the bad, which he has personally witnessed and chronicled. *EngageME Will Leaders Listen?* provides insight and analysis of the central issues confronting management as they attempt to energize and motivate their workforce, as well as the pitfalls and consequences of failing to do so. John is fearless in his documentation and criticism of the numerous failures of administrative leadership that he has personally encountered in his career.

Having articulated the problem, John proceeds to offer specific advice, including concrete methodologies and practical recommendations to assess an organization's preparedness and correct its deficiencies. He illustrates through real-life examples of events, how organizations succeeded or failed in their interaction with employees as well as then potential for such interactions to foster disengagement thereby compromising patient experience and optimal institutional function and success. He proposes recommendations including specific methodologies and metrics for initial and follow-up assessments, to restructure the very nature of organizations to improve access and communication between management and employees to promote and encourage employee engagement as well as to assess its impact on customers. He implores leadership to be proactive and accountable, and to create an environment of trust and confidence amongst its workers, whereby they do not fear offering suggestions or even criticisms of the organization.

EngageME Will Leaders Listen? ultimately is a guide for administrators and leadership to improve the quality and performance of their organization by enhancing engagement of their most valuable resource- their employees, as they attempt to navigate the rapidly changing, and sometimes unforgiving, health care environment of today.

R. D. G. Ferguson
Cleveland Ohio March 2015

When Home Isn't Where I Belong

"Heartbreak is lonely." Vizzuso

For some reason, defining moments keep finding me. I believe these moments seek me out like a moth seeks a flame. I cannot help but curse them and love them at the same moment. These moments challenge everything inside me. They seek out emotional connections that I sometimes forget I have. These connections start to spark and fire rapidly. It is as though my life falls from the sky, approaching a dead impact on the ground, yet I'm alive and focused more than ever before.

Organizations are a difficult entity to understand. Many move slowly and entrench themselves in mediocrity and misplaced decisions. They claim mission-linked core values guide the path, yet many times these values build a hollow wall from straw and paper. I sometimes wonder if organizations truly exist to reverse all that is good to savor what is bad.

At the end of *Shared Sacrifice*, my last book, I detailed a moral dilemma I was facing in my own choice of career paths. I work for a company that owns two hospitals. I am shared between both in an executive role. This corporation was splitting apart and I was fearful of making a choice of one over the other. My final choice was touching as many people as I could through leadership teaching and choosing both for the impossible task.

It has now been two days from a day that will be with me for years to come. It all started on a Monday afternoon. In my line of work, Mondays are filled with problems from a busy weekend filled with executive meetings that never seem to stop. My assistant was notified that I was to meet with both my bosses on Wednesday morning at 7:30. In most cases, this was not an unusual task, yet I've only had a handful of these types of meetings.

It wasn't more than an hour later that a notice graced my screen scheduling a special senior leadership meeting at one hospital for Wednesday at 8:00 am. In my field, special meetings usually mean one thing: employment cuts. Could this be really a setup to remove me? My mind started wondering about all the scenarios this could be. I actually convinced myself that this was just a fear in my head.

On Tuesday, another strange event occurred. My assistant was asked to come over on Wednesday for a special project. That had never happened before in my employment. At this moment I was convinced my doom was the next day. I had one more avenue to pursue to find out the truth. I work very closely with all types of physicians. In cases like this, the organization would surely communicate the change to the physicians. I sought out one physician whom I respect and told her about my fears. She had no knowledge of the transaction and felt pretty comfortable that I was just being crazy.

I walked out at the end of Tuesday and came across the head person in the human resources department. The HR Director and I joke around all the time and I asked him if he was coming to my meeting in the morning. He looked at me and answered no with his eyes to the floor. I then asked him if I should bring a box for my things and again he said no with his eyes trying to avoid my stare. I knew at that time he was lying to me. A man I respected and liked completely was disrespecting me and lying.

I went home tired and disgusted with the day. I did not tell my wife, for her sleep would be affected. The stress of the next morning was overwhelming and I went to bed very early for the "cut" day. I still held out hope that it would be different and more of a promotion day. How the mind can play tricks on you!

I was in my office when the lady I call "the General" called me to come up early. I walked into the room and there sat my new boss, Nancy, along with Ted and the HR Director. Sitting between them made me uncomfortable and uneasy. Nancy took the stage and announced she had some bad news. The corporation was eliminating my position. She then explained that she had some good news. There was a position I could take that would not be at the executive level and paid significantly less. In addition, the company was adding another executive role in another area and I could apply if I wanted to.

Let me say, you always need to remain calm in these meetings because emotions can cause a scene. I could feel my blood starting to warm like a simmering pot of tea. I stared at Nancy as she spoke and marveled at her uncaring and emotionless expression. I also had the right to my severance package if I did not choose my options. This package was excellent—it paid my salary and benefits for 12 months. It was then that remarks came from Ted, whom I respected, that I marvel at:

"John, this has nothing to do with you. Your people love you, you've done a great job. We just could not afford you in the budget."

Ted was unskillfully trying to justify the action at the same time he was passing an operating budget with an $8 million profit margin. I can safely say I did not make $8 million in salary. I politely shook their hands, gathered my things, and left the building.

The days that followed were filled with phone call after phone call from people devastated, crying and searching for an understanding of such a horrible decision. These people moved me in many ways:

- **Ken.** Ken called me first thing that morning when he heard. He was speechless on the phone. He could not believe what had happened. Actually, this was a good thing for Ken because he now had the opportunity he wanted. He was going to replace me at one of the hospitals. I made sure Ken knew that he should take this job; he was ready to spread his wings.
- **Dr. Smith.** Dr. Smith, the second person to call me, is a cardiologist who had been upset with the one hospital for many reasons. I had the pleasure to get to know him and his high level of integrity. It was he and I who worked through things over two years to make them right. He had just accepted a leadership

role in the Cardiology Department. He said some very nice things to me in my support.

- **Karen.** Karen called me with deep sighs in her breathing. Karen and I are like siblings. I love her for who she is and who she isn't. Together we took a department with equipment falling apart and in three years replaced it all with new technology. It broke my heart hearing her words of apology for an organization gone wrong.

- **Fran.** Fran called me with her famous introduction, "So how are you, Mr. Vizzuso?" Fran is a survivor. She was shocked and awestruck by the events. Fran has the world in front of her. She needs to forgive the past and embrace the future.

- **Cat.** Cat was probably the most upset of any of the callers. We had developed a bond of trust over the past several years. I think she knows I know the true Cat, who is caring, soft, and private. The Cat that everyone sees is a tough-minded, possibly aggressive personality. She vowed to get the decision reversed. I appreciated her thoughts but I knew it was too late for such heroics.

- **Joyce.** Joyce was my faithful and assertive assistant. I could hear tears in her voice as she listened to me about the day. I know this was very hard for her. She was placed in the middle of two forces and was scared about her own job. Joyce will always be okay. She has all the makings of a star.

- **Tom.** My favorite IT guy called and was floored. "How could they dispatch a person that made such a difference? How could they do that?" He had a hard time understanding the reality of the situation.

- **Frank.** The day before the event, I sat next to Frank in our weekly staff meeting. I leaned over at the end of the meeting and whispered to Frank that I thought I was going to be released the next day. Frank called me later that day and said he was sure that wasn't going to happen. I then bet him lunch it was going to happen. He called me and was lost with his words and thoughts.

- **Gail.** Gail called me several days later. I got an email from her that day that simply stated, "I love you." I had the pleasure of watching Gail grow in her job. She started as a new manager several years ago and has grown into the role. I could see her tears through the phone.

- **Dr. Man.** Dr. Man called me, outraged and disgusted at the decision. He has been in practice for 20 years and expressed a comment that I was the best administrator he ever worked with.

- **Dr. Kenworth.** Dr. Kenworth called me and was his crazy self. I love Dr. Kenworth because I could always count on him to be brutally honest with me. He expressed his sorrow over the issue.

- **Dr. Higgins.** Dr. Higgins called me, very angry. She was the physician I talked to the day before. She is a strong lady who felt helpless.

My entire career has been littered with years of service to organizations in need of direction and leadership. I would spend anywhere from four to six years putting my life on the line at every moment. This particular job was no different. I was given an impossible task with an impossible organization, and yet the outcomes were there. Through these organizations, I rise up, do the job, emotionally connect to the people around me and yet the same action occurs.

I went home at the end of the day and told my wife, who was shaken by the event. She loves and supports me and loathes organizations that do this. It creates a feeling of disdain for those who selfishly make these types of decisions. I would equate the decision with having surgery to cut off your arm, even though there is nothing wrong with your arm—it works, does the job, and supports the rest of your body.

The first two days were rough. But then you come around and accept your fate and start to understand that the path you take forward is your choice and no other's. What do you do? We had just moved to be closer to work and this happened. We were now faced with a new house, new mortgage, and no job. Irony is a subject that lives through time and space. A person can pick up any history textbook and find irony in human nature. This situation was no different. I was completely engaged in the success of the organization, yet the leadership failed me. My engagement could not save me from this cruel fate. My devotion, untiring energy, and belief in the mission of the organization failed to cement my position.

The recession of 2009 created problems for people across the United States. Lost work, home foreclosures, and despair hit the heart of American workers. Employee engagement is a simple concept. It describes the emotional commitment of an employee to the goals and objectives of an organization. Employee engagement is filled with intrinsic energy providing life-altering substance to an organization.

This book is my journey to discover the true nature of employee engagement. Through these chapters, I find my way through organizational heroes, unethical leadership, and wayward friends to functionally explain employee engagement and the strategies necessary to EngageME.

November 18th, 2009

Dear Mr. Vizzuso,

As a result of organizational restructuring at UHHS/CSAHS, your position is being eliminated effective November 18, 2009. We regret that this action impacts you personally. I wish to express my sincere gratitude for your contributions you have made to St. Vincent Charity Hospital and St. John Westshore Hospital. You will be provided with the severance benefits described in your agreement, provided you sign a separation agreement releasing any legal claims against the company and its affiliates. The separation agreement and general release is enclosed for your review.

Whether or not you sign the separation agreement and general release in return for severance benefits is entirely voluntary on your part. If the terms and conditions set forth in the separation agreement are acceptable to you, please sign and date the separation agreement and general release on the appropriate line and return the original to the undersigned within a specific timeframe. You should keep a copy for your own records.

Before deciding whether or not you wish to sign the separation agreement and general release, you may take up to 21 days to review and consider its terms. You are not obligated to take that full time, however, and may sign and return the separation agreement and general release any time prior to that date, so long as you are satisfied that you have fully reviewed and considered its terms and conditions, understand them and are signing the separation agreement and general release voluntarily. In the course of reviewing and considering the separation agreement and general release, you should feel free to consult with an attorney and/or any other professional advisors of your choice.

If you sign the separation agreement and general release by the stated deadline, you may still revoke the separation agreement and general release in its entirety within seven days after signing by sending a written notice of immediate revocation to the undersigned. If you revoke the separation agreement and general release within the seven-day period, it shall be null and void and no severance benefits will be provided.

If you sign the separation agreement and general release, you'll be eligible to receive the severance benefits. You must timely elect COBRA coverage to be eligible to continue your group health insurance during the severance provided for in the agreement. A COBRA notification election form will be forwarded to you. Your accrued PTO will also be paid out according to the paid time-off policy.

We appreciate your services at St. Vincent Charity Hospital and St. John Westshore Hospital and wish you well in your future endeavors. We recognize that you may have additional questions. Please contact the human resources department at 216–592–2820 if need more information or would like to meet.

A Hospital Home

"Finally home?" Vizzuso

One day I happened to come across a recruiter website and noticed that a local large acute hospital had a job opening for an administrative director of radiology. My entire career has been involved with radiology in almost every aspect except radiologic oncology. It hit me that not only did I need a job but I also needed an environment to test out my theories of employee engagement. I applied online to the recruiter for this position and immediately got a response and interview with the recruitment firm.

It was one of those interviews one tends to remember for years to come. I met the principal partner of the recruiting firm in a hotel in downtown Cleveland. He had a background as a hospital CEO and now was a managing partner of the recruiting firm. He described a hospital looking for new, fresh leadership in the radiology department. The department was in the midst of change, turmoil, and need of direction. He also said something to me that spurred my curiosity: "John, can you take a punch?" He then went on to explain that the chairman of radiology, who is a physician, could be a handful to work with.

Sitting at the hotel, I now had a mental picture of an organization in need of assistance and a perfect opportunity for me to test the effects of emotional connection in an organization. The initial meeting took a little over two hours. At the end of it, I realized this was a perfect spot for me.

The initial interview with the vice president of system services took over a month to set up. I learned later that the chairman of radiology was not supportive of bringing in a new administrative director of radiology, but would rather support the person currently in the interim role. I met Candice in mid-May and marveled at my meeting. Again, she portrayed a department in transition and trouble. She insisted that major change was needed in both operational structure and customer service. She echoed the recruiter in suggesting that the chairman of radiology needed to be managed and mentored.

In the second interview, I met the chief operating officer and the current director of operations of radiology. My interaction with the director of operations was really to ascertain what she thought she needed to be successful. In addition, I had my first meeting and interaction with Tom, the chairman of radiology. My time in the healthcare field has been centered on working with, coaching and protecting physicians from poor decisions and themselves. I remember clearly in the meeting that Tom gave me his background and his vision for radiology and in the same breath informed me that he was interested in being part of the management team of the radiology department. In fact, he made it very clear that he managed the entire department and needed that control to be successful.

I walked away from the meeting knowing that he and I would make a very formidable team in the management and direction of the department. Let me describe Tom. He is in his mid-50s, a world-renown neuronal interventional radiologist who moved to Cleveland to be closer to his wife's family. He is brilliant beyond comprehension, with a very good business instinct. I could tell from day one that he and I would be inseparable in the success of the department. I was offered the position, accepted the challenge, and began my career at the hospital home in June of 2010.

That month I began a new job and role with the hospital home. It is human nature when you walk into a new environment to be apprehensive and nervous. Just take a moment and think back to when you started a new school or a new job and how you felt. You're walking into a new environment where you have no relationships and your slate is clean. What I really mean is that you have no past to bring to the situation. As in most new employment opportunities, you first go to a full day of orientation. In this orientation, you find that everything is made to be simple, positive, and team-oriented.

The day after my orientation, I walked into my new office. It was my first interaction with my new administrative assistant, Barb. A 27-year veteran, Barb greeted me with a pleasant smile of confidence. In previous books, I described various administrative assistants and their job performance. In all those cases, I would not have been successful without their support. It took me only a few weeks to realize that Barb was the best of the best. She has an incredible work ethic combined with an almost compulsive desire to be organized.

This compulsiveness is extraordinary. In an attempt to be clean, I decided to place my empty food containers in Barb's wastebasket. Her compulsiveness exploded from her frame and she showed me where I should properly place these items. When I sit back and look at the situation, it brings a smile to my face. There isn't one thing that has occurred in the last 27 years in the radiology department that Barb doesn't know something about. She has an uncanny ability to read my mind before I even know what's in it.

The radiology department is significant in both gross revenue and contribution margin. Our gross revenues exceed $180 million, with contribution margins of nearly $30 million. The department produces 260,000 exams a year and employs 175 people. These people represent radiology technologists, nurses, physicians, residents, supervisors, managers, and ancillary personnel.

It was very important for me to start the process of emotionally connecting to the staff. I honestly believe the first impression is actually important to laying the foundation of commitment and context. I made a critical decision to meet every employee one-on-one as an introduction. I know when I told people that I was going to do this, they thought I was crazy.

Thus started my journey of meeting every employee who worked in the radiology department. This provided several key early components of emotional connectivity:

- **Respect.** This initial contact allowed me to respect the individuals of my department. I was able to give them some background about my history and also learn about their tenure with the organization, why they chose to be in healthcare, their families and what their expectations were of me. It was actually amazing that many of the employees thought that this meeting was wonderful. In fact, many expressed views that the previous administrator had been there five years and did not know their names.

- **Expectations.** This interaction allowed me to set my expectations of the employees. I reviewed and supported the chain of command. In addition, I wanted to know their expectations of me. This time also allowed me to set the expectation that I would be working in the department and not just sitting in my office.

- **Understanding.** This brief 15 minutes gave me great insight into and understanding of the people of my department. I was able to easily understand which individuals were engaged and which ones were disengaged.

- **The Sheriff Principal.** This interaction also allowed me to express that *the sheriff was in town*. I was able to articulate a vision and goals and demonstrate that this department was going to take the lead and be the most important department for the hospital.

I deliberately set up these meetings to start the bridge of connectivity. I first met with all the management team. This allowed me to set the stage to meet all their employees. In my meetings with the managers and supervisors, I made sure that they knew I supported the chain of command and I was going to meet with all their employees.

Make no mistake; it takes some time to meet 175 people. I believe it took over two months to finish the entire department. There were many interesting and important sessions:

- **Ms. Angry.** I met this individual through my sessions. She is a seasoned technologist who produces excellent quality exams. However, she does display an angry persona. When you look at her facial expression, it is that of a frown, a constant upside-down smile that doesn't go away. She was pleasant, respectful, and knowledgeable but she had a slight bite to her.

- **The Painter.** He was very interesting. He painted houses during the day and worked as a radiology technologist at night. He was pleasant, encouraging, real, and a generally good person.

- **The Comedian.** This person was female, blonde-haired and from another country. She had a thick accent when she talked and a fabulous personality. It didn't take me long to build an emotional connection because this person was really engaged in the organization and believed what she was doing. She was very comical in her impressions and views.

- **The Next-in-Line.** She is a supervisor in the department, bright and intelligent and someone who I think will be able to progress in her career. I'm hopeful that she will continue to learn the art of leadership while increasing her interpersonal skills.

- **The Biker.** This person was very interesting because she asked me strange questions:

    o   Did I ride a motorcycle?

    o   Did I have any tattoos on my body?

I have to admit these are really strange questions for a first meeting. However, I did learn about her son and husband. She was testing me, her new boss, in a way that nobody else did. She wanted to know the real me, not what was on my name badge.

- **The Computer Lady.** Computers are in our everyday lives. Some people thrive in the world of networks, cables, hard drives, and applications. The Computer Lady is the definition of a female geek with a twist. She is the IS manager of the radiology department. She is also a radiology technologist. I found her to be strong, knowledgeable, and confident, yet she had a very subtle emotional chip on her shoulder. This is a very interesting combination and one that would amuse as the days went on.

- **The Application Specialist.** This person had started only a few months before my arrival as the supervisor of our interventional radiology department. Her background for the past 20 years had been as an application specialist for an equipment vendor. These people come on-site and provide education and training to employees to run and operate new medical equipment. This particular department had a history of volatile interpersonal relationships, operational issues and overall respect problems. The application specialist was in for a rough road because her clinical skills were outdated, yet she was pleasant and open in my first interaction with her. Little did I know that this person would demonstrate to me true courage and focus in an incredible achievement which today is one of the most amazing situations I've ever witnessed. You'll have to wait until later on in this book for the gory details.

- **The Bookkeeper.** When I met the bookkeeper, I was surprised at how young he was. He was perfectly dressed, well-mannered and an all-around pleasant person. I could tell that he was well-liked and respected within the department but had issues with respect from his supervisors. This perception was created by a poorly communicated restructuring that occurred a year before my arrival. As I moved through the organization, I would find him facing some inner demons and coming to conclusions that I think he'll not only treasure but admire in years to come.

- **The Chameleon.** There are some people you meet whose first impressions never seem to leave your own mind. This person smiled and said all the right things, but my experience told me that not all was right in this particular situation. I've been involved in too many used-car sales situations! However, I was hopeful that my presence would either control the true personality or help the person improve.

- **The Checkout.** When I first met The Checkout, he was pleasant and polite in his demeanor and very likable. It didn't take me long to gain the perception that, even though he technically did his job, he had mentally checked out. This doesn't necessarily mean it is a bad thing, but I could tell where he was in his life and the stress of work was of no interest. Please do not get me wrong. He was technically sound and meeting the requirements of the job, yet you can tell when somebody is ready to retire, and he was the poster child for the walking retired.

- **The Professor.** The Professor was, by far, the most intelligent person that I met. His meticulous work ethic is one that I have not seen in my career. This is only matched by his willingness to help his coworkers in any endeavor. I am proud to have him as part of my department.

- **Super Resident.** The radiology department supports a residency program. Basically, for those of you that are not in healthcare, we train physicians to be physicians. My entire career has been based on working with physicians years after they finished their training. I had the pleasure of meeting one resident that I think has the ability, personality and drive to become one of the best doctors ever seen. It is unusual to find all these good qualities in one medical professional.

- **Two-for-One.** One of my last meetings was probably one of my strangest. Two employees came in tandem to talk to me. They were pleasant, funny, energetic, and engaged in the conversation. Still to this day I'm not sure how it happened, but it was sure an interesting pair and conversation.

This was a snapshot of the people I met through my initial contact. My overall impression of the department was very positive and encouraging. The employees and physicians were taking care of thousands of patients a week and doing it with pride and honor. One must not underestimate the power that people collectively can control.

OPERATIONAL CONNECTIVITY

Leaders in organizations have a responsibility and a duty to understand what their employees think and do on a daily basis. Too many times, leaders and managers are completely disconnected from what happens on a day-to-day basis, which I call Gap Connectivity. Gap connectivity is more common in large organizations with layered management structures. Basically, in normal speak, the administrations of organizations are not connected to day-to-day activities, which creates many challenges:

- **Poor decisions.** It is almost impossible to make good decisions when there is a lack of knowledge in process and practice.

- **Respect Issues.** The common frontline employee deserves respect from all levels of management. The lack of understanding and knowledge of jobs performed is the first step in disrespect. In most cases, especially in highly specialized fields, this can severely affect operational efficiency, outcomes, and overall morale.

- **Resentment.** People follow leaders who take the time to understand what they do and how they do it. Baseline resentment develops when this understanding is not present.

- **Confidence.** People generally follow those in whom they have confidence. It is vitally important to build confidence through actions, not words. The gap in connectivity creates low confidence levels in employees in the organization, which in turn makes leadership almost impossible.

In my one-on-one sessions with all the employees, I promised them three things:

1. **Department Orientation.** I promised that I would take the time after the initial meetings to come and work in their particular areas.
2. **Off-Shift Commitment.** I made a promise to work every four months with off-shift employees.
3. **Rounding.** My last promise was that I would periodically do rounds in the department to be visible and accessible.

My purpose for these promises was to build operational connectivity, which is the ability to directly connect where employees meet the customer. I cannot stress how important this connectivity is to the ability to emotionally connect and make a difference for the people that surround you. In addition, it sets the ground rules that build confidence, respect, knowledge, and the ability to make right decisions.

My days following the initial contacts were filled with working inside the department. I was able to see with my own eyes issues that I heard about during the initial contact sessions. This experience was invaluable because it allowed me to cross the barrier between manager and employee. In addition, it demonstrated that I was a man of my word and could be trusted. Please note that, even in the circle of trust, there is still a slight flavor of distrust.

I also had the pleasure of working with our off-shift employees. The night that I arrived, I walked into what I would equate to a war zone. The staff was challenged with level I trauma patients. It did not take long for me to jump in and start helping them perform radiology exams on these patients. I was totally and completely amazed at their teamwork, accuracy, and compassion for the patients in their care.

The off-shift experience again demonstrated that I was willing to work with them side-by-side in the difficult trench of delivering healthcare. I believe I won not only their respect but their trust at this moment. The art of operational connectivity is not so much walking in with a title but walking in title-less, willing to share in the burden of work.

Doing rounds in the department then reinforces the trench work and initial contact. It continues the circle of connectivity in the department. It allows the leader to stay focused on personal relationships while keeping a finger on the pulse of the operation. It has been my experience that many organizational leaders sit in their offices contemplating organizational success while their employees muddle through the day.

I truly feel sorry for leaders who do not connect with their day-to-day operations, because they lose sight of what really is important. The importance of connecting with frontline employees outweighs the importance of any title. It can be the most important aspect of creating the genesis of emotional connectivity. I would challenge scholars that a manager or leader cannot emotionally connect with his or her employees until the operational connection occur.

TURNING POINT

The new opportunity was an once-in-a-lifetime chance to expand my skills and test my theories on emotional connectivity and engagement. As the years rolled on, I built strong relationships with excellent performance results. Then, as always, I was approached to take on managing surgical services and apply for a vice president's position. Now I have to tell you, I had significant reservations about taking on more responsibility, for several reasons. First, I've done this several times in my career with bad results. As you move up the ladder of leadership, you are more vulnerable in terms of keeping the job. Second, the hospital home had a horrible reputation, with challenging senior leadership, trust issues with the medical staff, and a terrible history with turning over senior leaders. I had a meeting with a senior leader about the opportunity. He convinced me to take on the new duties and interview for the job. I had a significant advantage because I would be in the trenches. He went so far as to say, *"John, you'll be driving the bus. Nobody else is driving the bus."* I decided to take on the challenge.

Now, for those leaders who aspire to gain a promotion, it is never a good sign to have to go through an interview process for an internal job versus external candidates. If an organization really wants you in a position, it will promote you to an interim position. So I took on more work, with the same title, and went through an interview process of 7-9 interviews. It was narrowed down to an external candidate and me. The lead physician with whom I interviewed approached me and told me that the medical staff in surgery gave me support and told the senior leader they wanted me to have the job. My confidence was high and I was energized when I got the call from a senior administrator for a meeting. I walked in with high hopes and this is what I heard:

> *"John, you interviewed real well and it was a tough decision, but we are going with someone from the outside. I know that's not what you wanted to hear."*

When you hear bad news, a calm response is necessary to go back to your job. Ultimately, I believe I was a victim of diversity, as they offered the job to an African-American. In fact, the new vice president signed a two-year agreement and never moved to Cleveland, Ohio from New York. Nevertheless, I will let his job performance be the record of choice.

Interestingly, the conversation did not stop there:

"But we really need a business development function for the organization. We would like you to put together a presentation on how you would put this department together."

Okay, I didn't get the job, but they were showing their appreciation of my business development skills. I took that message and felt good and energized to put together a great department. This played out over several months, and I presented my plan to a senior leader and the gentleman that told me the original bad news. The plan had structure, process, and integration. It also had a sample of a new proposed organizational structure for the $1 billion company. After that meeting, everything went silent. This occurred because a new CEO was named to start in 30 days. Once the new CEO started, the communication channel dried up. I happened to be meeting with the bad news-giver about something else when he said:

"John, I should tell you we are moving forward with a business development function, but we are going to hire it from the outside. You can still be involved if you want to."

I politely declined and went back to my office. The next day a company-wide email went out with a new organizational structure. It was the structure that was in my plan. Devastated is not a strong enough adjective to use for the way I felt. Several months later, I was ignored for a simple bonus based on high performance. Once again, history will prove my department had a better budget performance than another department for three years running.

So what do you do? I was 43 years old, getting my doctorate in business administration, making decent money with great benefits. I'm usually a very energetic and engaged employee. The reason I joined the organization was to gain a full understanding of engagement. I was now the most disengaged leader in the organization. In fact, I secretly hoped for bad results, to stop big, fat bonuses going to unethical people. I found myself loving the people I work with but despising the people above. I found corruption, distrust, and greed. I saw people whom I wouldn't hire as employees in my department in high-level positions that made no sense. There were senior-level leaders who did not meet minimum industry standard educational requirements.

Engagement is important. I will go so far as to say it is vital for personal and professional goals. What are those ideals and strategies that influence whether you care or don't care about meeting the goals of an organization? Can an employee be successful without caring? I never believed the phrase "good guys finish last." I believed the record lives in the hearts of my coworkers and I would be viewed as a "good guy." Will I finish last by the end of this book?

Emails

Joe wasn't asked and destroyed everything and everyone in his path. I think sometimes when the real thing is in front of you, it scares people. From my experience, most people are not trustworthy, and you keep the real you locked up inside and maybe sometimes you let it out. Think about it—many people do not want to make that emotional connection. It takes a lot of energy and time to foster relationships and, if you keep it superficial and impersonal, it is easier to screw someone over. I have said I have an inner circle, and not many people will ever know what makes me tick, by choice or survival. You'd like to think you work for an organization that values hard work and dedication, but the more I see, the more I wonder why not everyone is held to the same standard. I do know one thing—I am glad that you and I connected.

Parsh

John,

I wanted to take a few minutes to say Thank You!

It was truly a pleasure to work with someone who put a personal touch back into administration. You have a very unique leadership style, which most administrators could learn from. It is a style that does not demand respect but gains it through the example you set, the work ethic you have and the way you treat people.

Your guidance showed me many different ways to look at and approach situations, how to think through a problem and create a solution. You taught me that no matter how bad today is, tomorrow is a new day and life is what you make of it.

Your approach, direction, problem-solving skills and personal touch will be deeply missed around the hospitals—it already is. From a personal standpoint, I'll miss the "Here comes trouble" comments when I walked into your office.

Cindy

Success Defined

"Success is defined by the internal eye." Vizzuso

Before understanding what and how employee engagement affects the workplace, I must first take a look and understand what true success tastes like in the corporate world. I want somebody, I mean anyone, to tell me what success is. Please read these lines and write down on a piece of paper the key measurements that define success, because today I cannot see them, hear them or understand why they somehow have lost me along the way. I just lived through another disappointing employment where my job was eliminated. How could this happen again?

Years ago when I looked back on job opportunities lost, I could always pick a defining moment that led to the end, but this time I could not seem to locate that moment. I performed the job flawlessly. The job itself was impossible, but only those very close to me knew that. I look back to those people who I would consider peers and my head shakes in amazement. Most, if not all, were having some kind of issue in the workplace. In fact, a former peer was feared and loathed by his peers, employees, and customers yet survived every day and left on his own accord.

I define success in an executive position as "The ability to emotionally connect with your peers, employees and customers as you meet the quality and financial goals of the organization." I am living proof this definition is absolutely wrong. It is a fatal vision of truth where truth has fallen off the edge of a cliff.

Thus, my journey has begun to define, understand, and grasp the concept of success and sharing that success with the people around me. I do not believe success is a definable term, nor do I think you can find it on the Internet. Success is an amoeba-like substance that flows from everything you do, everything in the environment, relationships and life in general. It is that shadow that shines on some individuals and shades others.

Success is personal, individualized, deep, satisfying and paralyzing. People feel they can conquer the world when success is around them and yet feel like the world has ended when it has gone. I cannot help but desire and hate success all in one emotion. Many wise people say that the world cannot have good without evil to compare it against. I believe this life cannot have success without the threat of failure.

I know a man whom I admire for his simple outlook on life. He has a family with a wife that should be jailed for poor interpersonal behavior. His kids are great but have been controlled by the mother and are finding it hard to find their own way. His financial state is a wreck. This situation was brought on by too many years of financial mismanagement. His goal in life is to work the least possible, claim bankruptcy, and die early.

He is amazingly happy and feels he is on a successful track. In fact, everyone around him sees him as a glowing success in the community. His ability to smile in the midst of muck and slime is truly remarkable. He is a success because he believes that his life is a success. He looks past all the issues to view his life and internally smiles because he is happy and successful in the living of life the way he wants to.

When I look in the mirror, I want to believe that success is staring back at me, but my employment history tells a different story. I have a wonderful family, financially secure, and live a healthy life, yet I do not feel successful. Then, in a rush, a bat hit me in the face with a marvelous revelation:

"I need to live my life. I need to be me and do what makes me happy"

My days as a slave to the corporations of fake core values and mission statements are over. I cannot believe the lies provided and will not adhere to rules they apply. There is a day in a person's life when common sense goes out the window and is replaced with a drive that equals rage. Today I do not have rage. It is beyond rage; it is a feeling of utter determination to change one's life. It is so powerful that not succumbing to it means a relative death.

PERSPECTIVES OF SUCCESS

It was a quiet night, after the flu ravished my household, when many perspectives of success floated through my mind. A main question kept me up all night:

What were the key traits, items, processes, and actions I would need to feel happy, successful and content with the life I lead?

I believe there are ten perspectives of success. These perspectives are absolutely necessary to attach yourself to the glow of success:

- **Vision.** You have to have a clear vision of truth, life, and actions. The road to success is paved in a layer of glass.
- **People.** It is vitally important to emotionally connect with the people around you.
- **Drive.** A drive must be strong to blast through negativity, fear, and self-doubt.
- **Faith.** You have to believe in something.
- **Trust.** The barriers to trust are far greater than the actual bonds that forge trust.
- **Fear.** Fear is a motivation.
- **Confidence.** Confidence is always pure.
- **Resolve.** The difference between success and failure is a measure of resolve.
- **Unselfishness.** Greed is unnecessary.
- **Price.** There is a price for success.

Take a deep breath, sit back in your chair, and get ready for a journey of self-discovery and hopefully successful outcomes. I cannot foretell the future, and when the day is done I may be in the unemployment line, but I will tell you, the reader, one thing—I will commit and give everything I have to give, feel, believe, and attack the concept of success and employee engagement, and I will not stop until I see both in the mirror.

Dear John,

You have one of the kindest hearts of anyone I've worked with in Administration. You have a special gift and talent for really connecting with people. Hold onto this. It is your strength. Don't take posturing that moves you away from being the person you are. I wish you the best in the future. Continue to keep the mission alive in all you say and do. Keep writing too.

Jeff

Vision Alive

"A strong vision breathes." Vizzuso

Many of you work in organizations that claim to have a vision and a mission to serve the greater good. These visions are portrayed by many words:

- **Visionary.** Is seen as being beyond its time.
- **Unique.** The vision is the only one of its kind.
- **Strategic.** The vision will outthink the competition.
- **Tactical.** The vision will be very organized.
- **Long-term.** The vision will last more than five years.
- **Short-term.** The vision will last only five years.
- **Cutting edge.** The vision is very secret.
- **Groundbreaking.** The vision will rock the marketplace

All organizations and families have three distinct parts to their overriding culture:

- **Mission.** The mission is the overriding reason to assist. It describes ethical and moral attitudes of an organization. The mission is the single factor that will propel the organization into successful outcomes.

- **Core Values.** The core values of an organization are the cornerstones that uphold the mission. These values are upheld at all costs. The words are usually meaningful and are demand statements. The words that are used are: Respect, Diversity, Truth, Fiscal Responsibility, Leadership, Quality, and Spirituality.
- **Vision.** Vision is the path an organization will take to carry out the core values, which in turn live out the overall mission.

I've been in various managerial roles throughout my 27-year career. These roles ranged in responsibility:

- Supervisor
- Manager
- Director of Operations
- Vice President of Operations
- Director of Radiology
- Business Manager
- CEO
- President
- Administrative Director
- Vice President, Cardiovascular and Imaging Services

I've also had the pleasure of working in different types of organizations such as:

- For-profit organizations
- Nonprofit organizations
- Hospitals
- Non-hospitals
- Physician practices
- Retail
- Faith-based
- Non-faith-based

The number of organizations that have employed me had reached seven as of November 2009. All these organizations have vision, mission, and core values. I'm sad to write these words, but only one—that's right, only one—truly lived out those values and traits. If you're like me, you are sitting there, talking to yourself, and shaking your head up and down, because you are in a situation where you know your current employer is falling completely short of the vital obligation of vision, mission and core values.

My Black Book

I have a special black book to share with all who read these words. This book doesn't have my romantic conquests but describes the seven organizations that I've shared my life with.

Hospital A (1989-1990). Hospital A was the first hospital where I worked out of college. I was a young radiology technologist who was promoted to afternoon supervisor at the age of 21. This was the most enjoyable job in my history. I was in the position for four months when

I was called in for a meeting. That meeting was with HR, and I was notified that my position had been eliminated due to budget issues. I walked away into a new opportunity.

Hospital B (1990-1992). I took a job with another hospital doing mobile x-ray. This service was not located inside the walls of the hospital. I worked with the local management and soon found myself in a political environment I wasn't ready to handle.

Mobile X-ray Service (1992-1997). I left the hospital and started a small company in Canton, Ohio doing mobile radiology. The company was sold and I became a branch manager in Canton. I was promoted to Director of Operations several years later. I saw more horrible things in this job than any other. In this company leadership defined the negative attitude.

Imaging Center Company (1997-2002). The Imaging Center Company was a faith-based organization in the medical imaging world. I started with the company as an operations manager for five imaging centers across the country and left as a Vice President of Operations with 13 imaging centers. I would say this was more extensive job experience but also a disappointment on the value side. They fell short on many issues regarding the people who were employed but also the consumers they served.

Hospital C (2003-2004). Hospital C is my winner to date. This county hospital is still standing today in a competitive hospital environment. The senior leadership is still in place six years after I left the organization. The organization and the management staff live the core values in the way they act and what they do. The people are kind, sensitive, and warm, and deliver the best care in the area. I drove two hours one way for eight months to work at this hospital. I thoroughly enjoyed my time with the employees and management of Hospital C.

Group Practice (2004-2009). The Group Practice was a 13-member radiology physician group. I loved these doctors and would do whatever was necessary to protect them from the environment and, many times, from themselves. There wasn't a real mission, vision or core values. This is not uncommon in physician groups. However, I was amazed at how they treated each other. They would verbally harm each other, reading people's weaknesses by behind-the-door meetings. Their disdain for each other was only matched by their skill level.

Unfortunately, over time many members left the group, and the remaining physicians became employees of the health system. I sometimes wonder if they would have survived if they did have vision, mission and core values. That will be a question that will never be answered.

Hospital D (2006-2009). Hospital D is a Catholic health care system, with two hospitals and two large physician practices. Hospital D has vision, mission, and core values that are hanging all over the organization. This is the organization from Chapter One, so I have to be as objective as possible on their success rate living the mission. I truly believe that the organization wants to live the values and mission in everything they do. I also believe they do accomplish this at times.

Unfortunately, they also fall from grace way too often. I worked with the senior leadership of both hospitals and I believe they are pure in their thoughts but the process of action claims the organization as a victim. When you look at my situation, I was at the top of my game, my people loved me, my relationships with the physicians were strong, and there were very few issues in my area. I can tell you that the most senior people had many issues, including poor processes, marginal performance, and arrogant behavior. Yet they chose me as the one to move on and did it in a very disrespectful manner. I could list all the crazy decisions that came from this organization, but that would just leave more bad taste from an entity that I loved and adored. The Catholic nuns are human and make mistakes just like anyone. I give them credit for trying to get it right.

John,

I wanted to take a moment to write you how sorry I am that things worked out the way they did. We miss you and your wonderful sense of humor and personal sharing with our team that said…. I truly believe all things happen for a reason and months from now you may realize this was all for the best. Perhaps it will allow you to follow dreams you never thought to pursue.

I wish you the best always and will miss your smile. Take care and God bless you.

Carol

Drive

"Ready.…..Set.……Go." Vizzuso

Energy of the soul is a unique concept and property. Human nature in general has both flight and fight responses. Our ancestors had that same instinctive choice when they faced adversity, turmoil, and defending a way of life. These life experiences define the durability of the human spirit and determine success or failure.

There have been many historical situations in which people, countries, and common heroes faced the choices of charging or retreating:

North Vietnamese People. The North Vietnamese people fought several devastating wars to finally unite the entire country. The Vietnam War was costly for the United States but was devastating for the population of both South and North Vietnam. These people focused on the objective and drove the resolve of a nation.

General George Armstrong Custer. General Custer was considered heroic in his service to the United States and faced danger and certain death many times, yet he faced his last battle overwhelmed and outnumbered to the last man.

Nelson Mandela. Nelson Mandela served 27 years in prison for his anti-apartheid activities in South Africa. His determination, will, and vision produced a revolution that propelled him to the presidency of South Africa and the freedom of his people.

Bill Gates. Bill Gates had a vision of what computers could look like. His vision and assertiveness transformed an entire world of information technology.

DRIVE

We all have drive in our lives. Drive itself is the ability to move an ideal, process, relationship, purpose and principle in a direction with energy, cause and purpose. It is a divine right to make something happen, no matter what obstacle may face the individual. There are several properties one must understand to truly build unbeatable motion:

- **Energy.** Energy is necessary in nature as we know it. Energy propels movement of objects, people, and ideals. There are several forms of energy all around us:
  - **Constant Energy.** Constant energy is energy that remains steady and unchanging. The output is predictable, measureable, and never-ending.
  - **Free-Flux Energy.** Free-flux energy is energy that suffers from environmental barriers. These levels can climb dangerously high or fall morbidly low.
  - **Hypo-Flux Energy.** Hypo-flux energy is energy that remains very low and never appears to challenge the day.

- o **Adaptive Energy.** Adaptive energy is energy that adapts itself to the given situation. It attempts to regulate based on expected outcomes.
- o **Hyper-Flux Energy.** Hyper-flux energy is energy that climbs to elevated levels.

Today my energy level is completely in a hyper-flux mode. This energy mode has been live and building since the day my latest employer eliminated my position. There are several key areas of focus when you're in a state of mind of no retreat, no surrender:

- o **Purpose.** You must develop a purpose to latch yourself to. It allows a drive to have a goal or outcome to work towards. The purpose is critical to the journey. I cannot think of a path taken where gold was not at the end of the road.
- o **Critical Thinking.** Drive is supported by critical thinking. This concept develops reason in the fog of high energy. The reasoning abilities control irrational thought and behaviors.
- o **Vision.** Vision is necessary to move a drive. You must be able to see beyond the day's activities.
- o **Creativity.** A strong drive propels the creativity that swells deep inside one's own mind. The path to success will be found no matter what direction is taken.
- o **Edge.** The edge of success or failure needs to be felt. Today I feel very hungry—starving, one could say. I will do whatever is necessary to succeed.
- o **Cause.** The cause must be pure, void of need or want.

o **Proof.** The drive needs to be able to prove the fine point of directions, leadership, and self-awareness.

The Gas Tank Is Empty

There are those people in life for whom the *Drive Tank* is on the big red "E." These people are all around us every day. All you need to do is take a step back and look around you. I bet there will be handful of people you see who walk slowly, care little about the life they lead, and try anything just to get by. Does this sound familiar? Families, organizations, education systems, and government entities are full of the disengaged. People who crawl through life just to get by seem to fill the ranks of the employed.

There are several key traits to look for in someone to see if the drive is gone:

- **Depression.** People with little drive will seem depressed all the time.
- **Fakeness.** People with the drive on "E" will tell you how much they hate their jobs, yet they never seem to leave or find a new job.
- **Retirement.** These people will threaten retirement around every corner.
- **Performance.** The overall performance in a job or family is weak at best.

In most cases, people with low drive are not harmful and just walk their own journey through life. However, it can become very dangerous when heads of families, executives in the workplace or any leader loses the drive, which I call **Empty Leadership**. Empty leadership can happen to any leader, in any situation. It is when you are in a leadership role that you have to defend your drive at all costs. Empty leadership is dangerous because survivability is still very strong in the human soul. Leaders with empty leadership will do anything to keep the role, pride, and riches of the life position. They will stop at nothing to hide this and keep the status quo.

I worked with a gentleman who had this issue. Tim was older, in an executive role, and definitely at the end of his work career, but he was in position to survive at all costs. I witnessed Tim laying off people so that he would have a safer position. He would always talk about his unhappiness, his desire to retire, and his dislike of the organization, yet he survived at the expense of others. He was the worst kind of leader because he sacrificed people for his own salvation.

Dear John,

I AM DEVASTATED!!! How dare they take you away from me!

I just wanted to thank you for everything. Your optimism and general "good will" attitude has actually worked on me. Well......sort of......?

I've appreciated all your patience with my "mouth" and my "feistiness." You must be a saint to put up with all that.

I have never had a boss who has ever done more for a department, thank you. Congratulations on a superb job! I wish you and your family the best. I'll miss you.

Pam

Faith

"Believe in something or fall for anything." Vizzuso

How is your faith today? Do you believe in something more than life itself? The faith-based organizations I've worked for believe in core values and mission that place the bar on a high plane of existence. These entities used prayer in the morning, prayer before meetings and regular prayer emails to send thoughts for people who were having a tough road. These religious actions may seem strange to Corporate America but deliver a refreshing take on business life.

In the three books I've written, I've really never commented on my own belief and view on faith and the world. I absolutely believe in God and the influence on my life as it stands today. I believe in His word, His light, and the difference between good and evil. However, I do not believe in organized religious orders in any way shape or form. I have many reasons for this thought, which I would like to share with you:

- Organized religions have been the catalyst for wars, death, and destruction throughout the history of man. These organizations use the word of God in the defense of creating hell against man himself.

- The acts of clergy on innocent people throughout the years have been both disturbing and despicable.

- The extremists use their religious beliefs to teach hatred to everyone around them. It is as though people become what they preach against.

- There have been too many people who preached the words of the gospel only to fall to human behaviors of distrust and deceit.

- Faith-based organizations seem to fall short of living God's core values in a human world.

- I had dinner with a born-again Christian several years ago. Denny believed 100 percent that he had accepted Jesus Christ as his savior and that he was saved. This made him ready to go with God when the world died. I asked him a simple question:

"So you are telling me that if I am not saved and live a good life, I will not go to heaven, yet a murderer who claims he or she is saved will go before me?" He said yes, I would not go to heaven.

With this said, I want to also clarify that faith is not in an organization, it is in the person. The person is where one finds God. I believe you find this by acting pure, doing the right thing and making a difference for the people around you.

ASPECTS OF FAITH

There are aspects of faith that bore into my body and take root in the soft confines of my stomach. Faith to me is a natural feeling, just like breathing air. I feel as though faith is behind my eyes looking out at everyone. Adhering to the aspects of faith creates this enlightenment:

- **Truth.** Truth is essential to fully realize faith. A person has to be true to the self and true to the people and environment around him or her. The truth will always position a person in the right place and time to do the right thing.

- **Calmness.** Calmness is a deep-rooted sense of settled composure and feeling. If you can imagine a feeling where nothing bothers you, no matter how bad or strange something is, that is calmness.

- **Self-Awareness.** Self-awareness and self-expression become like an evenly flowing stream. When you have faith, you can share yourself without shame or doubt because peace has found you.

- **Empathy.** Empathy is the ability to truly care for someone without judgment. This caring can bend the will of any person.

- **Wisdom.** Wisdom comes from the attainment of self-awareness. To be wise does not mean that you know everything; it just means that you have lived a life and are better for it.

- **Generosity.** The ability to give back is an essential part of faith. It allows people to give back to the community.

- **Love.** Love is important to keep in people's hearts. A person needs to be able to feel and share this strong emotion.

- **Respect.** All people deserve to be respected, but they also hold the burden to earn that respect.

THE FAITH ZONE

I have been in what I call "the faith zone" for many years. I have faith, believe in the aspects of faith and I am at peace. The faith zone is the place you find yourself when life has slowed to a calm, peaceful pace. It is a place where fear is on the outside and you somehow know the direction you're walking.

This zone is special because it allows a clear vision, clear conscience, and clear internal voice. It is a place where the feeling of comfort and resolve seem to coexist together. The belief is strong and soft at the same time.

I am not proud to say that I've not always been in this zone. In fact, for many years I had lost my faith because of life's cruel lessons. Those years seem like a long-lost memory of times that went bad.

I look back on why faith escaped me through those years and I can point the finger at one reason and one reason only—I am human and I am imperfect. I suffered through those days with resentment, fear, and despair.

John,

Hope you enjoyed the holidays with your family. I know I did—it was nice being home last week. Got a lot accomplished. Just wanted to say thank you again for all you have done for me these past few years. I would never have gone back to school without that extra push (or was it more like a shove? Ha-ha-ha, just kidding). It's been a great ride so far. Looking forward to reaching my goal—only 13 more months!! Seriously though. I really do appreciate all your efforts and for believing in me. Looking forward to what lies ahead. These are indeed exciting times!!!

Thanks again - Dawn

Fear

"Fear is the real four- letter word." Vizzuso

Fear, the dreaded four-letter **"F"** word in my life, still searches me out. It has been my enemy since birth and continues to try to damage me even today as I write these words. Successful outcomes are always challenged by fear of the unknown, fear of failure, and fear of embarrassment. Today fear hangs over me like a fog that freezes on your skin as it touches you.

The loss of the job was expected and actually desired in some respect. The building of a new future is exciting and vibrant until fear edges into my mind. It challenges the good things that have already happened:

- **Clients.** As I look for a job, I already have two consulting clients and two excellent potential clients in a four-week period. The attainment of consulting clients will provide much-needed cash flow as the company grows. It is amazing I have four prospects in four weeks—this is a great sign! Then fear crawls out of the sewer and questions the strength of these clients. It questions if they really will turn into dollars, because if they don't the cash flow will come out of my savings account and push me to financial ruin. It makes me look at my cash forecasts and my bank account totals on a daily basis.

- **Seminars.** I filmed my first commercial, which will air the week after Christmas for three weeks. It was awesome, fantastic, and hard all at the same time. I need people to attend the first four seminars to meet financial goals next year. The total cost was $11,000, not bad from my point of view. Then fear sneaks into my mind. What happens if no one signs up? You just socked $11,000 into an idea that is flawed. It tells me to start looking for a job instead of following my dream.

- **Home.** My wife is very supportive of my career decisions. Her eyes sparkle with the thought of not going through another downsizing. She never talks about money or investment but spoke very strongly to me to follow the path before me. Yet fear is just around the corner, waiting to say rude things. It tells me that I'm wasting my time—look for a job or run the risk of putting my family's financial security at risk. It forces me to add up all the money I've spent to move my family north, home improvements, and two mortgages for a year to prove how much money I lost.

Fear stops people from finding their dreams and changing their lives and keeps them in the status quo. It prevents a person from changing for the good to stay in the bad. I believe that any individual brave enough to face fear by using it against itself can conquer fear:

Force to Focus

Equal Leverage

Anticipation

Resolve

FORCE TO FOCUS

Force is the will to make something happen. It stares fear down and places actions in motion. For me, it is meeting with potential clients and networking. I have a special knack for communicating with other professionals. I had several meetings with people who may want to work for me as I look for a job:

- They were reasonably priced. I used this firm for another business and found them to be honest and respectable.
- This group only does accounting services. Many accounting groups also offer operational services to their clients. This will allow me to network with them and possibly open the door to hundreds of potential healthcare clients.

The meeting went well and I could see their interest in helping their clients with medical operation issues. We left that meeting feeling good and setting up a follow-up meeting with their healthcare accounting partner.

EQUAL LEVERAGE

You can never forget where success has found you before. There were years when consulting was a big piece of my life. It was time to get back to my roots and find my groove, to leverage my old contacts while leveraging new ones and new products. Three days after my job was eliminated, I hopped on a plane to fly to Chicago to attend the largest healthcare tradeshow in the world, RSNA.

At RSNA I met several prospective consulting clients but, most importantly, hooked up with a dear friend of mine, Gordon. Gordon started his own company several years ago and was doing great. Gordon and I work with the same type of clientele and can network with each other for winnable situations.

In addition, I contacted a former client who lives near Gordon to see how the company was doing. I was the lead consultant that built a 14,000 square-foot imaging center for this physician group. They were very eager to talk and I then made flight arrangements to see them both in the coming weeks.

Fate works in mysterious ways. The day after the layoff, I got a call from an old friend named Jim, a radiologist in Pittsburgh. He wanted me to come over for dinner and talk shop. Jim wants to develop his own group and he wants me to put it together. Jim became my first client.

ANTICIPATION

I must be realistic and anticipate that not all my future clients or jobs will become successful. I need somehow to see into the future and come up with plans that will deliver home-run business proposals. Dan, another physician I know, approached me to do a company together. He wanted to start up a company that electronically reads for health care organizations. The problem is that this market is full of competitive organizations much stronger then he and I together. I anticipated that this would be a bad business decision and quietly convinced him it would not work. But through this conversation I did foresee a business that Dan and I could make work together; one that used my skills in business and his skills as an interventional radiologist. We decided to look into building a clinic for people with chronic pain.

RESOLVE

I have to have resolve in my approach and never give up. Don't get me wrong, businesses do fail and do close. The law of going out of business is universally sound. There is a distinct difference between giving everything you have to a company and closing it and just quitting in the middle and throwing in the towel.

I cannot live with the fact that I quit on myself again, as I described in *Shared Sacrifice*. I would not be able to live the rest of my life knowing that I am a coward. I need to follow this path to the end, knowing I gave it everything I have and stopping with no regrets, I can live with that.

THE PICTURE FRAME

I did several things with organizations to limit my emotional connections to them. These tasks should be used wisely:

- **Name Plate.** If emotional connection is foreign to you, never place a nametag on your door.
- **Business Cards.** I never kept business cards in my office.
- **Knowledge of Organization.** I would limit the number of people who knew me, which limited my appearance.
- **Diplomas.** Never display diplomas on the walls. It's hard to pack those things when you leave.
- **Family Pictures.** Under no circumstance do you place family pictures in the office. Keep your family away from the organization.

Fear comes on with everything you have. I'm not afraid, nor am I scared to fail because I've already won.

John,

Thank you for all you have done for our department and for being so inspirational. You will truly be missed.

Jodi

John,

Out of all the administrators I've worked with, you were the best.

Pat

John,

Thank you for everything you did for St. Vincent. We all learned so much from you. Good luck to you in the future.

Leslie

Confidence

"Confidence is cockiness with respect." Vizzuso

F ear is in front of you, people are around you that you believe are in your way and enemies are hiding in the shadows to take away what is yours. Are you confident? The first sentences seem like a scene from a "Terminator" movie, but it is real life when everything you have is on the line. Confidence is embedded in success. Success cannot be obtained without confidence in purpose, mission, values, and skills.

Leaders from all ends of society develop confidence at a young age. It is the ability to know your strengths and limit your weaknesses. As life matures, people will follow you if they know you have pure intents but they will believe in you when your confidence secures their hearts.

Growing up, my confidence was present yet weak. It was always there, sometimes buried, battered, and bruised, but grew as I became a man. My levels of confidence grew both at work and at home as I started to build a family of my own. I look back through the years and my level of confidence has always been high.

At work it bulged as a muscle with a healthy blood supply. It matured as a separate being inside of me as work experiences grew and I began to make motivation and inspiration a tool to help others.

PEACE WITH CONFIDENCE

High levels of confidence correctly used can create calmness and peace for the people around you. It allows people close to you to realize that, no matter what happens, the person with the high confidence will save the day and make the outcomes successful. People can sense this peace and strive to flock to it.

Amy is a special person I used to work with. Amy today lacks the confidence level to make her feel comfortable. I remember the day when she caught my eye. She seemed bright and energetic as she whipped around the department putting out fires every day. There was something about her that made me look twice. I'm not sure if it was her eyes or a slight confidence streak that sat beside her. I soon offered Amy the opportunity for a management role, much more than she was doing. I could see her wondering if she could really do the job.

She accepted the job and was thrown into **Confidence Hell**. This confidence hell is seen by all people learning to be a good leader. In fact, I think I had a room in this hell on a daily basis as I learned my trade. I watched and guided her over the years as she grew, fought, cried, and sacrificed to become who she is today.

Unfortunately, since the downsizing, I will not have the pleasure of watching her continued growth. I saw her recently and, with tears in her eyes, she explained how I had lied to her. I told her when I left that she would do just fine and it was time for her to excel. A teacher educates a pupil in hopes that the pupil one day will do things better than the teacher. She was having a horrible time of it with the change and stated that she was not going to be okay without me.

Amy has confidence that is not yet matured, but these are the times when confidence takes that necessary next step and pushes its way to the surface. Amy now has the opportunity to be a teacher and find her own path. She always said that I made things look easy. I suppose she is right, but I made them look easy because I'm at peace with my confidence. Amy needs to look deep inside and find her peace.

CONFIDENCE PATH

There is a path that we all take to build our confidence over the years. The **Confidence Path** is a journey that people take to build a level of assurance that leads to successful outcomes. This path can be both fruitful and deadly:

- **Judgment.** To build confidence, a person must first utilize good judgment and pick situations and scenarios that are easy building blocks. This allows for a safe practice field where failure is nothing more than a learning exercise.
- **Street Knowledge.** Confidence is nothing more than enhanced street smarts. Instinct and gut feelings are the founding fuel for

confidence. It is this basic primal urge that separates confidence from catastrophe.

- **Observation.** The observation path is probably the most important piece of the journey. It is vitally important to learn from others' special traits, tendencies, and flaws. This will allow a person to absorb the significant traits of others while improving his or her own confidence.

- **Courage.** Trial-and-error is necessary to build confidence levels. Failure is okay as long as lessons are learned. The fear of failure will destroy confidence levels.

- **Short-Term Memory Loss.** The path is wide and narrow at the same time. The ability to fall off the path and fail is very easy. The short-term memory buttons in the brain need to erase failure from our thought patterns in order for confidence to build.

- **Emotional Depth.** The confidence path is more than a mere journey; it leads to self-discovery and knowledge. One must realize this and have enough emotional depth to succeed.

PITFALLS OF CONFIDENCE

The path to confidence is not contained in one moment or tied to any time frame. It is consistent and always there. However, there are obstacles in this path that can not only stop it temporarily but stop it on a permanent basis. The pitfalls of confidence can be self-generated or induced by others. These holes in our confidence surround us every day:

- **Extreme Self-Criticism.** In nature, self-criticism is a normal pain-producer followed by gentle pain relief. As with anything in life, self-criticism can be taken to extremes and tarnish confidence going forward. It is important to learn and move on.

- **Emotional Criticism.** We are not a perfect species by any stretch of the imagination. The mistakes we make in life try to define who we are. I hope that people can stop being defined by their mistakes and instead forgive themselves for wrongs of the past to build confidence for the future.

- **Empathetic Judgment.** The hurtful words of others can be very damaging. These words can rip away confidence and bury it for good. There has to be a time in one's life when empathy needs to leave and the words of others hurt no more.

- **Failure.** The act of failure can be the most devastating pitfall. There are too many times that a significant job failure ends a person's career. It is important to understand and realize that failure and success happen throughout one's life and will continue until death.

CONFIDENCE VS. COCKINESS

Yes, there is a difference between confidence and cockiness. Confidence is the emotional experience of using knowledge wisely. Cockiness is the barbaric use of ego as a weapon. For example, I am a very competitive business person. I might add that I would stop at nothing to win. My mind set is moving in three general areas:

- **Assertiveness.** I will work harder than my competitors. I want their business and I will have it. They cannot out-think, out-work or play me in any way, shape or form.
- **Assets.** I want all their assets, including customers, vendors, and employees. For example, I will search out and hire their best employees.
- **Humility.** I will be humble with my intentions, for I will one day have everything they own.

The concept of cockiness is not much different, except that the person will openly challenge the competitor and question integrity, stance, and purpose. A high level of confidence will allow me to take everything before they even know things are gone.

The high-confidence person does not need to boast or brag, for the outcome is always at hand. The person who is cocky always has to verbalize strengths for everyone to see. How many times have you known a person who does nothing but complain about how busy he or she is? This verbal diarrhea is a bi-product of cockiness. I guarantee these people are not busy at all.

Success is the sum of confidence, courage, and heart. Confidence has to be obtained, maintained, and cultivated over years of practice and mentoring. There is confidence in all of us that sits hidden away ready to mature and seize the moment.

Amy,

The hardest part of leaving an organization is seeing the people you care about upset. It has been my pleasure and honor watching you grow as a leader. It is unfortunate that endings happen so suddenly.

As your mentor, I know you now have to realize that it is time to mature and lead your people. It is time for you to build your confidence and expand your role. I realize things may be different and strange, but that is when true leadership surfaces to serve the common good.

I have the utmost faith that you will face these times and flourish, for you have the natural traits necessary to become successful. I look forward to the day when I can look at you and see the leader you will become.

John

Deb,

What can I say; Mr. Vizzuso has left the building! Deb, please continue down your path of self-discovery and forgiveness. Your people are now looking at you for direction, support, and calmness. You need to look in the mirror and you'll see confidence you didn't think you had. This may never make you feel comfortable in public speaking, but it sure will make you a better leader.

John

Resolve

"When the going gets tough, the tough get quiet." Vizzuso

Is resolve real? Is resolve something people inherently have or is it learned over time? These are questions that I have to ask myself over and over again because I question my own resolve over the years. I absolutely believe the concept of resolve in the human condition. Resolve is the ability of an organism to develop the mentality to survive and overcome obstacles. It demonstrates the will necessary to weather poor decisions, bad outcomes, and overall negative karma.

I recently watched a "20/20" episode about four people trapped in a car for nine days after they took a wrong turn down a snowbound road and got stuck. The family—husband and wife and two small children—were stuck in a real horror situation. They struggled the long days and nights as the mother resorted to breast-feeding to keep her children alive.

I can only imagine what must have gone through the father's mind as he sat trapped, his family in jeopardy, and how helpless he must have felt. A father and husband have an inherent drive to protect the family unit. This protection is fundamental and just in its honesty. The frustration of getting lost surely ate at him and begged him to resolve the situation. As the days wore on, he got more desperate to find a way out. He resorted to removing all four tires and setting them ablaze in an attempt to signal rescuers.

He then made the decision to leave his family in an attempt to find help. He walked off in a direction he felt would find the nearest town. This decision had to be hard and sickening, but he made it. His resolve for his family compelled him to risk his life in the cold depths of the winter to find the much-needed resolution.

His wife was now alone with her children, hanging onto the last visions of life it self. Her children were showing signs of dehydration and starvation as two days past with no news of rescue or communication from her husband. The wife made a critical decision to leave their stranded car and forge into the cold, dark forest to look for her husband. As she walked with her children in the snow and cold, she soon realized this might be their last walk together. It was then that a search-and-rescue helicopter noticed the family walking in an opening within the forest. The mother's daring resolve, courage, strength, and instincts saved her family's life.

Do you have resolve? Can this attribute be learned or is it inherent in people? I often wonder, as I see employees, managers, senior leadership, customers, patients, and common people in the community, if resolve is real. My experiences with people in general dictate that resolve is something feared and admired. To truly understand resolve, one must be able to tactically understand, respect, and describe the important attributes.

RESOLVE'S SEVEN LAYERS

The concept of resolve can be dissected into seven distinctive layers:

- **Cost.** For resolve to be true, there must be a value or cost at risk. This cost has to have inherent value to the person. This value needs to be real and tangible, not only to the person but also to the environment. It also has to have a significant emotional weight.

- **Value.** The ultimate outcome needs to provide significant value to the stakeholder. The value itself is not based on some number or amount but on an emotional factor scale. In fact, the more emotional value creates higher resolve levels. These resolves have a direct correlation to successful outcomes.

- **Vision.** Resolve cannot be blinded. It has to have sight, perspective, single vision, and depth perception. A person with blind resolve is no different than a poetry reader with no sight and no voice.

- **Touch.** Resolve is not in a vacuum. It lives in both our consciousness and the environment we live in. It has to be massaged, flattened, inflated, and felt. True resolve has a contour to its exterior. It can be both harsh and uncomfortable while at the same time soft and comforting.

- **Justice.** All human beings at one time or another seek justice, sometimes through the actions of others, organizations, government, and sometimes from ourselves. Justice allows resolve to renew and begin again. It allows regenerating for future events.

- **Resistance.** Resistance is the letter of resolve that shows individualistic compassion and indifference to self-inflicted wounds. In the modern world and its history, resistance has been seen, fought, and welcomed.

- **Foundation.** The foundation of resolve is not easily seen. As in any old structure, the foundation is the key to keeping resolve from crumbling. The foundation is composed of our character, integrity, values, and determination, and is its soul. A crack in the foundation can sincerely inhibit one's ability to have resolve.

My career in management started when I was 21 years old. In the years since that time, I've seen about every type of resolve, human emotional response, human judgment, human character, intrapersonal relationship, behavior, and emotional connectivity. In regard to having the strongest resolve I've ever seen in my career, one person comes to mind. Joseph was a leader among leaders. He inspired others and had strong character and integrity in addition to a keen business sense. Joseph's resolve was remarkable. He demonstrated the seven layers of resolve in everything he did.

There wasn't a time when I saw him angry, depressed, or frustrated. It was as though he operated in a different dimension. It followed him no matter where the journey was leading. Yet the organization Joseph worked for was fraught with poor leadership, aspiring dictators, low employee engagement, and poor operational performance. This did not deter Joseph. It actually made him focus even more on making his area the best it could be. I realize as you're reading about Joseph, you're looking at your own area of your own company and realizing that there are a lot of major issues going on. Let me tell you how Joseph dealt with adversity.

Joseph was both confident and arrogant, wrapped up in the same package. This combination is called "Confidence Squared." It allows an individual to operate with no fear of defeat, for even in defeat one is confident. In meetings with Joseph, I always marveled because there was never a time he was on the defense. His motion was always forward, not backward, even with the opportunity of failure.

His resolve to make a difference for his peers was evident in his relationship-building techniques and self-discovery and his ability to emotionally connect with the people. Followers, employees, soldiers, and citizens are attracted to people like Joseph for many reasons:

- *Direction.* People seem to gravitate toward leaders who provide them direction.
- *Respect.* People follow those who use titles as a position to deliver respect with no guarantee of respect returned.
- *Stamina.* People follow leaders who don't tire easily.
- *Drive.* The strong **drive** of poised leaders attracts people ready to follow.
- *Discipline.* Internal discipline is both strong and flexible.

Joseph was an individual whom I could follow and not worry about the direction he was taking us. His leadership skill, combined with a strong resolve, created a person like no other. I'm sure that wherever he is today he is continuing his path of inspiration and leadership by making a difference for the people that surround him. I'm sure he is using his strong resolve to produce outcomes that will stand for generations to come.

Dear John,

I'm sorry I missed your get-together. I was actually relieved when the code was called on CCU. I wanted to thank you for all the support this past year. When it comes to senior management, you are a rarity with your sincerity and sense of integrity. I truly enjoyed working for you. Not only do you talk the talk but you walk the walk.

I wish you the best with your new business venture. Please stay in touch.

Linda

Unselfishness

"Can you give without any returns?" Vizzuso

Greed is a human emotion that is deep within all of us. This emotion, or what I call flaw, is prevalent in our society today. One only has to watch the latest news program to see how greed has transformed our society. There have been many instances where greed, low moral character, and criminal influences have affected millions of people around the world. Let me remind you of a few:

- **Enron.** Enron was a complete and utter disaster, not only for the investors but also for the employees of the company. This company falsified financial projections, inflated the cost of bulk electrical sales, and defrauded their employees. In many cases the employees lost every dollar of retirement savings because of a false belief in the company.

- **Mortgage Crisis of 2009.** The financial crash of 2009 was rooted in unsound lending practices by financial organizations providing mortgages. The greed of the financial organizations overshadowed smart lending practices. This led to giving loans to home buyers who had no means to repay the loans once interest rates increased. This then lowered home values across the United States, which harmed those individuals who could afford their debt.

- **Ponzi Schemes.** The criminal mind can be disguised as a fully functioning, rate-returning investment firm. In these types of schemes, people are rewarded with profits from capital that is secured from new investors. These programs tend to attract large investors to secure large profits; unfortunately, when financial times are tough, the schemes fall apart. In many cases people lose total retirement fortunes.

In 2008 I had the pleasure of working for Catholic Hospital in Cleveland Ohio. One day in my office, the director of marketing and I had a heated discussion about her opportunity for advancement within the company. She was upset that she was still the director instead of being promoted to vice president.

On a Friday some time later, a memo went out for a conference call. During this call, my peers and I were notified that the marketing director had been suspended due to questions about marketing invoices being paid. It appeared that she had created a fictitious company that provided marketing and advertising resources. Either the services were not being delivered or she and her husband were providing the marketing services.

The following Monday, I was again summoned for another conference call. On this call we were informed that both the marketing director and her husband had committed suicide. The investigation now moved forward very aggressively. It took several months for the investigation to conclude that she had embezzled over $4 million over a seven-year period.

This situation really bothered me for some time. I could not comprehend why she would steal from the people she was working with. The hospital served the poor of Cleveland and needed every dime to complete that mission. This person I trusted, worked with, believed in, and listened to was nothing more than a thief! I felt betrayed, sorry for her family and very angry at her actions. Their greed and disregard for the organization and the people it served will go down as one of the most selfish events that I've ever been acquainted with.

What does it take to be unselfish—I mean something totally unselfish that in every case you're looking for someone else's best interests and not your own? I may be crazy for thinking this, but I believe that there are people in this life who are truly unselfish in everything they do. To really understand this premise I think we first have to look at the characteristics of unselfishness:

- **Perspective.** People who are unselfish have a different perspective of what is needed to be happy. This perspective allows individuals the opportunity to do for others instead of doing for themselves.
- **Values.** Values seem to wrap themselves around the unselfish person. These values of goodness, right, justice and honesty seem to encircle one's inner being to make sure one's needs are met without taking them from others.

- **Affirmation.** The act of being unselfish is not done in a vacuum. The feeling one gets when giving is appreciated and seen, which leads a person to actually want to be unselfish. It is as though the high feeling one gets through giving is no different from a drug that makes you feel better. That feeling is wanted and needed by those who are unselfish.

- **Confidence.** A high confidence level can increase the likelihood of unselfishness. However, confidence cannot do this alone. In many aspects, confidence has to be combined with high values to keep an honest balance in one's mind. A highly competent person with poor moral values can be very selfish in actions and words.

- **Servant Leadership.** The most important characteristic of unselfishness is the ability to live servant leadership. One must believe that it is better to serve the common good of people instead of serving self-interests. I believe that servant leadership is not a learned trait but inherent in human DNA.

I can imagine right now you're thinking of that one person you've worked with, live with or interacted with who is completely selfish. The completely selfish individual derives this flaw from both inherent qualities and environmental situations. Through my years of experience in management and leadership, I have identified several key types of selfish people:

- **The Bull.** The bull is that person who shows his or her true identity and selfishness in the open. These people do not care nor do they fear repercussions based on their actions. There is no sense in beating around the bush—the needs of this type of selfish person must be met, no matter the cost to friends, family, coworkers, or the general public.

- **The Silencer.** The silencer portrays an unselfish façade. This façade traps other individuals and provides a false level of confidence and trust. And, just as the spider snares the fly, these people at the appropriate time incorporate their needs to fulfill their selfish personalities.

- **The Manipulator.** The manipulator combines genius and strategy used for the wrong purposes. This person will manipulate others around the particular item so that other people provide the price. In other words, the manipulator uses other people as tools to secure items that are desired or needed.

The real question is: How do you deal with these types of people? Right now, picture a person in your mind who fits one of the three categories. I can honestly say I've dealt with all three right through my entire career.

The worst one I ever dealt with was a combination of a bull and a manipulator. I first met a predator on the opposite side of the conference table. She was the chief operating officer for an acute care hospital and I was the chief executive officer of a physician group serving that hospital. She has an assertive, aggressive, and abrasive personality at times. She was the perfect corporate predator.

Corporate predators are people who will do anything to influence, control, possess, and defend the acquisition of power. In this particular situation, my physician partners were having service issues. She had reasons to improve change. The main issue wasn't around trying to improve the operations of the hospital; it was her methods and demeanor in dealing with physicians.

It was the first time in my career that I witnessed complete disrespect for another human being. She demonstrated a ruthless personality and was almost impossible to deal with. My partners eventually lost their service contract and became employees of the hospital. That was the last time that I would see my first corporate predator, or so I thought.

Several years later I had what I thought was the perfect job at the hospital home. I was again running a large radiology department in Cleveland, Ohio. It was then I learned, six months into my job, that the organization had hired this predator to run inpatient operations. I learned this by accident from one of my direct reports. I could tell from my own reaction that my direct report knew there was something wrong. Luckily for me, I reported to a different person in the organization who had no dealings with this person.

As always in my career, when I think everything's okay, that's when everything just changes. The person I reported to decided to leave the organization and retire. Now, those of you who watch the National Geographic Channel know how a predator acts. In most cases, predators seem to congregate around areas where their prey seeks substance. The local watering hole provides not only much-needed H2O but also the best hunting grounds. This is no different for corporate predators.

My particular division, which was now without leadership, also happened to be generating 60 percent of the organization's profit. During this transition, my medical director offered to become the executive director and manage the division. In these types of negotiations, timing can be very political. In the process of decision-making, this person forwarded to me an e-mail with a quality report attachment. In addition, she requested an opportunity to do rounds within my department. This was the perfect opportunity for the predator to get close to the prey. At this point I do have to make note that she and I had a reasonable relationship with this organization. In fact, my impression of her had changed since she joined the organization, but I was still cautious.

She arrived for her visit and was very gracious, interested, polite, and positive. I gave her a tour of the department and she left. There was one interesting aspect of the visit that haunted me—her reason for the visit was to review the quality reports. There was not one mention of the file reports, nor did we review any reports. The whole trip was a reason to infiltrate my department.

No more than a week later, my medical director was promoted to executive director and had his first verbal communication with the predator. This communication developed into a disaster within 15 minutes. In fact, it was the catalyst that kept her from running my department. However, that same day she instructed one of her direct reports to continue to listen for issues in my area because there were problems there. Her manipulative, abusive, and underhanded ways were now very apparent.

This situation was ongoing as I wrote these lines. I'm sure by the end of this book I will have played out the final outcome of this situation. There really were only two outcomes that could possibly happen:

- She now had several enemies within the organization, would not survive.
- Her manipulating ways would undo me within the organization.

The moral of this paragraph is that unselfishness has a longer-lasting effect than greed's affect on our society. In addition, it is always good that life's prey always know where the predators are lurking in the weeds, for a predator is only a predator if the prey allows it.

Dear John,

Thank you so much for mentoring and guiding us during these challenging times. We so appreciate your time and support. We wish you only the very best. We'll miss you!

Fondly,
Lori

John,

Thank you, John, for all your work with our team! We appreciate the time you spent over the past few weeks. It was great getting to know the ins and outs of the center. Good luck in your future. I am looking forward to reading your book I won at the health fair.

Dawn

John,

Thank you for everything you did for St. Vincent. We've all learned so much from you. Good luck in all your future endeavors.

Leslie

Price

"There is a price for success." Vizzuso

Let me clarify the quote at the beginning of this chapter. Let no person misunderstand me, there is a price to be paid for being successful. I do not care if the success is in a career, marriage, sports, education, finances, or anything else in life. The real question is not about accepting the price but about whether the individual is willing to sacrifice his or her own interests to become successful.

The price is a generic term with specific personality input. For instance, price may be different from individual to individual. What I consider my price for success may not be equitable to another person's definition. For example, I personally have found and have written about the lack of balance in my life. My inability to connect emotionally at home has been the main price to be paid for success in my profession. I am not proud of it, nor would I suggest to anyone reading this text that you should be disconnected from your home life.

This disconnection started midway through my career. At one point I traveled extensively around the United States. This travel schedule allowed me to disconnect easily from certain aspects of my own life and focus on my career 100 percent of the time. Yet I would never talk about my job with my wife and family. There wasn't a moment or a time that the job wasn't on my mind in some form or fashion.

I can say that this devotion to my job did create both financial and professional sustainability in an era when job security was a thought of the past. It allowed me to mold my leadership and management style into a thing of perfection. My management style has drastically changed over the last 30 years, making me more effective and efficient in leading my troops to the finish line.

The price of this success—my inability to connect with my family at times—is my greatest shame. Please realize I'm very happy at home today; my marriage is strong and loving. My children are good people and do good things. My emotional connection at home today is stronger than it has ever been. My shame is centered on all those years when my mind was not home even when my body was. I call this type of shame Priceless Shame. Priceless shame is that emotional feeling that one feels when motivation overcomes sensibility. This feeling develops over time and, at least to my knowledge now, never goes away.

There are distinctive symptoms of priceless shame:

- **Depression.** At times I find myself looking through old photos of events I missed mentally. It's comical that I look at small things such as pumpkin-carving as grave mistakes. I've now been married for 26 years and I can safely say I've never carved a pumpkin with my kids. I do realize that my wife played this role for our family, but that does not release my responsibility.

These types of looks back generally throw me into a depression. I realize at times that my wife will ask me if everything's okay and I always tell her everything's fine. I've become a good liar.

- **Regret.** When you pay the price of success, regret is like drinking water—it's always with you but, when it's not, you don't realize it until it's too late. An individual learns over a significant period of time to live with regret. You only hope that the amount of success in your life outweighs the number of regrets.

- **Judgment.** People with priceless shame can find it easy to judge other people who seem to be inferior, unsuccessful, lazy, and malcontented. It is hard for me to watch the evening news and see people not being assertive in their lives. I seem to judge them for what they haven't done instead of accepting them. I find it very frustrating that some people refuse to develop a plan for their lives—in fact, there are times I find it disgusting. I have this reaction because there are times when I wish I could be like them.

- **Loneliness.** It is possible for an individual to be around people all the time and still feel alone. I know that sounds impossible, but sometimes reality is undeniable. I have all kinds of people around me and yet there are times, because of the shame, that I feel utterly alone.

I would like to take this opportunity to apologize for the morbid description of the price of success. I do think, after all these years, that there is a better way to pay the price without sacrificing yourself. The analogy for my keen insight is no different from a recovering alcoholic's providing advice to an individual suffering from the disease. There are several steps that a person can take to prevent the excessive price:

1. **Communication.** The act of communication is vitally important in the pursuit of success to ensure that listening, understanding and nonverbal communication does not cease or lessen, but rather increases as successful outcomes become evident. I cannot underscore the importance of communication.

2. **Emotional sharing.** It is critical, as success builds for the individual, that the person is able to share this experience with the family unit. Having personal success without emotional sharing is like celebrating your wedding anniversary by yourself. It is important not to fear this emotional connection, because it allows the family to share in the success, It also allows the door to remain open when failure happens.

3. **Perspective.** The sense of knowing when the road is too hard and too long needs to be experienced sooner rather than later. One must be able to recognize when the price is starting to be too high. There is one truth, that an individual has power over the journey of life. A change in direction is available to all. The secret is knowing when to make the change.

4. **Expectations.** It is imperative to set realistic and achievable expectations. Successful individuals have a tendency to rush their success, which in turn sets unrealistic goals and objectives. Unrealistic expectations set the stage for increased cost in one's personal life.

5. **Reflection.** The ability to review one's path and journey is critical to controlling the cost for the next successful endeavor. Reflection is different from hindsight, because reflection is a mirror to one's actions that leaves an everlasting impression for future events. Hindsight is a simple look back to what went wrong, instead of understanding what went right.

In this journey we call life, we sometimes come across people who remind us of our youth. I recently met a young John.

Paul was an up-and-coming financial protégé. His built-in legacy was very interesting indeed. He was in his mid-20s and a senior financial director of a large corporation. People in the organization perceived Paul to be a workaholic. The urban legend in the organization was that of Paul working himself to death. He worked so many hours that his manager purchased a flat-screen TV for his office so that he could watch the World Cup soccer tournament while he worked. In meetings, Paul displayed a slightly arrogant confidence that could almost be felt on his skin. I often wondered whether he was really that cocky or whether it was all a façade to protect his ego from his lack of age and experience.

However, I found Paul to be very knowledgeable, polite, opinionated, and task-oriented and an efficient manager of resources. Yet I could also tell he was not patient with his career. It wasn't long after I met Paul that he resigned from the organization to accept a position as chief financial officer across the country.

Paul is not abnormal. Rather I believe he is more the norm for young, aspiring, and inpatient leaders we have in our society. He is one of many people in my past about whom I wonder if one day he'll realize the price for his success. In some respects, I see a lot of me in him. I remember the days of working more hours in a day than I slept. I was in an extreme rush in my career to find both the title and financial reward that would fill my cup of success.

I hope one day Paul will realize that success is not measured by what you know and how much money you have in the bank but rather by the difference you make for people around you, including your family and friends. I'm sure that ten years from now he will be the chief executive officer of some company. I can only wish that he will read this book and realize the price before it's too late.

Hey, old man,

Hope this e-mail finds you well. I never thought I'd see the day, but it has finally arrived. Finished my last class on Sunday—algebra. I am so relieved, I can't begin to tell you. Not sure where all the time went, but I do know it went by very quickly, surprisingly enough. Now I can focus on what is really important—my family. Mark will be coming home from a weeklong hospital stay. His therapy has been progressing very slowly, so I asked that he get a complete workup to make sure there were no additional major problems. Had to have some minor surgery—debridement—and now he is on a wound vac. Doc said that the wound should heal in about four to six weeks. I certainly hope so, because it has been quite a detriment to his recovery. I am certainly more than ready to move forward and get him back on his feet. Has been very frustrating for all of us.

I had a very nice surprise on Friday. Chris was cleaning her office for the big move and found an envelope with my name on it. She placed it in the interoffice mailer and when I opened it, I smiled—it was the dollar bill you and I signed right before my educational journey began! I guess I did win that bet—sorry I wasn't able to share that moment with you. I really do appreciate all the encouragement. I am grateful to be where I am today. Hoping to put my studies to good use.

Heard you are back at school, going for a Ph.D.—wow! I was asked to contemplate continuing my studies for a master's degree. Unfortunately for now, I will put that on hold until I can get my other affairs in order. That education has done wonders for my self-esteem, too. What a world of difference to actually have confidence in your abilities. Life followed by some home chores, so I'll close for now.

Talk to you soon!
Dawn

Engagement: The Study

"Engagement begins with me." Vizzuso

Abstract

The Patient Protection and Affordable Care Act of 2010 created an environment for health care reform by decreasing hospital reimbursement by $500 billion. Hospitals face a 27% decrease in profitability because of patient dissatisfaction. With an absence of leadership strategies, employee disengagement may decrease patient satisfaction and consumer loyalty. The purpose of this phenomenological study was to explore the lived experiences of health care leaders in their desire to design strategies to engage employees in order to provide better patient care. Improving patient care provides opportunities to capture new market shares, which increases sustainability of health care organizations. The research question guided inquiry to understand strategies health care leaders might implement in order to engage employees and enhance patient care. Expectancy theory shaped the conceptual framework of this study to explore the connection between employee motivation and personal expectations. Inquiry consisted of personal interviews with 23 leaders in health care. Data analysis occurred with a modified Van Kamm data analysis process, which entailed descriptive coding and sequential review of the interview transcripts. Member checks and data saturation ensured integrity of the data. The findings from these personal interviews led to four distinct leadership strategies that influence employee engagement. These strategies are (a) improving psychological commitment, (b) expectation realization, (c) trust actualization, and (d) reduction in the power distance of leadership. By applying employee engagement strategies, leaders influence patient care. This study contributes to social change by increasing healthcare quality for patients leading to a positive influence on medical care and societal health.

Section 1: Foundation of the Study

Health care reforms have led to financial uncertainty in health care organizations (Aslin, 2011). Leaders, physicians, and patients await changes in health care reimbursement practices that may lead to an economic shift from a focus on health care volume to value in health care (Bennett, 2012). With these new reimbursement guidelines, health care consumers have the ability to choose health care services based on price and quality metrics (Cassalty, 2011). This creates a competitive environment for health care organizations while decreasing the overall cost of health care (Aslin, 2011). Employee engagement and patient satisfaction now influence consumer loyalty (Albdour & Altarawneh, 2014). Patient dissatisfaction places the sustainability of health care organizations at risk (Bonias, Leggat, & Bartram, 2012).

Background of the Problem

Historically, health care delivery systems in the United States have lacked oversight in cost management and customer service (Aslin, 2011). In 2011, health care costs represented 12% of the gross national product (GNP) with no sign of cost reduction (Roehrig, 2011). Improving financial performance for health care organizations depends on cost containment, increased market share penetration, and improving the patient experience (Roehrig, 2011). The Patient Protection and Affordable Care Act, otherwise known as ACA by the federal government, creates an opportunity for health care reform and improvement in consumer health care experiences (Devore & Champion, 2011). The federal government created health care coverage for all citizens, which provided incentives for health care organizations to lower costs and improve the quality of care. Health care organizations that do not become customer-focused may be at risk of market share loss because health care consumers have choices and have become cost sensitive (Devore & Champion, 2011). Market share loss may also occur due to demand changes in health care delivery and decreases in the total cost of care (Lowe, 2012). Legacy operational processes and price insensitively creates an environment for market loss and health care consolidation (Devore & Champion, 2011).

Health care organizations face economic pressure to decrease cost while improving quality of care. The Baby Boomer segmentation, which represents the segment of the population born from 1946 to 1964, will increase the retirement population through 2029 (Chiesl, 2012). This will lead to a flood of educated consumers using health care. Health care leaders must provide high-quality services at the lowest possible cost or risk market erosion. Improved customer satisfaction and loyalty drives sustainability.

Meeting employee expectations positively affects employee motivation, which increases employee engagement and job effort (Lunenburg, 2011). These expectations trigger either personal satisfaction or dissatisfaction, and influence the emotional connection between employee satisfaction and organizational goals. Employee engagement is the connection between the emotional well-being of the employee and organizational commitment (Nasomboon, 2014). Employees who are positively engaged in their jobs are more likely to excel in their work; these satisfied employees perform and work well with patients, which can improve consumer satisfaction and loyalty (Dikkers, Jansen, De Lange, Vinkenburg, & Kooji, 2010). Emotional connectivity and employee engagement increase productivity, which improves profit margin and consumer satisfaction (Dikkers et al., 2010).

The role of employee engagement in health care is critical in maintaining quality care. Employees must engage patients at an emotional level to increase satisfaction and create an optimized patient experience (Wessel, 2012). Patients may face uncertainty, a lack of medical knowledge, financial insecurity, and life and death decisions when using health care services. These patient experiences may make it more difficult for health care workers to create a positive experience for the patients. Therefore, with the onset of new health care delivery options, it is important for health care organizations to engage their employees and provide a positive work environment that can lead to increased patient satisfaction.

Problem Statement

Hospitals are in a precarious position with declining reimbursement, eroding profit margins, and low patient satisfaction (Alrubaiee & Alkaaida, 2011). ACA reform may decrease hospital reimbursement by $500 billion from 2010 to 2020 (Petasnick, 2011), while low patient satisfaction may decrease profitability for hospitals by 27% (Alrubaiee & Alkaaida, 2011). As of 2013, Medicare paid out $850 million in incentive payments on an annual basis to hospitals that improve quality and patient satisfaction (Petrullo, Lamar, Nwankwo-Otti, Alexander-Mills, & Viola, 2013). Employee engagement, the display of commitment between employees and their work environment, can influence patient satisfaction (Hewison, Gale, Yeats, & Shapiro, 2013). The general business problem is that health care organizations face decreasing Medicare reimbursement funding due to low patient satisfaction. The specific business problem is that some health care leaders lack strategies to engage their employees in order to provide better patient care.

Purpose Statement

The purpose of this qualitative, phenomenological study was to explore the lived experiences of health care leaders in their desire to design strategies to engage employees in order to provide better patient care. The population for this study consisted of 23 health care leaders in Midwestern U.S. hospitals. This population was appropriate to this study because health care leaders influence health care employees.

This study may lead to positive social change by influencing the quality of health care services. Improving employee engagement may increase the likelihood of improving patient satisfaction, which directly influences financial stability of health care organizations while improving a manager's ability to lead (Alrubaiee & Alkaaida, 2011). Contributions to the business environment may involve improved sustainability of health care organizations.

Nature of the Study

This study was a qualitative, phenomenological exploration. A qualitative research method is a research strategy for exploring cognitive views, social interaction, and interpersonal perspectives (Moustakas, 1994). Uncovering personal experiences through the interview process provides researchers with a unique perspective on the participants' lived experiences (Moustakas, 1994). Qualitative research provides an opportunity to capture a wide diversity of population characteristics (Anyan, 2013). Through questionnaires, interviews, and focus groups, qualitative researchers provide data reflecting personal perspectives, experiences, and cultural backgrounds. A qualitative research design offered the best method to grasp the social impact of meeting employee expectations on an organizational level. For this study, the phenomenological design provided an opportunity to review and understand employee experience as it pertains to meeting employee expectations in a health care environment. The importance of gathering the personal experiences of the participants eliminated other designs. I did not consider grounded theory since my study would not generate or discover a theory. Case study design includes the entire group dynamic, but this may leave out the perspective of the individual (Yin, 2009). Ethnographic researchers focus on behaviors and language of culture, which were beyond the scope of my study (Sangasubana, 2011).

Quantitative researchers provide insight into correlations between variables (Frels & Onwuegbuzie, 2011). In my study, I focused on strategies necessary for health care leaders to improve employee engagement. Employee perspectives and experiences created a foundation for research analysis. However, quantitative researchers cannot provide a personal base of information, thus eliminating the use of a quantitative research approach.

Mixed method research includes a combination of aspects of quantitative and qualitative research in an attempt to answer how and what affects a topic (Heyvaert, Maes, & Onghena, 2011). Mixed method research is an extension of quantitative research and focuses on a complex matrix of variables and experiences (Heyvaert et al., 2011). The complexity of using both quantitative and qualitative methods was beyond the scope of my research intent, thus eliminating the use of the mixed method research process.

Research Question

The major research question in this study was: What strategies should health care leaders implement to engage employees and enhance patient care? Through a phenomenological study design, I analyzed the personal experiences of leaders to describe strategies that influenced employee engagement. Personal demographic, targeted research questions, and follow-up questions provided an opportunity for data collection and analysis.

Interview Questions

To develop initial rapport with the participants, I asked the following questions:

PQ1. What is your name?

PQ2. What is your job title?

PQ3. What is your age?

PQ4. How long have you been in the health care field?

PQ5. What is your educational background?

PQ6. How many jobs in health care have you had in your career?

PQ7. What do you do in your job?

PQ8. What does health care reform mean to you?

The following conceptual and follow-up questions related to the proposed research inquiry and formed part of the discussions.

C1. How do you define employee engagement?

C2. How does employee engagement affect the day-to-day operations of your department?

C3. What expectations do you have as an employee?

C4. How does your attitude affect you meeting employee expectations?

C5. How does your personal ownership of the workplace influence your performance as a leader?

C6. How does trust influence your employees' engagement within the organization?

C7. How does leadership influence engagement in your workplace?

C8. How is your motivation affected by your leader meeting your expectations?

Targeted follow-up questions were as follows:

C1F1. What examples do you have of employee engagement?

C1F2. What are the components of employee engagement that influence your employees?

C2F1. What are your key operational tasks?

C2F2. What are the specific drivers of employee engagement that influence the job tasks of your employees?

C3F1. What expectations do you have that are reasonable?

C3F2. What expectations do you have that are not reasonable?

C4F1. How can the attitudes of employees be improved?

C4F2. How can you improve your attitude to improve engagement?

C5F1. How do you improve your personal ownership of your work environment?

C6F1. How do you improve trust between you and your employees?

C6F2. How might a decrease in job security affect your engagement?

C7F1. How can your leadership skills improve the likelihood of meeting the expectations of your employees?

C8F1. How does communication affect your relationship with your supervisor?

C8F2. How does a strong interpersonal relationship with your employees affect your desire to meet organizational goals?

Conceptual Framework

The basis for this study was expectancy theory. Vroom developed the expectancy theory in 1965 in an attempt to understand personal motivation of people in the workplace (Lunenburg, 2011). According to expectancy theory, a relationship exists between personal effort, performance, and rewards (Bembenutty, 2012). Workers join organizations with expectations, make behavioral choices, and create life goal options to maximize personal outcomes (Faleye & Trahnan, 2011). Expectancy theory has associations with employee satisfaction and engagement. Influence from an environmental context, organizational culture, and social interactions affect employee expectations, which increases or decreases employee engagement (Chou & Pearson, 2012). The purpose of this qualitative, phenomenological study was to explore the lived experiences of health care leaders in their desire to design strategies to engage employees in order to provide better patient care.

Definition of Terms

Definitions create a basis for understanding the information contained in a doctoral study. In this definition section, I focus on health-care-related terms. However, some word meanings can be contextual.

Accountable care organization (ACO). ACO is an organization accepting reasonability for cost-savings programs in health care reform (Bennett, 2012).

Employee engagement. Employee engagement is the act of an employee emotionally connecting to the success of the organization (Nasomboon, 2014).

Expectancy theory. Vroom suggested that performance increases when workers understand the job requirements and predicted outcomes occur (Lunenburg, 2011).

Fee-for service. Fee-for-service is a reimbursement method that provides health care organizations with a fee per unit of service rendered (Bennett, 2012).

Psychological ownership. Psychological ownership is the ability of a person to take an ownership view of work related tasks (Avey et al., 2012)

Transformational leadership. Transformational leadership is a leadership style that focuses on positive feedback and interpersonal relationships, while recognizing follower performance and contribution (Yuan & Lin, 2012).

Assumptions, Limitations, and Delimitations

ASSUMPTIONS

In this study, assumptions included the thought that the influence of leadership on employee engagement plays an important role in increasing organizational productivity, efficiency, and financial success. A further assumption focused on improving employee engagement may create an environment for improving patient satisfaction in health care while participants view employee engagement as a positive driver for organizational performance. A final assumption was that all participants would respond to the interview questions in a forthright manner.

LIMITATIONS

The limitations of this study included (a) lack of ancillary stakeholders, (b) geographical limitations, and (c) shift variability. I focused on health care leaders. Ancillary stakeholders in health care such as commercial payers, suppliers, and vendors may provide perspectives on challenges in health care but will not be included in this study. Lack of ancillary stakeholder perspectives limited the scope of this study because their services may influence patient satisfaction and employee engagement. There were geographical limitations with the selected population. The sample size represented leaders from several health care organizations. This limits the ability to view perspectives from other organizations. Views and perspectives of the employees focused only on one employer.

An additional limitation was shift variability. Interview scheduling might have led to limited access to off shift workers. Hospitals operate day, evening, and midnight shifts of employees creating different work environments, which may create different employee experiences. These variations in experience may limit a complete understanding of the full range of employee expectations (Nasomboon, 2014).

DELIMITATIONS

Delimitations help clarify the focus of a study by indicating the areas that are included and excluded from the study. For example, a delimitation of this study was to select participants with direct patient care duties. This ensured that interview responses would provide data from employees who had influence on patient satisfaction. It is conceivable that employees without patient contact might provide different perspectives. The final delimitation was excluding employees with less than one year of service. Research was dependent upon reliable, credible, and accurate presentations of data from participants. This exclusion increased the likelihood that the participants had an understanding of the organization and a familiarization with the management team.

Significance of the Study

Understanding the impact of meeting employee expectations is necessary for improving the social impact of health care on patients. Many health care organizations fail to meet the requirements of consumers, which hampers service quality in health care (Angelova & Zekiri, 2011).

The findings of this study may contribute to positive social change by enhancing employee engagement and improving service quality in health care. In turn, this may improve medical outcomes.

VALUE TO BUSINESS

Employee engagement in health care provides value for businesses by improving profitability, productivity, and customer satisfaction (Marini, 2013). Improving patient satisfaction increases consumer loyalty while improving the quality of health care services. Improvements in financial performance provide value in improving shareholder return and organizational sustainability (Nasomboon, 2014).

CONTRIBUTION TO BUSINESS PRACTICE

Health care reform creates an environment in which consumers will have more choices on who provides their health care. With this competition among health care providers, health care organizations must find ways to ensure patient satisfaction to increase revenue for health care organizations. Increasing employee engagement and psychological ownership creates opportunities for organizations to improve their competitive advantage, gain market share, and improve patient satisfaction, as well as increase consumer loyalty. Improvement in engagement provides more opportunities for patient satisfaction (Lowe, 2012).

IMPLICATIONS FOR SOCIAL CHANGE

Employee engagement plays a role in supporting the continuum of care, which may improve patient satisfaction. Health care employees work in a unique continuum of care, being present from birth to death (Dorval, Rey, Soufflet, Halling, & Barthelemy, 2011). Consumers may emotionally connect with health care providers during life and death situations. In addition to better meeting patient needs, improving patient satisfaction may also increase financial stability in health care (Metha, 2011).

Successful health care organizations provide a wide range of services that meet the needs of the community. Low employee engagement may negatively affect the sustainability of health care organizations, which may decrease service offerings, limit access, and lower the quality of services (Lowe, 2012). Decreases in access and quality of care may have a negative influence on medical outcomes, which would impact society as a whole.

A Review of the Professional and Academic Literature

The purpose of this qualitative, phenomenological study was to explore the lived experiences of health care leaders in their desire to design strategies to engage employees in order to provide better patient care. Poor employee engagement may increase the likelihood of financial distress. The research question for this proposed research was: What strategies should health care leaders implement to engage employees and enhance patient care?

The literature review involved conducting content searches using a search strategy focused on Walden University Library Databases and Google Scholar by reviewing peer-reviewed journal submissions in the following health care databases: Business Source Compete, ABIFORM, Premier, and ProQuest. The following keywords guided database searches: *expectancy theory, psychological ownership, leadership, employee engagement, patient satisfaction,* and *hospital reform*. Research information from the literature review included articles from 124 academic journals. The review included 192 references (see Table 1). Of the 187 journal articles examined, 165 were peer-reviewed sources published within the last 3 to 5 years, representing 85.94% of the literature review (see Table 2).

Table 1

Subject Matter Review

References	Books	Journal Articles
Health Care Reform	1	27
Research	4	14
Leadership	0	34
Psychological Ownership	0	15
Expectancy Theory	0	7
Employee Engagement	0	52
Patient Satisfaction	0	38
Total	5	187

Table 2

Numbers of Sources for Literature Review

Category	Books	Peer Review 3-5 Years	Not Peer Reviewed	Total
Books	5	N/A	N/A	5
Journal Articles	N/A	165	22	187
Total	5	165	22	192

EXPECTANCY THEORY

Employees meet performance goals when organizations meet or exceed employee expectations. According to Vroom's expectancy theory, there is a link between effort and the expected outcome (Lunenburg, 2011). Organizations that meet employee expectations positively influence employee motivation (Faleye & Trahnan, 2011). Organizations have a duty to create a culture that provides an environment in which leaders can foster clear expectations for their employees (Faleye & Trahan, 2011).

Expectancy is an estimate of the effort that results in a desired level of performance (Lunenburg, 2011). Vroom suggested that motivation is the product of expectancy (Lunenburg, 2011). A collaborative culture creates an environment for clear communication and expectations (Spurgeon, Mazelan, & Barwell, 2011). An organization that does not promote a collaborative culture may not meet employee expectations.

Researchers applied the expectancy theory to study workplace motivation (Bembenutty, 2012). Westover, Westover, and Westover (2010) found that the work environment creates opportunities for both employee work motivation. Bembenutty (2012) found that students scored higher test results by focusing on understanding the expected goals, as opposed to those in the control group not having knowledge of the general expectations. When an individual understands and meets expectations, he or she is more likely to have increased engagement. Leaders who do not encourage goal setting with employees may negatively influence employee engagement and motivation (Bushra, Usman, & Naveed, 2011).

PSYCHOLOGICAL OWNERSHIP

Psychological ownership is the act of feeling emotional ownership of work tasks and responsibilities (Avey et al., 2012). Shuck, Rocco, and Albornoz (2011) commented that interpersonal relationships of the employees played a role in their emotional ownership or commitment to the organization. The leader-employee relationship plays a role in organizational commitment (Yuan & Lin, 2012).

Organizations should value fairness, respect, and emotional connectivity in the workplace (Avey et al., 2012). Psychological ownership occurs when the value of equity exceeds expectations (Avey et al., 2012). A high organizational value for equity, combined with respect for the employee's ideas, creates psychological ownership (Avey et al., 2012). Transformational leaders provide employees with the opportunity to communicate problems they are experiencing, or any other input within the workplace, which fosters psychological ownership (Yuan & Lin, 2012). Sieger, Zellweger, and Aquino (2013) suggested that a shared mindset among employees created the sense of ownership for the group. All employees in high-performing organizations experience psychological ownership collectively. The genesis of ownership feelings begins at the individual level. However, employees may experience difficulty with individual commitment and being motivated in their jobs without strong leadership, decreasing their likelihood of taking psychological ownership of their positions (Ghafoor, Qureshi, Kahn, & Hijazi, 2011).

Feelings of ownership emerge at the interpersonal level when there is personal motivation and self-identity with a job (Sieger et al., 2013). Work structure, job design, and improved communication create an environment that promotes psychological ownership. Bushra et al. (2011) believed that transformational leaders provided employees with vision, clear communication, and support. This created an environment in which to foster psychological commitment. When an employee feels psychological ownership, group dynamics converge to create a sense of possession and ownership of the environment, organization, and outcomes (Avey et al., 2012). Dollard and Bakker (2010) defined the personal safety climate (PSC) as policies, practices, and procedures for protecting workers' emotional wellbeing. An improved sense of security and a decreased risk of job loss influence employee psychological commitment (Nasomboon, 2014). Workers who feel anxiety about job loss are more likely disengaged from meeting expectations of the customers (Dollard & Bakker, 2010).

Increased PSC and an efficient organizational climate lead to employee engagement and psychological ownership. Organizations should allow employees to share their perceptions of organizational policies and procedures in an effort to create a safe emotional work climate (Dollard & Bakker, 2010). Shuck et al. (2011), however, claimed that the environmental climate alone does not create engagement. Shuck et al. looked for a correlation between resources, demands, psychological well-being, emotional exhaustion, and employee engagement and found that there was significant correlation between psychological stress and work demands with $p < .01$. Engagement can only happen when an employee and a leader create a safe climate together.

Power sharing between leaders and employees increases employee satisfaction and an employee's sense of control over his or her personal workspace. Psychological ownership and transformational leadership affect employee decision-making (Han, Chiang, & Chang, 2010). Transformational leaders can create an environment in which to increase employee motivation (Muchiri, Cooksey, & Walumbwa, 2012). A motivated employee is more likely to have a personal investment in the organization (Zhu, Chen, Li, & Zhou, 2013). Perceived ownership provides employees with an incentive to achieve successful results. Han et al. (2010) found that workers who felt psychological ownership demonstrated a positive association with the organizational commitment, $p < .01$. Individual informational sharing correlated with psychological ownership, organizational commitment, and personal knowledge with $p < .01$ (Han et al., 2010). Psychological ownership and transformational leaders positively influence overall employee attitudes and job performance.

Stewardship is the mental commitment from an employee to the company (Hernandez, 2012). According to the stewardship construct, psychological ownership influence behaviors that change the organizational governance from an agency model toward a stewardship model (Hernandez, 2012). Psychological ownership ultimately influences stewardship (Hernandez, 2012). Employees who are emotionally connected demonstrate stewardship to the organization. Stewardship leads to improved engagement between the employee and the organization (Caspi & Blau, 2011).

Emotional connectivity increases the likelihood of improved consumer loyalty. There is a relationship between psychological capital, employee engagement, and organizational identity (Liu, Wang, Hui, & Lee, 2012). Lowe (2012) suggested that employee engagement created opportunities for improved customer-supplier relationships. Psychological capital is the ability of an employee to develop emotional ownership of his or her job (Liu et al., 2012). Psychological capital and organizational identity influence positive organizational behavior (Liu et al., 2012). However, employee deviance can affect psychological capital and organizational identity (Baumard, Andre, & Sperber, 2013). Organizational performance and positive behavior ultimately result from the attitudes and personal choices of the employee. Rothmann and Welsh (2013) studied the psychological conditions for employee engagement in the developing country of Namibia. Rothmann and Welsh found that work-role fit, job satisfaction, and available resources affected employee engagement through psychological availability. Work engagement improves customer loyalty, employee productivity, and profitability (Rothmann & Welsh, 2013). Psychological commitment is the first step in the process of employee engagement.

LEADERSHIP

Transformational leadership. There is a connection between transformational leadership, employee engagement, and employee performance (Ghafoor et al., 2011). Transformational leaders meet the needs of employees by offering employee incentives for meeting organizational goals. Psychological ownership creates belongingness, self-identity, and responsibility at a personal level, while transformational leaders provide a foundation of trust, expectations, and an environment for psychological ownership (Avey et al., 2012). A relationship exists between transformational leadership and employee engagement (Krishnan, 2012). Transformational leaders develop a connection with their employees, encouraging employees to become engaged in their jobs. Mozes, Josman, and Yaniv (2011) suggested personal responsibility was an essential part of employee motivation, regardless of environmental situations. Ineffective leadership influences engagement, but employees still have a social responsibility to meet job expectations (Mesu, Riemsdijk, & Sanders, 2013). Transformational leaders influence work engagement over time (Warrick, 2011). An increase in employee engagement influences service performance, productivity, and improved customer relations (Simola, Barling, & Turner, 2012). Improvement in customer relationships leads to customer loyalty.

A leader's most valuable commodity is his or her ability to engage employees (Bushra et al., 2011). Transformational leaders promote employee commitment and respect. Employees treated with respect feel more attached to the organization (Bushra et al., 2011). Welch (2011) determined increased company communications influenced employee engagement, creating opportunities for building trust between employees and senior leadership (Bushra et al., 2011). Bushra et al. (2011) used a Likert-like scale questionnaire consisting of 35 items designed to measure the effect of trends from transformational leadership on employee engagement and found that transformational leadership had a positive impact on job satisfaction in the commitment of employees. Decreased job risk and fear fosters psychological ownership (Dollard & Bakker, 2010). Transformational leaders create an environment to enhance interpersonal relationships and psychological ownership (Birasnav, Rangnekar, & Dalpati, 2011).

Transformational leaders influence employee engagement at the interpersonal level, which includes increased empathy, interpersonal relationships, and effective communication (Tims, Bakker, & Xanthopoulou, 2011). Psychological empowerment creates higher employee engagement (Karkoulian, Mukaddam, McCarthy, & Messarra, 2013). Leadership has the responsibility for the development of a stable emotional work domain. Day-level transformational leadership has a significant, positive correlation with work engagement and optimism of employees (McKnight, 2013). Overall, transformational leaders have a positive effect on employee engagement.

Other leadership attributes. New age leaders should understand and shape employee engagement, shareholder perceptions, and customer requirements (Baird & Gonzalez-Wertz, 2011). Organizations focusing on understanding consumer insights in the digital era have value in a virtual marketplace. Leadership styles should align with the mission of the organization (Darbi, 2012). Centered leaders create a mission for innovation and organizational adaptability. New business models should include business units focused on the changing demands of consumers, information relevance, and innovation (Meng & Berger, 2011). Effective leadership provides vision and direction for market-driven development (Souba, 2011).

Middle-manager leadership is crucial to the overall success of health care organizations (Birken, Lee, & Weiner, 2012). Effective leadership creates positive team environments (Guay, 2013). Middle management should use senior leadership approaches in everyday work duties (Birken et al., 2012). Darbi (2012) suggested that successful leadership at all levels in an organization should include a focus on both the mission and vision statements, which created a culture of accountability. Middle managers work closer with frontline employees (Birken et al., 2012). With this proximity, middle managers have the opportunity to create strong work-related relationships. The relationship between a middle manager and his or her employees affects employee engagement.

Authentic leaders influence the engagement of employees (Nichols & Erakovich, 2013). Leaders balance moral perspectives with interpersonal relationships to create a dynamic leadership personality. Improved employee engagement is a by-product of the direct relationship with leadership (Lowe, 2012). Authentic leaders focus on improving interpersonal relationships (Nichols & Erakovich, 2013). Proactive leaders positively influence work engagement and increase an employee's sense of empowerment (Nichols & Erakovich, 2013). Authentic leadership plays a role in ensuring work engagement and empowerment (Nichols & Erakovich, 2013).

Ethical leaders support the development of task importance, job autonomy, and job performance (Krishnan, 2012). A leader with a strong moral center can enhance employee engagement and job performance (Kottke & Pelletier, 2013). Employees with ethical leaders are more likely to place more effort into their jobs, leading to better job performance (Krishnan, 2012). Leaders with an ethical code of conduct influence employee engagement by developing trust (Den Hartog & Belschak, 2012).

Ethical leaders offer personal initiatives to their employees (Den Hartog & Belschak, 2012). Ethical leadership is the expression of a moral identity. Ethical leaders send clear messages to followers and stand by an internal code of ethics, which may make an employee more engaged with the organization (Den Hartog & Belschak, 2012). Employee engagement is a strategic objective for organizations (Lowe, 2012). Improved employee engagement leads to increased financial performance. Ethical leaders have the ability to influence the engagement of employees (Derr, 2012).

Employee Engagement

Stakeholder development. Communication plays a role in employee engagement (Welch, 2011). The focus on employee engagement developed over time through interval waves. The first wave of engagement occurred in 1980 where businesses examined the need to engage employees in organizations (Welch, 2011). During the second wave, (1990-1999) academics began defining employee engagement as a movement to promote employee satisfaction and organizational success (Welch, 2011). In Wave 3 (2000-2007), researchers defined how an engaged employee could lead to increased productivity, which results in decreased costs and an improved the financial foundation for organizations (Welch, 2011). The ability of leadership to communicate effectively creates a basis for employee engagement. Ghafoor et al. (2011) defined engagement as a positive psychological attitude. Transformational leaders support this approach to improve engagement.

Psychological engagement begins at the board of director leadership level within organizations (Guerrero & Seguin, 2012). The board of directors should provide motivation for the management of the organization. Guerrero and Seguin (2012) examined engagement at the board level and found that organizational motivation achievement, self-motivation, identification, and engagement had a significant relationship to achievement.

Employees, leadership, and shareholders should hold a general interest in the stability and success of the organization (Adelman, 2012). Faleye and Trahan (2011) examined the relationship between stakeholders and shareholders and found that the creation of business-friendly environments promoted improved relationships. Leaders created a psychologically safe workplace, which creates a culture of psychological ownership and engagement (Dollard & Bakker, 2010). The ultimate goal should be a focus on improving shareholder return while improving the stakeholder's work life.

According to the stakeholder theory, stakeholder and shareholder relationships are necessary for creating value for the corporation (Faleye & Trahan, 2011). Faleye and Trahan (2011) reviewed four measures of operating performance: employee productivity, firm-level factor productivity, return on assets, and Tobin's q. Faleye and Trahan found that return on assets increased from 2.15% to 3.89% over a 4-year period because of increased productivity in a labor-friendly environment. Employee engagement provides a return on investment for shareholders while increasing the prospect of sustainability (Nasomboon, 2014).

Employee engagement influence on outcomes. Employee engagement is the individual's feeling of satisfaction and enthusiasm in work-related activities for the organization (Nasomboon, 2014). There is a statistical correlation between high employee engagement and improvements in productivity, profitability, and job satisfaction (Nasomboon, 2014). Job involvement and trust are the primary determinants of organizational effectiveness (Nasomboon, 2014). Trust in expectations creates employee motivation (Swarnalatha & Prasanna, 2013). Problems arise in employee engagement when there is dysfunctional leadership and dissatisfaction with the workplace.

Employees dissatisfied in their work domain produce less and may have decreased customer service skills. The work environment can affect employee job satisfaction and engagement (Westover et al., 2010). Work domains should be places where employees can build trust and communication without fear of losing their job (Dollard & Bakker, 2010). Satisfied employees support the mission of the company. Westover et al. (2010) used an ordinary leased square correlation with descriptive statistics to examine employee satisfaction and commitment and confirmed a statically valid connection between work domain and employee satisfaction. Organizational trust, passion, and gender had a relationship with $p < .01$ (Westover et al., 2010).

Employee engagement has a U-shaped relationship with job requirements and demands (Sawang, 2011). Job demands place stressors on employees. Companies need to have healthy environments to improve employee satisfaction while achieving organizational goals. Karkoulian et al. (2013) suggested job demands combined with job insecurity created difficulties in engagement. Significant correlations exist between psychological empowerment, job demand, job insecurity, and employee engagement. Social drivers and work demands are predictors of higher engagement (Sawang, 2012). However, the longer the employee works, the more likely their relationship is going to erode, which suggests that trust fades with tenure. Employee engagement is the ability to harness emotionally cognitive attributes to improve organizational performance. Consistent and honest communication is an essential requirement for employees (Sawang, 2012). Leader-follower relationships affect levels of engagement in an organization (Shuck et al., 2011). Changes in employee empowerment, recognition, and training affect employee engagement.

Employee engagement positively influences business outcomes (Hynes, 2012). Hynes (2012) claimed that improved communication and interpersonal relationships between leaders and employees provided a foundation that fostered engagement. Nasomboon (2014) suggested increased communication and employee empowerment increased employee engagement. Increased engagement positively influences organizational performance and psychological ownership (Nasomboon, 2014). Leaders must identify skills that influence employee performance and engagement, such as interpersonal communication, flexibility, corporate culture, team skills, and proactive problem solving (Hynes, 2012). The organization should develop training programs focused on improving these elements. Employees who enroll in this training program experience improved engagement levels. Coca-Cola's leadership believed that engaged frontline employees influenced customers daily (Fritz, Kaestner, & Bergmann, 2010). Coca-Cola's leaders invested capital funds and technology to improve the on-boarding process for new employees. Kompaso and Sridevi (2010) determined engaged employees have an emotional connection with the organization. Increased emotional connections influence consumer satisfaction. Learning solutions create opportunities for frontline employees to understand communication tactics, vision collaboration, and self-study (Kompaso & Sridevi, 2010).

Employees who interact with customers must have a sense of engagement with the organization to be effective (Slatten & Mehmetoglu, 2011). Job autonomy, role benefit, and strategic attention influence employee engagement (Slatten & Mehmetoglu, 2011). Garg (2014) examined additional factors that influence engagement in frontline workers. Slatten and Mehmetoglu (2011) found employee engagement had a positive correlation with strategic awareness with a path correlation of .250, while innovation behavior had a positive correlation of .636. Companies that stressed role importance had better employee engagement.

Individuals who take the initiative for improving their current situations create new learning environments (Sieger et al., 2013). Organizations that focus on interpersonal attitudes allow psychological ownership to take hold, grow, and develop into a team-oriented mentality (Sieger et al., 2013). The Dutch government examined a proactive personality as it relates to employee engagement and job demands and found that a proactive personality increased employee engagement after an 18-month interval (Dikkers et al., 2010). Employees with improved social support demonstrate higher engagement scores. An employee with a proactive personality defines his or her job demands, while improving his or her engagement (Dikkers et al., 2010).

Joint goal setting and understanding of on-the-job requirements provides a foundation for a positive relationship. Employee engagement in a recognized organization, known as a preferred employer, demonstrates improved worker productivity (Shuck et al., 2011). Management should encourage open lines of communication, employee recognition, and goal setting (Shuck et al., 2011). Rashid, Asad, and Ashraf (2011) demonstrated that the manager-employee relationship influenced job satisfaction and engagement. The leader-employee relationship plays a role within the organization. Leadership philosophy and hiring practices create an environment for employee engagement.

Workplace interpersonal injustice and workplace deviance negatively affects employee engagement (Cheng, Huang, Li, & Hsu, 2011). Low self-esteem can also affect the attitude of employees. Nasomboon (2014) suggested that engagement had a direct relationship with improved organizational performance. Decreased employee morale influences engagement. Cheng et al. (2011) found a negative relationship between daily interpersonal injustice and workplace defiance, while daily interpersonal injustice had a negative relationship with self-esteem. Overall, increased interpersonal injustice decreases self-esteem and increases workplace deviance (Cheng et al., 2011). Real or perceived unfairness between employees leads to employee disengagement outcomes (Cheng et al., 2011).

Improved employee development strengthened employee engagement and work performance. Pendleton and Robinson (2011) examined the relationship between employee shared ownership and employee development. Service quality influences patient satisfaction (Metha, 2011). Service quality depends on employee engagement and employee psychological ownership improves the likelihood of employee satisfaction (Metha, 2011). Pendleton and Robinson claimed that involvement in ownership plans influences employee training. Improved training increases the likelihood of employee satisfaction and engagement. In direct focus groups, Granatino, Verkamp, and Parker (2013) demonstrated that service training increased engagement to 77% and increased customer satisfaction to 82%. Improved engagement has a direct effect on customer satisfaction.

There is a relationship between employee satisfaction and increased efficiencies (Fearon, McLaughlin, & Morris, 2013). Satisfied employees decrease labor costs, increase efficiency, and influence customer satisfaction (Abel, 2013). Fair compensation, available resources, and fair treatment influence employee satisfaction (Abel, 2013). Ghadi, Fernando, and Mulla (2013) suggested leadership plays a role in employee satisfaction.

Trust influences interpersonal leader-employee relationships, which leads to improved communication, work performance, and employee retention (Xu & Thomas, 2011). Organizations must create strategic objectives focused on increasing employee satisfaction and engagement. Transformational leaders provide an effective environment that fosters inspirational motivation, which increases employee engagement (Abel, 2013). These leaders focus on improving employee relationships and building trust.

Improved operational efficiency occurs when employees engage (Lee, Lee, & Kang, 2012). Companies that provide a high quality of service create consumer loyalty. Lee et al. (2012) demonstrated a significant relationship with $p < .01$ for an efficient relationship with an employee's well-being, a positive influence on service quality, and customer loyalty. Kompaso and Sridevi (2010) suggested meeting employee expectations provided the best opportunity to increase engagement. Engagement directly influences operational performance.

Sutharjana, Thoyib, Taroena, and Rahayu (2013) described organizational citizenship behavior (OCB) as positive personal behaviors that supported the mission of the organization and service quality. OCB has a relationship with service quality, while service quality has a positive relationship with patient satisfaction and loyalty (Sutharjana et al., 2013). OCB directly affects service quality, which improves the overall patient experience. Self-motivated employees have organizational attitudes, leading to better outcomes (Shahid & Azhar, 2013).

Motivation. Many people work to feel motivated and satisfied (Abadi, Jalilvand, Sharif, Ali Salimi, & Khanzadeh, 2011). Improved training techniques can affect employee motivation, increasing employee satisfaction. Shorbaji, Messarra, and Karkoulian (2011) examined the correlation between the Core-Self Evaluation (CSE) instrument and employee engagement. CSE is useful when examining how self-esteem plays a part in employee engagement. In a three-part survey answered by 150 people focused on aspects of CSE and employee engagement, Shorbaji et al. (2011) found that individuals with high CSE scores for self-esteem demonstrated high employee engagement. Kompaso and Sridevi (2010) also described a significant correlation between employee engagement and the organizational citizenship of the employee. As employee self-respect increases, so does the organizational commitment (Kompaso & Sridevi, 2010). Employees with higher self-esteem, self-efficacy, and an internal focus are more satisfied with their organizations (Kompaso & Sridevi, 2010).

Corporate social responsibility (CSR) influences employee engagement, satisfaction, and motivation. CSR is the business of monitoring corporate compliance with ethical standards (Mozes et al., 2011). Eisele, Grohnert, Beausaert, and Segers (2013) examined intrinsic motivation and employee engagement. Employees committed and engaged improve operational performance. Intrinsic motivations develop within a contextual environment (Eisele et al., 2013). Employees who have a sense of pride have an increased personal motivation to succeed. Improving motivation creates opportunities to better employee engagement (Eisele et al., 2013). CSR is important for ensuring ethical behavior and connects integrity with personal actions (Mozes et al., 2011). Psychological connections create employee commitment and improved employee motivation that enhanced the culture of the company (Van Rooy, Whitmen, Hart, & Caleo, 2011). Motivational drivers included skill use, relationship to leadership, work duties, meaningfulness, and job flexibility (Van Rooy et al., 2011). Meaningfulness of work and self-worth influenced employees' overall motivation improves CSR.

The manager-employee relationship is necessary to foster employee satisfaction and engagement. Performance management influences employee engagement and motivation (Mone, Eisinger, Guggenheim, Price, & Stine, 2011). Performance awareness provides an environment for setting goals, expectations, recognition, and development (Mone et al., 2011). Understanding expectation and relationship requirements provided a solid foundation for employee engagement (Mone et al., 2011). Lunenburg (2011) found a link between expectancy theory attributes and positive employee motivation. Motivated employees who understand expectations met goals and became more engaged in the organization (Robertson, Birch, & Cooper, 2012).

Human resource activities such as performance appraisals influence employee engagement (Jose, 2012). Jose (2012) suggested the social exchange theory described the process of social exchanges between parties in an effort to create and foster relationships. These social exchanges affected employee engagement because interpersonal relationships affected attitude and commitment (Jose, 2012). In 2011, 90,000 workers from India took an employee engagement survey with only 21% demonstrating positive engagement (Jose, 2012). Overall, engagement is declining globally by 4% on an annual basis (Jose, 2012). Bushra et al. (2011) dismissed workplace influences on engagement because direct leadership drove engagement. Leaders of organizations must develop sound human resources functions. These functions create a foundation for communication and trust.

Non-health care employee engagement. Coca-Cola employs more than 73,000 people on an international basis (Fritz et al., 2010). Employee engagement was a major issue for Coca-Cola due to the size and logistics of the employee base (Fritz et al., 2010). The hiring process of Coca-Cola failed to provide the necessary information on expectations creating disengagement. The Coca-Cola management changed the on-boarding process by providing peer-coaching support for new employees. The learning process focused on reinforcing learning through reflection while increasing the knowledge base. The on-boarding process does not end after employment but continues with support from leadership. The onboarding process lowered training costs and increased employee retention rates. Increased employee turnover increases organizational cost and decreases employee productivity (Chat-Uthai, 2013).

In 2007, 58% of Ritz-Carlton employees lacked engagement in the success of the organization (Gallup, 2007; Timmerman, 2009). Ritz-Carlton developed an approach to leverage employee engagement (Timmerman, 2009). Leadership fostered an environment that inspired vision, stimulated ideas, and touted ideas for effectiveness. Ritz-Carlton developed employee focus groups to concentrate on increasing employee engagement and innovation. These focus groups described drivers that influenced employee engagement. Employees suggested that empowerment, use of best practices, leadership involvement, and inspiring vision influenced employee engagement (Erkutlu & Chafra, 2013).

The Gap is an international retailer that focused on employee and stakeholder engagement in an attempt to increase sustainability and social responsibility (Smith, Ansett, & Erez, 2011). Increased stakeholder engagement directly influenced economic performance (Smith et al., 2011). Stakeholder engagement created opportunities to improve trust, communication, and political influence (Smith et al., 2011). Lack of supplier engagement resulted in reduced labor results, environmental pollution, and tarnished company image (Smith et al., 2011). The Gap developed an engagement strategy by creating objectives such as developing leadership collaboration, resolving material problems, and increasing transparency. This created an increased level of stakeholder engagement.

Employee engagement is the act of an employee or group becoming more enthusiastic and passionately committed to the best interests of the organization (Vaijayanthi, Shreenivasan, & Prabhakaran, 2011). Sieger et al. (2013) suggested that psychological ownership existed in a group setting, and groups of employees created a positive influence on engagement. Vaijayanthi et al. (2011) studied the effects of employee engagement at General Electric (GE) Water and Process Technologies. Personal interviews and self-reflection questionnaires provided a method to collect data (Vaijayanthi et al., 2011). The results demonstrated a significant relationship with $p < .001$ between engagement and specific drivers (Vaijayanthi et al., 2011). Drivers included communication, workforce management, work environment, accountability, and lack of training (Vaijayanthi et al., 2011).

There is a relationship between employee engagement and financial performance in the banking industry in Pakistan (Rashid et al., 2011). Researchers used a five-part Likert-like scale questionnaire and structured equation modeling to survey 250 bank employees (Rashid et al., 2011). The instrument included topics of engagement, training, positive reinforcement, and development. There is a powerful connection between employee involvement and performance reward systems with $p < .001$ (Rashid et al., 2011). A significant correlation exists between employee appraisals and training with $p < .05$ (Rashid et al., 2011). Recognition and rewards supported expectations of employees while increasing personal motivation (Ugah, 2011). Employees perceived engagement as a positive factor in the profitability of the organization.

Employee engagement in health care. Improving engagement increases employee satisfaction, which directly improves patient satisfaction (Spurgeon et al., 2011). Medical engagement is a critical part of operational performance in health care (Spurgeon et al., 2011). Medical engagement decreases mortality ratios, raises safety standards, and improves medical outcomes (Freeney & Fellenz, 2013). Spurgeon et al. (2011) reviewed a systematic approach and found that engagement-improved performance. The main thrust of engagement is in the hands of the stakeholders of the organization (Guerrero & Seguin, 2012).

There is a connection between patient satisfaction and employee engagement (Gemmel & Verleye, 2010). More than 1,000 patients and employees took a survey, which demonstrated strong emotional connections within a health care organization (Gemmel & Verleye, 2010). This emotional connection created increased loyalty from both patients and employees (Gemmel & Verleye, 2010). Jose (2012) suggested the emotional bond between the employee and customer created long-term sustainability for organizations. Employee engagement delivers the necessary drivers to create consumer and employee loyalty.

Customer-organization linkage is the degree of loyalty between a service organization and their customer base (Handa & Gulati, 2014). Customers and employees share common drivers of pride, integrity, confidence, and emotional attachment (Gemmel & Verleye, 2010). Correlation for employees demonstrated that confidence significantly connected to integrity with $p = .000$ (Gemmel & Verleye, 2010). The trust and confidence between patients who had prior contact with the hospital versus those new to the system was not significant (Gemmel & Verleye, 2010). This suggested that the hospital delivered a less-than-optimal patient experience. Granatino et al. (2013) developed a secret shopping method designed to measure employee engagement in health care. Employee engagement and satisfaction directly affected the effort of the employee (Granatino et al., 2013). Welch (2011) ascertained that good communication created opportunities for employee empowerment and engagement. Feedback information pathways develop leader-employee trust.

Work environment, job characteristics, and organizational support increase with employee engagement (Lowe, 2012). Employee engagement is a strategic goal for health care organizations (Lowe, 2012).

Nasomboon (2014) demonstrated the connection between meeting customer expectations and increased consumer satisfaction. Employees consistently met expectations when engagement existed (Timms, Brough, & Graham, 2012). Lowe (2012) surveyed health care workers on several dimensions of engagement drivers, which built a unique engagement scale. Low engagement employees represented 33% of the sample total with 39% in the medium range of engagement (Lowe, 2012). High levels of engagement correlated with high increases in service quality, which directly influenced patient satisfaction (Springer, Clark, Strohfus, & Belcheir, 2012). Increased employee engagement directly influenced improvement in organizational performance (Lowe, 2012).

Low engagement decreases worker productivity and lowered profitability. Burnout and high work volume negatively affect employee engagement (Poulsen, Poulsen, Khan, Poulsen, & Khan, 2011). One-third of the workers surveyed reported significant burnout and decreased engagement (Poulsen et al., 2011). Spurgeon et al. (2011) demonstrated that decreased engagement negatively affects an organization. Survey data provided insight into the drivers of burnout (Poulsen et al., 2011). These drivers included shift work, 40-hour-plus workweeks, and marital status. Health care organizations can create better work environments to decrease burnout and improve employee engagement.

Patient-centered health care can create an improved patient experience by placing the patient in the center of the health care process. Nursing experienced a gap between engaged and disengaged employees; leadership influenced this gap (Rivera, Fitzpatrick, & Boyle, 2011).

Nursing engagement directly affected the patient experience in this process. Nurse longevity has a significant relationship with engagement with $p < .001$ (Rivera et al., 2011). Shift, manager, and tenure at the hospital all had significant relationships with nursing engagement with $p < .01$ (Rivera et al., 2011). Improved engagement created an environment for better care by focusing resources on the patient experience.

Psychological empowerment was important to both nurses and patients (Rivera et al., 2011). Purdy, Laschinger, Finegan, Kerr, and Olivera (2010) used a multilevel study questionnaire to collect data from 679 nurses and 1000 patients. Researchers focused on work and patient environments (Purdy et al., 2010). Opportunity for personal development, work challenge, and employee empowerment influences overall structural employee empowerment (Purdy et al., 2010). Avey et al. (2012) described psychological ownership as the feeling of ownership over the work domain and environment. Psychological ownership motivates employees to strive to achieve both personal and organizational goals.

Ideals of change such as communication, vision, urgency, and collaboration create opportunities for employees to engage in meaningful ways (Gerst, 2013). There is a connection between engagement in health care and aspects of change in management (Bleicher et al., 2012). Leadership roles within a hospital setting connected with the development of engagement (Bleicher et al., 2012). A review of top talent identified the top three employees from a salary perspective who had the biggest challenges of engagement (Bleicher et al., 2012). Darbi (2012) suggested leadership has a direct role in promoting a healthy work environment. Organizational leaders went through an eight-step process to improve change management and goal setting (Bleicher et al., 2012). Overall, operational performance and patient satisfaction increased in these areas (Bleicher et al., 2012). Leadership influences the opportunities for increasing the likelihood of improved employee empowerment.

Strong leadership creates an atmosphere of trust. According to Shuck et al. (2011), an atmosphere of trust created positive employee engagement, which all minimized a negative personality influence. Health care executives, patients, providers, and health care employees provide a wide range of views on employee engagement in health care (Luxford, Safran, & Delbanco, 2011). Interview groups focused on aspects of information that included technology, engagement, service delivery, communication, and work environment (Luxford et al., 2011). Luxford et al. (2011) identified several characteristics that create a patient-centered environment. These attributes focused on strong senior leadership, clear communication, active employees, engagement, focus on staff satisfaction, and patient satisfaction. The primary goal for health care organizations is to focus on transforming from provider-focused care to patient-centered care.

PATIENT SATISFACTION

Patient-centered care. Attention to the feelings of the patient results in an increase in patient satisfaction (Blakley, Kroth, & Gregson, 2011). Patient-centered care meets the emotional needs of the individual by placing the patient first (Pelzang, 2010). This care methodology started with engagement from the board of directors and the senior leadership of health care organizations. Senior leadership created the vision of patient-centered care and clearly communicated employee requirements in the delivery of care (Andrew & Sofian, 2011). Health care organizations created supportive work groups, measurable benchmarks, and focused on service quality (Pelzang, 2010). Lack of employee resources, miscommunication, and low employee engagement creates barriers to implementation of a patient-centered care model (Pelzang, 2010).

Stakeholders in a primary care practice should focus on creating educational models focused on improving patient awareness. Patient-centered care begins with the primary care practice setting (Farin & Nagl, 2013). Communication creates the ability to make emotional connections with patients (Tims et al., 2011). Improvements in communication, outreach services, and service quality provide a basis for patient compliance to medical treatment plans. The physician-patient relationship improves the opportunity for improving care (Farin & Nagl, 2013). Communication skills on both sides of the physician-patient relationship improve the likelihood of emotional connectivity. Improving the care plan significantly improves medical outcomes.

Strong leadership is necessary for transitioning to a patient-centered care model. Patient-centered delivery health care systems rely on delivering all services based on the needs of the patient (Cliff, 2012). Historically, delivery systems focused on operations around providers and hospital systems. Transition to patient-centered care creates a cultural shift in health care systems (Cliff, 2012). The nucleus of the patient experience centers on employee engagement (Needham, 2012). Employee engagement creates an environment that fostered consumer satisfaction.

In 2011, the Institute for Healthcare Improvement focused on understanding drivers that transform health care into a patient centric model (Cliff, 2012). Leadership, communication, and employee engagement created the best possibility to change to the new paradigm. Patient satisfaction flourished in the patient-centered design (Cliff, 2012). Cliff (2012) concluded that the key factor to achieve a patient-centered experience is the ability of leadership to establish a patient centric culture. Patient centered design places the patient in the center of the hospital operational focus with the intention of meeting the consumer's requirements (Cliff, 2012).

Service quality. High valued services in health care organizations positively influence financial sustainability (Angelova & Zekiri, 2011). Increased patient satisfaction increases profitability in hospitals (Shoemaker, 2010). This connection occurred regardless of medical outcome. Improved customer satisfaction facilitated volume growth and improved profitability (Shoemaker, 2010). Researchers collected data based on customer expectations, satisfaction degree, and comparison to similar services (Angelova & Zekiri, 2011). One-sample t test demonstrated $p < .05$, which reflected the significance of the relationship between satisfaction and customer expectations, while service quality had a significant relationship to customer expectations with $p < .001$ (Angelova & Zekiri, 2011).

Drivers of service quality in patient satisfaction are empathy, response, access, and safety; these drivers influence the perception of service quality for patients (Atta, 2012). Degrees of service quality influence patient satisfaction (Atta, 2012). Improved service quality created opportunities to influence consumer behavior (Leicht, Honekamp, & Ostermann, 2013). Shuck et al. (2011) determined that engaged employees consistently met key drivers that increased consumer satisfaction and improved service quality. Improved consumer satisfaction increases the likelihood of increased consumer loyalty (Detsky & Shaul, 2013). There is a distinct relationship between service quality and customer satisfaction with $p < .01$ while responsiveness, safety, empathy, and facilitations all had a significant relationship to service quality with $p < .01$ (Atta, 2012). Service quality was a key driver in influencing patient satisfaction.

Metha (2011) focused research resources on attempting to find a correlation between service quality and patient satisfaction. Patient satisfaction had a better correlation with service quality than the degree of the medical outcome (Shoemaker, 2010). Patient satisfaction related to meeting the expectations of the patient (Metha, 2011). Patients and employees shared common drivers that overlapped between satisfaction and engagement (Lowe, 2012). Metha used regression modeling between patient satisfaction and service quality. The sample size consisted of 400 patients in a hospital located in India (Metha, 2011). Promptness of service had the highest total variance of 35.738, while drivers such as problems with emotional handling, courtesy, response to questions, and physician availability all scored high (Metha, 2011). Overall linear regression demonstrated $p < .001$ between patient satisfaction and service quality (Metha, 2011). Collaboration between employee engagement and service quality provides a stable environment for improved patient satisfaction (Yousapronpaiboon & Johnson, 2013).

In Bahrain, service quality and patient satisfaction had an interesting relationship (Ramez, 2012). Ramez (2012) focused on the behavioral intentions of patients. A sample of 235 patients participated in a survey questionnaire that collected data about the patients' perceptions and insights (Ramez, 2012). Insights from the surveys revealed relationships between tangibles, reliability, responsiveness, and empathy.

Engaged employees demonstrate skills that affected overall service quality (Storch, Makaroff, Pauly, & Newton, 2013). Improved service quality increased consumer satisfaction (Slatten & Mehmetoglu, 2011). There were significant differences between service quality and the four insights (Ramez, 2012). Responsiveness had the biggest impact with a coefficient value of .364, while service quality had a significant correlation with patient satisfaction and a correlation value of .779 (Ramez, 2012). Improved patient satisfaction increases the likelihood of consumer loyalty and organizational profitability.

Service quality influences patient satisfaction and loyalty (Ramez, 2012). Service quality, customer satisfaction, and customer loyalty interconnect with each other (Chahal & Kumari, 2011). More than 400 inpatients answered survey-structured questions through a personal contact approach (Chahal & Kumari, 2011). Chahal and Kumari (2011) used structured equation modeling for data interpretation. Physical environment, expertise of the staff, and communication provided a significant relationship to consumer satisfaction and loyalty (Chahal & Kumari, 2011). Improvements in the physical environment and improved service quality give the best opportunity for increasing consumer loyalty and satisfaction (Chahal & Kumari, 2011).

Patient satisfaction can be a vague ill-defined concept with low validity, reliability, and standardization (Amin & Nasharuddin, 2013). Amin and Nasharuddin (2013) reviewed aspects of patient satisfaction research and literature in an attempt to compare patient satisfaction with service quality. Amin and Zahora compared and contrasted patient satisfaction theories on aspects of service quality and focused on patient satisfaction perception versus service quality issues. The correlation between patient satisfaction and quality of care is vague.

Health care organizations continue to focus on patient satisfaction rather than improving aspects of perceived service quality issues (Shannon, 2013). Alrubaiee and Alkaaida (2011) described health care quality as the perceived quality of care by patients. This perceived quality focused on metrics of communication, respect, cost, and empathy but not medical outcomes. Improved patient satisfaction leads to improved financial performance (Alrubaiee & Alkaaida, 2011).

Improvement in quality and service offerings increases the likelihood of improved patient satisfaction (Irfan & Ijaz, 2011). There was a difference between quality and patient satisfaction of public and private health care systems in Pakistan (Irfan & Ijaz, 2011). Improved service quality perceptions increased the likelihood of improved patient satisfaction

(Irfan & Ijaz, 2011). Empathy had a significant relationship with p < .000 in the private sector hospitals while public sector hospitals demonstrated p < .000 for tangible benefits for quality service (Irfan & Ijaz, 2011). Private hospitals provided more assurance in service quality and timeliness of services with p < .000 (Irfan & Ijaz, 2011). Private hospital systems in Pakistan created a better environment for overall service quality.

Drivers of patient satisfaction. There is variability in the drivers of the patient health care experience (Holzer & Minder, 2011). Holzer and Minder (2011) used the Picker Institute Methodology of data collection while reviewing information from 24 acute care hospitals. Information consisted of six classifications in communication, care, respect, discharge, cooperation, and the organizational process. Patient demographics of age, gender, and educational level were variables that influenced the classification scores (Holzer & Minder, 2011). The six classifications created a better mechanism for measuring of patient satisfaction. Classifications covered the spectrum of provider-patient interactions. Respect for patients and discharge management had significant correlation with patient satisfaction (Holzer & Minder, 2011).

There is a connection between patient satisfaction and improved communication in the patient-physician relationship (Holzer & Minder, 2011). Holzer and Minder (2011) created a cross-sectional questionnaire study to evaluate the extent to which continuity of care influences patient satisfaction. Psychological ownership builds a foundation of trust between people (Avey et al., 2012). Increased trust and longevity is dependent on the patient-provider relationship (Dorval et al., 2011). People who reported seeing their provider on a regular basis had a mean patient satisfaction 17.3 points higher than the average patient satisfaction score (Dorval et al., 2011). Relationship building provided a foundation team structure that fostered engagement for both parties (Ncube & Jerie, 2012). A strong continuum of care improves patient satisfaction. Improved patient-physician relationships create positive health care environments.

Community clinicians and providers are essential for producing quality health care services to the local population. The continuity between medical providers and quality outcomes influenced patient satisfaction (Beal & Hernandez, 2010). Community health care centers are more likely to provide services to low income and uninsured populations. Low-income patients are less likely to seek preventive care in a community health care clinic when compared to a private physician practice (Beal & Hernandez, 2010). Community health care centers struggle with communication with patients with only 53% of the patients expressing satisfaction with instructions, communication, and satisfaction with treatment plans (Beal & Hernandez, 2010). Community health care centers struggle with patient satisfaction, because of inconstancy with provider coverage and communication.

Different climates influence patient satisfaction on many levels. The orientation of managers in an organizational climate contributes to increasing patient satisfaction (Ancarani, Di Mauro, & Giammanco, 2010). Leadership provides key engagement drivers that influenced meeting the expectations of customers (Bushra et al., 2011). Human relationship climates augment patient satisfaction.

Improving communications, employee engagement, and shared values improve patient satisfaction (Kompaso & Sridevi, 2010). Ancarani et al. (2010) indicated that improved patient satisfaction occurs when the orientation of managers coincided with a perceived organizational climate by both the medical and nursing staff. Kompaso and Sridevi (2010) focused their research on strong predictors of communication, employee commitment, and positive behavior in employee engagement and customer satisfaction.

Health care conditions dictate consumer needs. There is a difference in patient satisfaction between critically ill patients and non-critically ill patients (Otani, Waterman, & Dunagan, 2012). Customer requirements changed based on the overall medical condition of the patient. Patient satisfaction was the goal for health care organizations. Data from five, large health care systems in St. Louis, Missouri provided a sample of participants in the study (Otani et al., 2012). Participants provided a dependent variable rating on quality of care and the possibility of recommending of services to other people (Otani et al., 2012). An independent, variable mix consisted of room accommodations, nursing care, and the overall admission process (Otani et al., 2012). Nursing care, physician communication, and room cleanliness had a significant relationship with $p = < .001$ for quality of care while quality of staff service, physician interaction, and nursing care was $p < .001$ for likelihood to recommend (Otani et al., 2012). Severity of illness did have a significant relationship with satisfaction (Otani et al., 2012).

Clinician communication plays a main role in promoting patient satisfaction (Oliveira et al., 2012). Physician communication and interaction, patient education, and service quality influences patient satisfaction within health care (Oliveira et al., 2012). Improved communication creates the possibility of improving customer service and meeting the needs of the consumer (Johansen, 2014). Oliveria et al. (2012) suggested that 38 communication factors consistently improved patient satisfaction ratings in health care. Verbal and nonverbal communication creates style interactions with patients.

Effective triage of patients marginally increases patient satisfaction for emergency room patients. Crane, Yerman, and Schneider (2012) compared patient satisfaction scores between days with and without physicians. Gemmel and Verleye (2010) suggested physicians create emotional connections with patients. The results did not demonstrate any significant difference in mean patient satisfaction scores based on the availability of a physician (Crane et al., 2012). Crane et al. suggested short examination times affected the strength of the patient-provider relationship. Improving provider-patient relationships depends on the amount of time for social interaction between the physician and patient (Crane et al., 2012). However, provider-patient relationships differed between types of specialties (Holzel, Kriston, & Harter, 2013). Primary care physicians have a much stronger and longer bond with patients than emergency physicians have because of the time and frequency of the provider-patient relationship (Mercer, Jani, Maxell, Wong, & Watt, 2012).

There is a relationship between proactive communication and patient satisfaction while admitting patients from the emergency room (Gemmel & Verleye, 2010). Ferguson, Ward, Card, Sheppard, and McMurtry (2013) used convenience sampling on adults and pediatric patients in an effort to gain an understanding of the relationship between communication and patient comprehension of health issues. Ferguson et al. used analysis variances to gain an understanding of the significant differences between patient satisfaction and the ability of a patient to understand his or her medical treatment. Oliveria et al. (2012) studied communications between medical providers and patients. Verbal and nonverbal communication creates pathways for the transfer of data. Researchers focused on a central hypothesis that increased dialogue translated into increased patient satisfaction.

Verbal communication improves direct communication with patients improving patient satisfaction (Oliveria et al., 2012). Oliveria et al. (2012) reviewed a wide range of studies associated with reviewing the influence of communication in health care. Nonverbal drivers of time spent, body position, facial expressions, and tone of voice influences the perception of patients on the delivery of their health care (Oliveria et al., 2012). Information demonstrated that 90% of patients rated their care as excellent (Oliveria et al., 2012). A total of 22% of the patients did not understand the reasons for admissions, medical tests or results (Oliveria et al., 2012). Slatten and Mehmetoglu (2011) suggested that frontline employees formed the first line of communication for customers. Communication developed early in the patient experience. Errors in communication created issues through the cycle of medical care. Paired *t* test demonstrated $p < .01$ between understanding and patient satisfaction, which demonstrated a significant correlation (Slatten & Mehmetoglu, 2011). Lack of understanding creates negative perceptions with patient satisfaction.

There is a relationship between high nurse-to-patient ratios and patient satisfaction. Organizations with a nursing ratio of seven patients to one nurse had higher patient satisfaction when compared to a ratio of 10 patients to one nurse (Fujimura, Tanii, & Saijoh, 2010). Fulimura et al. (2010) compared profitability between these same organizations. Health care environments with high nurse to patient ratios influenced high nursing turnover (Purdy et al., 2010). Smaller nursing-patient ratios created a more manageable nursing care environment that improved job demands and nursing engagement, which in turn led to improved patient satisfaction (Fujimura et al., 2010). The mean patient satisfaction score for 10:1 ratio was four on a scale of one (low) and five (high) while the mean patient satisfaction score for a 7:1 ratio was 4.38 on the same scale (Fujimura et al., 2010). Employee satisfaction scores were slightly higher for the 7:1 nurse ratio model. A lower patient-to-nurse ratio increased patient satisfaction (Fujimura et al., 2010).

The Consumer Assessment of Healthcare Providers and Systems (CAHPS), which created surveys to measure drivers of the patient experience (Hays et al., 2014), provided data from patients on aspects of the care delivery system. Driver metrics on appointment scheduling, wait times, communication, and provider engagement focused on indicators of the patient experience (Lis, Rodeghier, & Gupta, 2011). There was a connection between meeting customer demands and service quality (Ali

& Ndubisi, 2010). Drivers of consumer needs created opportunities to meet consumer demands. Health care organizations can efficiently use CAHPS as a management tool (Hays et al., 2014). Data use can focus on health care operational issues, set-up provider incentive plans, and improving the quality of patient care.

The Dutch Health Care System underwent dramatic changes in 2006 with changes in quality standards, processes, and delivery of medical care (Ikkersheim & Koolman, 2012). The Dutch system adopted pay-for-performance based on quality metrics (Ikkersheim & Koolman, 2012). Ikkersheim and Koolman (2012) studied drivers of health care quality factors from 2006 to 2007 in the Dutch delivery system. Factors included infection rates, patient satisfaction, communication, safety, and discharge data. Hospitals improved overall quality outcomes by .034 (p < .05) to .060 (p < .01) (Ikkersheim & Koolman, 2012). Hospitals that agreed to publish their data increased quality scores higher than those who did not (Ikkersheim & Koolman, 2012). Pay-for-performance, consumer-oriented services and increased competition improved the patient experience. Stephens and Ledlow (2010) suggested improving the patient experience increases financial stability.

Patient satisfaction is an international objective. Camgoz-Akdag and Zineldin (2010) examined the factors that affect patient perceptions of health care quality in Turkey. Baird and Gonzalez (2011) concluded organizations that focused on meeting the requirements of the consumer-increased sustainability. Improvement in consumer loyalty influences long-term viability. The quality of the infrastructure, atmosphere, and medical service ranked at the top of the scale for patient-perceptions

(Camgoz-Akdag & Zineldin, 2010). The primary problem in health care in Turkey is the lack of a sense of well-being. Over 32% of patients in Turkey perceived the health care system as needing improvements in food quality, family accommodations, and communication (Camgoz-Akdag & Zineldin, 2010). Improved patient satisfaction is an indicator of quality of care.

Relationship quality and rapport create opportunities for building strong consumer relationships. Health care organizations must establish an interpersonal relationship with patients to increase their market share (Ali & Ndubisi, 2010). This emotional connection increases satisfaction. Respect and rapport building had a significant relationship to interpersonal relationship building with $p < .001$, while results also indicated a significant relationship with responsibility, report building, and the quality of the relationship with $p < .001$ (Ali & Ndubisi, 2010). There was not a statistical difference between attention and valuing with the quality of the relationship (Ali & Ndubisi, 2010).

HEALTH CARE REFORM AND SUSTAINABILITY

In 1965, President Johnson signed the Social Security amendments, which created Medicare. Medicare legislation created a provision that would provide health care for senior citizens (Petasnick, 2011). Petasnick (2011) also suggested that Medicare created social change in the role that government played in the health coverage of its citizens. Robinson (2011) analyzed the fundamental idea of Medicare because of the significant inability of Medicare to keep up with growth in medical expenses. The mission of Medicare faced questions as health care changed. The role of senior citizens in society changed with the passage of the law.

Through the years, Medicare transformed from being a simple medical coverage to becoming a more inclusive health care coverage. Approximately 77 million, or one third of the people in the United States, will retire by 2029 (Chiesl, 2012). Baby Boomer retirees represent the single largest population segmentation in history (Chiesl, 2012). Medicare accounted for 15% of the federal budget (Petasnick, 2011). Health care reform predicted reducing provider payments by $500 billion by 2020 (Petasnick, 2011). An increase in the Medicare population may increase health care costs while reimbursements decline creating sustainability issues for health care organizations.

A current challenge for Medicare lies in the expanding constituency, with an estimated 53 million beneficiaries enrolling by 2015 (Petasnick, 2011). Successful Medicare transformation occurs by implementing appropriate safeguards, linking reimbursement to quality results, and adjusting the age eligibility (Petasnick, 2011). Early government intervention provided a basis for future health care changes. Life expectancy in 1965 was 67 years for men and 74 years for women (Petasnick, 2011). In 2015, experts predict to see a life expectancy of 76 years for men and 82 years for women (Petasnick, 2011).

The ACA created an environment for health care reform by creating the Accountable Care Organization (ACO) (Bennett, 2012). An ACO is an organization that combines primary care physicians, hospitals, and specialists into an entity to focus on managing health care services for a patient population. The main goals of an ACO are increasing quality, decreasing cost, and improving patient satisfaction. Bennett (2012) articulated that shared saving programs provide ACOs opportunities to save money and improve profits. Shared savings programs provided incentives to any businesses that participate in lowering the cost of health care. Certain incentives decrease costs and increase competitive advantages for an ACO. In addition, reform created health care exchanges that provided all citizens with health care coverage. Kaufman (2013) agreed that health care reform provided universal coverage, but the central goal focused on improving the quality of care, lowering costs, and improving the patient experience.

Quality outcomes and patient satisfaction determine payment schedules for health care services. The ACA transformed the historic in-patient reimbursement methodology to pay for performance (Cliff, 2012). Patient satisfaction results affected 30% of reimbursement exposure in the new payment model (Cliff, 2012). Lowe (2012) determined high performing hospitals created environments that fostered employee engagement that supported the eventual outcome of improving the patient experience. Improved patient satisfaction directly affects the profitability of health care systems (Cliff, 2012).

The federal government planned to reduce reimbursement to health care organizations by $600 billion over the next 10 years (Orszag & Emanuel, 2010). The goal of ACA was to reduce federally covered health care expenses (Orszag & Emanuel, 2010). Reducing expenses alone would not increase the economic stability of health care (Singh, Wheeler, & Roden, 2012). Improvements in revenue cycle management provided a balanced approach to fiscal health for health care organizations. Capital investment in information technology has become a strategic objective for hospitals (Singh et al., 2012). The development of the electronic medical record provides an opportunity to recover overpayments because of medical necessity for decreasing revenue (Singh et al., 2012).

Unhealthy patients with severe health care conditions create an uneven expense distribution with 10% of patients representing 64% of overall health care costs (Orszag & Emanuel, 2010). Cassalty (2011) claimed that health care reform would even out the distribution of payments for services by changing the reimbursement model from fee-for-service to quality-driven metrics. Healthy wellness programs develop methods for dealing with the health of the person before chronic concerns could persist in an attempt to lower the overall cost (Cassalty, 2011).

ACOs review information technology for meaningful use, value management, payment policy, and garnishing arrangements in an attempt to develop cost-sharing activities (Devore & Champion, 2011). Lack of institutional knowledge, practical experience, and proven results inhibits the process of collaboration, which increases the likelihood of sustainability issues in health care. ACOs provide opportunities to increase hospital profitability, decrease costs, and improve quality metrics (Devore & Champion, 2011). Devore and Champion (2011) suggested creating an ACO is difficult because of a host of legal issues that create reasonable concerns. Aslin (2011) recommended that hospital leaders must understand the criteria for success as ACOs continue to influence health care delivery systems.

Bennett (2012) suggested ACO models focus on improving patient satisfaction while decreasing costs. ACOs focus on sharing cost savings with health care consumers. ACOs must provide a wide range of services to patients in order to control quality and cost of the services (Bennett, 2012). ACO development created patient loyalty with over 75% of patients staying within an ACO environment (Antos, 2014). Service variety, cost savings, and provider confidence influence the success of the ACO model.

Primary care development is the initial step in creating health care reform and cost control (Stephens & Ledlow, 2010). Zwanziger, Khan, and Bamezai (2010) suggested that lowering the overall cost of care would reduce the overall quality of health care delivery systems. New technology and services create an increased cost associated with improving overall patient care. Primary care physician networks provide oversight for patient care while lowering the cost of health care by improving patient wellness services (Stephens & Ledlow, 2010).

Health care insurance coverage and increases in deductibles negatively influence patients. Woolhandler and Himmelstein (2011) reviewed aspects of health care reform in the United States and suggested that more than 45,000 Americans die annually because of lack of health care insurance coverage (Woolhandler & Himmelstein, 2011). Americans with insurance are unable to pay the deductibles of their medical bills (Woolhandler & Himmelstein, 2011). Troubling economic factors, low literacy rates, and service quality negatively influenced the health care environment in the United States (Woolhandler & Himmelstein, 2011). The Massachusetts health care system provided a snapshot of the new health care model. Some residents in Massachusetts still cannot afford the care offered by the state (Woolhandler & Himmelstein, 2011).

Patient loyalty translates into improved profit margins (Kaufman, 2013). Patient satisfaction and loyalty is the ultimate goal for health care leaders (Kaufman, 2013). An emotional connection exists between employee engagement and patient satisfaction when service quality meets the expectations of the patients (Kaufman, 2013). Ali and Ndubisi (2010) suggested health care organizations must differentiate their service quality from other health care firms in an effort to improve patient loyalty. Service quality produces an environment in which health care organizations must capture market share.

Hospital ownership models have an impact on hospital service offerings and profitability (Horwitz & Nichols, 2011). Nonprofit hospitals offer fewer services than for-profit organizations (Horwitz & Nichols, 2011). Data used and gathered from the American Hospital Association provided key financial ratios for Horwitz and Nichols's analysis. Cassatly (2011) explained irreversible changes in health care reform influenced how hospitals receive payment creating cash collection issues that led to negative cash flow and financial distress. In addition, nonprofit hospitals are more likely to give unprofitable services to patients. For-profit hospitals are less likely to provide unprofitable services, such as psychiatric emergency room services and home care (Horwitz & Nichols, 2011). Increasing patient satisfaction lowered overall risk while improving revenue (Horwitz & Nichols, 2011). Nonprofit and for-profit organizations need changes in consumer offerings and service quality.

Researchers between 1990 and 2009 gathered data on the attributes and deficits of paying businesses based on meeting performance goals. Pay-for-performance will affect health care organizations (Emmert, Eijkenaar, Kemter, Esslinger, & Schoffski, 2012). Cliff (2012) suggested patient-centered health care provided the best opportunity to meet the needs of customers and influence performance metrics. Researchers found the current payment system in the United States had a minimal effect on clinical effectiveness, cost-effective operations, and continuity (Emmert et al., 2012). Effects varied based on program design and payment methodology. Pay-for-performance systems work best when the organization demonstrates stakeholder engagement, development of core metrics, payer collaboration, and team-based financial incentives (Emmert et al., 2010). Researchers compared hospital profitability with corresponding patient satisfaction scores. A 20% increase in patient satisfaction produced an 85% increase in hospital profitability without a correlation to the medical outcome, which creates a connection between patient satisfaction and financial stability of hospitals.

Engaged employees have an inherent desire to be productive members of the organization while increasing productivity and improving profitability. Employee engagement increases organizational performance and service quality (Kompaso & Sridevi, 2010). Service quality and innovation play a significant role in organizational efficiency in the delivery of health care services (Barnett, Vasileiou, Djemil, Brooks, & Young, 2011). Improved service quality influences consumer loyalty and satisfaction.

Barnett et al. (2011) suggested four fundamental themes exist in regards to service quality and innovation. Barnett et al. described these themes as organizational partnerships, human-based influence, impact of contextual factors, and the rule of evidence affecting organizational service and innovation. Interaction between intrapersonal and intra-organizational networks facilitates the four central themes. Dollard and Bakker (2010) suggested the failure of leaders to create an environment supporting psychological ownership decreases human based influence. Improvements related to increasing the impact of the four themes create an opportunity to meet the expectations of the health care consumer (Barnett et al., 2011).

Gregorio and Cronemyr (2011) used the Kano Model to categorize product and service standards by focusing on consumer requirements. Understanding the requirements of the consumers increases the likelihood of consumer loyalty (Gregorio & Cronemyr, 2011). Alrubaiee and Alkaaida (2011) suggested improved customer satisfaction and loyalty increased hospital profitability. Hospital sustainability depends on increasing consumer loyalty and thus, improving financial performance (Rao, 2012).

Improvement in the quality of service creates opportunities for increasing patient satisfaction (Weinberg, Avgar, Sugrue, & Cooney-Minor, 2013). Improvements in the work environment, team performance, and service quality create positive financial outcomes (Weinberg et al., 2013). Shoemaker (2010) connected increased patient satisfaction with hospital profitability. High performance teams had a significant correlation with employee satisfaction with $p < .000$, while low retention demonstrated a significant relationship with a high performance work climate with $p < .012$ (Weinberg et al., 2013). The work climate demonstrated a significant correlation with patient satisfaction with $p < .008$, while improved work performance and work climate positively influenced overall patient satisfaction (Weinberg et al., 2013). Increased profitability provides opportunities for organizational investment and improved sustainability.

Safety-net hospitals provide care for the low income, uninsured patient population. Kane, Singer, Clark, Eeckloo, and Valentine (2012) collected financial data from 5,299 hospitals and demonstrated three critical financial benchmarks. Kane et al. reviewed total patient revenue, average total margin, and negative margin operations that determined safety net hospital status. More than 50% of the 526 safety net hospitals operated in metropolitan statistical areas (Kane et al., 2012). Safety net hospitals focus on providing care for those individuals without insurance coverage. Many publicly owned health care organizations received subsidies covering the cost of health care services. Graduate medical education is also a major component of safety net hospitals. The combination of medical education and federal subsidy offset portions of uncompensated care for safety net hospitals.

Retaining and attracting new customers creates strategic objectives for sustainability. Starting in 2007, the safety net hospital system in San Francisco, California transformed itself into fully integrated health care delivery system (Katz & Brigham, 2011). By 2010, the health care system enrolled 89% of the uninsured population with a 94% patient satisfaction score (Katz & Brigham, 2011). Healthy San Francisco created a competitive advantage by increasing information technology, establishing primary care base, and improved customer service (Katz & Brigham, 2011). Strong medical engagement and a clear vision created an opportunity for a financially successful delivery of community health care coverage. Healthy San Francisco created a formula for employee engagement, medical leadership, and community involvement that improved health care coverage.

Medicaid patients' choice of provider increased because of the ACA. Safety net organizations face increased pressure to keep costs under control while attracting low risk Medicaid patients (Zwanziger et al., 2010). Zwanziger et al. (2010) used the Annual Survey of Hospitals as the primary data source for analysis of financial performance of safety net health care organizations. Safety net activities have little to no effect on profit margins (Zwanziger et al., 2010). Overall, expenditures were lower for safety net organizations, which created a perception that safety net hospitals provide a decrease in service quality.

Kane et al. (2012) reviewed data that supported how safety net hospitals financially thrived before the last recession. Health care organizations with significant Medicaid discharges demonstrated healthy profit margins in competitive environments. Devore and Champion (2011) suggested that health care reform created opportunities for businesses to thrive. Increased market share produced improved profitability while overall revenue decreased. Medicaid payment systems and subsidies are vulnerable to decreases during challenging economic environments (Kane et al., 2012). A stressed economic climate created an opportunity for issues with sustainability for safety net hospitals. Decreased political support and increased population created a situation in which medical care comes with higher costs and decreased reimbursement.

The federal government reviewed the reimbursement shift between nonprofit and privately owned hospitals by studying cost versus reimbursement rates. Medicare planned a reduction in reimbursement rates as patients signed up for ACA insurance plans (Robinson, 2011). The ultimate goal of the legislation is to decrease cost while improving quality. Robinson (2011) indicated that health care organizations in concentrated markets attempted to increase reimbursement from private insurance companies while health care organizations in competitive marketplaces focused on cutting operational costs. Decreased cost improves profit margins, which provides capital for reinvestment.

Grants, gifts, and contributions affect the profitability of hospitals (Bailey, 2013). Fiscal ratios determined fiscal viability. Urban and rural health care facilities created a sample pool of data to examine the impact of grants and contributions. Kane et al. (2012) demonstrated that contributions, gifts, and grants did not play a significant role in the total hospital revenue. However, these items did have a more positive impact on urban hospitals than for rural hospitals. Kompaso and Sridevi (2010) suggested employee engagement created a solid foundation for positive operating performance. Increased employee engagement is a predictor of increased productivity and profitability. Motivated employees develop opportunities for gifts and grants. In addition, the impact of non-operating revenue was greater for larger-sized facilities.

Transition and Summary

Low employee engagement in health care is a business problem because employee engagement negatively influences consumer satisfaction. Health care reform mandates improvements in cost control, improving quality, and increasing patient satisfaction. The new strategic objective of hospitals and health care systems focuses on improving the patient experience to increase consumer loyalty. The general research question for this study focused on how meeting employee expectations influenced employee engagement in health care.

The literature review focused on aspects of health care reform, expectancy theory, psychological ownership, transformational leadership, employee engagement, and patient satisfaction. In the literature review, I confirmed that specific drivers influence employee engagement. Enhanced psychological ownership developed strong emotional connections to the organization. In Section 2, I provide detailed information regarding research design and methodology for approaching the problem statement while, in Section 3, I present the findings from this study and the significance of the study as it relates to a business practice.

Section 2: The Project

In this section, I provide information on the research method and design, and I chose to address the business problem that some health care leaders lack strategies to engage their employees in order to provide better patient care. I describe the role of the researcher and the participants, and provide justification for the selected research methodology and design, as well as information about the population and the sampling. I also cover ethical concerns, data collection instruments, and steps taken for the assurance of reliability, and validity.

Purpose Statement

The purpose of this qualitative, phenomenological study was to explore the lived experiences of health care leaders in their desire to design strategies to engage employees in order to provide better patient care. Increased employee engagement may influence patient satisfaction in health care. The population for this study consisted of 23 health care leaders in Midwestern hospitals. Improvements in patient satisfaction create opportunities to improve revenue, consumer loyalty, and sustainability. This study may provide insight into understanding engagement from the perspective of the employee, which ultimately could lead to creating strategies focused on increasing patient satisfaction, improving business sustainability, and increasing the quality of care. Improvements in the quality of health care may have a positive effect on social change by improving the overall health of the members of the community.

Role of the Researcher

In this qualitative phenomenological study, I had a direct role in the research design, data collection, and analysis of the study findings. I was the data collection instrument. My interest in understanding strategies that increase work motivation came from my personal experience as an engaged employee. I chose qualitative phenomenological research based on the nature of my topic and main research question.

Bias is the influence of a particular culture, background, and experience that may influence personal and external views (Bernard, 2013). I mitigated bias through my understanding of the presence of a personal lens related to my personal views and work experiences. This facilitated an objective interpretation of responses. The interview protocol was the same for each participant by (a) holding the interviews in a safe, off site location, (b) allowing adequate time for a response and, (c) conducting the second interview to document response validity. This consistency prevented my personal bias from entering into the interview process.

As the researcher, in an effort to mitigate bias, I selected health care systems in which I had no contact with the leaders ensuring that my leadership views would not influence the participants. Bracketing is a useful technique used to separate the research topic from the contextual world (Patton, 2002). I used bracketing to eliminate external influence by taking the research topic out of the environmental context by using well-written questions and focusing conversations on topic analysis as research orientation instead of corrective action. Covell, Sidani, and Ritchie (2012) suggested that the interviewer has an obligation to protect participants from interviewer interference and ensure confidentiality in the data collection process. Bracketing also assists with reducing interviewer interference by putting aside my own beliefs on the research topic (Chan, Fung, & Chien, 2013). It was important to find hospitals that provided an environment where employees interact with patients. This provided the necessary environmental context in which to study employee engagement in health care. Employee engagement played a major role in my personal experience and success as a leader. Increasing patient satisfaction had been a major focus of my career goals and job expectations.

Epoche is the process by which a researcher takes on a phenomenological attitude to eliminate personal bias by looking at internal personal involvement in the subject matter (Patton, 2002). In Epoche, researchers set aside personal knowledge, judgments, and general perceptions (Moustakas, 1994). I was able to obtain Epoche by withholding judgment and personal ego on the research topic in a search for knowledge from lived experiences of leaders.

Participants

Twenty-three health care leaders of hospitals located in the Midwestern United States participated in this study. The participants managed and led employees in health care, holding the responsibility of meeting the expectations of employees. Leadership approval for employee participation in my research study created an environment for development of a working relationship with the participants. I accessed participants by working with department management and developed a system for volunteer participation.

I applied a snowballing sampling technique to select participants who could offer in-depth insights and information-rich data about this topic (Jawale, 2012). An appropriate sample size for a qualitative phenomenological study is 20 participants (Bernard, 2013). I selected a sample size of 23 health care leaders. This sample size met the Walden University DBA requirement.

I ensured a good working relationship with participants by providing a statement of purpose and intended results in an effort to share the importance of their engagement to increase the validity of the research. In addition, I discussed the ethical issues pertaining to the participants' confidentiality and rights. I selected numbers instead of names to identify the participants and present the results of this study meeting confidentiality guidelines. I provided an informed consent document (see Appendix A) to ensure confidentiality. I ensured that the environment would provide a safe, nonthreatening atmosphere that allowed for each participant's comfort by providing comfortable chairs, soft lighting, and use of a soundproof room. All information and consents will reside on an external hard drive and a separate flash drive stored in a locked and secured place for a period of 5 years. I will destroy all information after the 5-year period.

Research Method and Design

In this section, I describe the research method and design and provide justification for using the selected approach. The decision to apply qualitative phenomenology stems from a need for an in-depth understanding of the triad of health care leader actions, employee expectations, and employee engagement. A qualitative research method allows for in depth discovery of individual perceptions and motivations.

RESEARCH METHOD

Qualitative research is an appropriate method to explore the perceptions and lived experiences of health care leaders improving employee engagement (Moustakas, 1994). Employees create interpersonal and emotional connections to an organization that builds personal perspective and knowledge (Nasomboon, 2014). A qualitative study provides an opportunity to interview health care leaders to gain perspective, understand emotional connectivity, and view an organization through the eyes of the health care leaders.

Qualitative researchers expose important points surrounding a topic (Anyan, 2013). Strong employee engagement positively influences consumer loyalty and increases revenue (Abel, 2013). Discovering why employees engage in their work environment may influence positive changes in the workplace. Qualitative researchers use conversation, active listening, and the merging of thought in an attempt to gain understanding (Branthwaite & Patterson, 2011). Interviews with health care leaders may create an environment to foster truthful dialogue about how meeting expectations affects work motivation. Personal experience gathered from interviewing individuals provides a unique perspective not found in the quantitative or mixed method research.

A quantitative approach would not provide the necessary investigation style and form needed to capture the nature of an employee's experience (Moustaka, 1994). Quantitative researchers use statistical correlations in an effort to explain how variables interact in an effort to document what happens. The goal of my research was to focus on understanding how health care leaders' strategies affect employee engagement, which eliminated quantitative research.

A mixed method approach combines both qualitative and quantitative methods. I eliminated the mixed methodology because of research found in the literature review. There was no need for the quantitative portion of the mixed method approach because of the past documented research in the literature review.

RESEARCH DESIGN

I selected a phenomenological design for this study. A phenomenological approach allowed me to focus on how meeting employee expectations influences employee engagement. Phenomenology is a science that focuses on understanding the subjective perceptions of participants (Eberle, 2012). A focused phenomenological approached develops an understanding of employee engagement from health care leader experiences. Moustaka (1994) suggested seven qualities of phenomenological design: (a) combining and clustering of ideas and themes from experiences, (b) observation through listening with connection to experience, (c) viewing experience and behavior as a critical part of the whole person, (d) focusing on the wholeness of the experience in total rather than individual parts, (e) creating questions that demonstrates the passion and interest of the researcher, (f) reviewing the meaning of experience rather than a measured response, and (g) gathering first-person accounts provides true perceptive reasoning.

Phenomenological analysis creates an in-depth review of personal perspective and insight (Eberle, 2012). Employee engagement is a personal choice influenced by an environmental context, interpersonal relationships, and experience. Experience holds the hidden keys to the reasons why behaviors occur. A phenomenological heuristic approach focuses on understanding how personal experience influence behavior (Moustakas, 1994). The personal experience of an employee provides insight into understanding the influence of meeting employee expectations on engagement.

I selected a phenomenological design for this study following an evaluation and review of five design approaches. The five qualitative designs were case study, grounded theory, narrative, ethnography, and phenomenology. Although grounded theory is systematic, it may not lead to new discoveries or new information about the research topic (Jones & Alony, 2011; Licqurish & Seibold, 2011). Case study design focuses on a group in a real life setting that studies related events over time (Yin, 2009). Case study design was not compatible with my doctoral study because group dynamics can influence an individual not to express personal experiences and views because of peer pressure (Yin, 2009). The purpose of a narrative research design is to structure experiences as narratives. A narrative design would not be preferred for my study because a narrative design can have broad reach, and would not offer the narrow focus on how lived experiences may influence leadership strategies (Bernard, 2013). The purpose of ethnography is to study people and cultures by observation. An ethnographic approach would be excessive and beyond the narrow scope of my doctoral study (Sangasubana, 2011).

Population and Sampling

The population for the study consisted of 23 health care leaders who influence employees. The group mix also included front office supervisors, nursing leaders, managers, lead technologists, directors, and physicians. I selected a snowballing technique for the selection of participants. Snowballing is a chain referral system that works by using current social networks (Jawale, 2012). Participants referred other possible participants through social interaction and interpersonal relationships. Bernard (2013) suggested that the appropriate sample size is 15 to 20 for a qualitative phenomenological study. Saturation occurs when newly acquired data does not lead to new information and themes (Walker, 2012). I reviewed the data to determine if saturation occurred within the first 20 participants. The data did not clearly indicate that saturation occurred, therefore I interviewed 3 more participants until no new information or themes occurred (Walker, 2012).

Sample size justification in interviewing studies occurs by interviewing participants until saturation occurs (Walker, 2012). Saturation occurs when interview responses provide no new data, coding, or themes, and the study is easily replicated (O'Reilly & Parker, 2012). There are several principles in evaluating saturation: (a) initial sample size, (b) interviews needed, (c) reliability analysis conducted by multiple coders, and (d) ease in evaluation (O'Reilly & Parker, 2012). I interviewed 23 leaders. The leaders consisted of physicians, nurses, technologists, and clerical workers until saturation occurred with no new data, coding or themes emerging from interview responses. Diversity in the sample pool provided a rich texture of experience from different levels within the organization. The sampling size of 23 health care leaders provided a diverse make up of leaders, which creates a reliable data collection pool. The tenure requirements of participants for this study effectively narrowed the pool of participants to people employed for at least one year and who work more than 10 hours per week. To be eligible, participants must provide supervision to employees who have direct patient contact. Patient interactions provide a connection to the emotional connection between employee engagement and patient satisfaction.

I selected a quiet place for the interview sessions creating a safe environment for the discussions. The environment had adjustable lighting, comfortable seating, and a table for personal items. All windows had shades ensuring a confidential environment. The ambiance of the setting enhanced the chance for a safe environment for honest dialogue. I held the interviews away from the job site in a neutral location to increase the comfort of the participants.

Ethical Research

Researchers have an obligation for ethical conduct while doing human research (Seppet, Paasuke, Conte, Capri, & Franceschi, 2011). Ethical challenges persist in qualitative research in health care when researchers bring personal emotions in the research process (Haahr, Norlyk, & Hall, 2013). Participants decided to join the study on a volunteer basis and could have withdrawn from the study at any time by providing verbal or written notice. I provided the mandatory informed consent form for participation in the study. The consent form outlined the purpose of the study, the procedures of the study, and the communication channel with me throughout the study. I discussed the role of the participant by reviewing the informed consent form with each participant, ensuring confidentiality and an understanding that participants could withdraw from the study at any time without penalty. A sample of the informed consent form is in Appendix A.

I held all data, communications, audio files, and transcripts in strict confidence. A participant's naming structure used position type rather than names to ensure confidentiality. I stored all data on a password-protected external hard drive and after 5 years will destroy all information related to the study. All interview results will remain confidential.

Data Collection

In this section, I describe the data collection templates, the collection techniques, and the organization techniques that I used in the study, and refer to the alignment of specific interview questions with themes from the literature review. Participants reviewed transcribed manuscripts of the interview sessions. As the researcher, I took notes of their comments and reactions while not changing the transcripts. I also describe the processes for assessment of reliability and validity.

INSTRUMENTS

I was the data collection instrument. An in-depth list of open-ended, semistructured interview questions created an appropriate instrument for gathering perspectives from participants (Bernard, 2013). I used a recording device in conjunction with the paper instrument. My personal journal allowed me to take notes while listening to employees. I took into consideration the goal of the study by designing the primary collection instrument to solicit answers to my research questions. My analysis of the interview answers may provide insight on general themes listed in the literature review.

I asked each participant the same set of questions ensuring consistency. I held interview sessions in the same location and over a constant time duration. Participants provided demographic data and answers to the open-ended questions. I asked permission to record the interviews before each session. As the participants answered the questions, I kept a personal journal to take relevant notes. Participants returned for a follow-up interview to review transcribed interview notes and provided additional information on the original set of questions. All information gathered from the interviews is stored on an external hard drive and will remain in a safe and secure location in my home for 5 years. After the 5 year time duration, I will destroy all data associated with the study.

Well-thought-out interviews provide a valuable tool kit for researchers (Lampropoulou & Myers, 2013). Interviews provide valuable insight into the experience of a person. Face-to-face interviews provided me with the ability to interact with the participants, observe nonverbal communication, and express my gratitude for their participation.

DATA COLLECTION TECHNIQUE

In this qualitative phenomenological study, I relied on health care leaders' answers to open-ended semistructured interview questions and my interpretive analysis. I completed a member check by conducting a transcript overview and reviewing the findings with each participant. Member checking provided an opportunity to validate findings by sharing interview analysis and interpretations with participants (Miles, Huberman, & Saldana, 2014). Along with recording each interview and the transcription of the responses for analysis, I also kept track of data and emerging understandings through reflective journals. I focused on themes of psychological ownership, leadership, expectations, and employee engagement. These themes related to the main research question of this study. The semistructured format allowed participants to provide answers and creates opportunities for follow-up questions and answers.

DATA ORGANIZATION TECHNIQUES

Data organization is an important aspect of a data management system. I used reference numbers instead of names for participants, which insured confidentiality of each participant. I created a separate file for each reference number. Participant files contain the informed consent form, interview voice files, transcribed journal notes, and transcribed interview sessions. I used NVivo 10 software in conjunction with Microsoft Office products on a Macintosh operating system for data management. All items will exist on an external, password- protected hard drive stored up to 5 years after the completion of my doctoral study. After 5 years, I will destroy the items. I used a coding system to identify positive words and themes associated with the subject matter. Review of themes created an opportunity to understand the experiences of employees as it relates to employee engagement. I analyzed the data and provided insight for understanding themes and for learning more about employee engagement.

Data Analysis Technique

Qualitative data analysis is a complex process that requires clear critical thinking (Bergin, 2011). Well-constructed interview questions aid in the thought process, and provides for substantive data collection leading to robust data analysis. I completed a member check by reviewing the interview transcripts and data interpretations with the participants. Interview questions complemented the overarching question: What strategies do health care leaders need to engage their employees to provide better patient care? Data analysis led to themes related to meeting employee expectations and employee engagement.

I used a heuristic method of review and the modified Van Kaam method of data analysis in this study. Researchers use heuristics ultimately to focus research on introspective views from the participants (Nikookar, 2013). Experience and individual perception creates a personal perspective. The modified Van Kaam method of data analysis provided a systematic process of data analysis (Moustakas, 1994). The data analysis consisted of: (a) creating list of experiences, (b) testing of each experience, (c) clustering like experiences into a theme, (d) reviewing the compatibility of the themes, and (e) constructing a description of the essence of the themes. The following interview questions provided an instrument for data collection and analysis:

Interview Questions

PQ1. What is your name?

PQ2. What is your job title?

PQ3. What is your age?

PQ4. How long have you been in the health care field?

PQ5. What is your educational background?

PQ6. How many jobs in health care have you had in your career?

PQ7. What do you do in your job?

PQ8. What does health care reform mean to you?

The following conceptual and follow-up questions related to the proposed research inquiry and formed part of the discussions.

C1. How do you define employee engagement?

C2. How does employee engagement affect the day-to-day operations of your department?

C3. What expectations do you have as an employee?

C4. How does your attitude affect you meeting employee expectations?

C5. How does your personal ownership of the workplace influence your performance as a leader?

C6. How does trust influence your employees' engagement within the organization?

C7. How does leadership influence engagement in your workplace?

C8. How is your motivation affected by your leader meeting your expectations?

Targeted follow-up questions were as follows:

C1F1. What examples do you have of employee engagement?

C1F2. What are the components of employee engagement that influence your employees?

C2F1. What are your key operational tasks?

C2F2. What are the specific drivers of employee engagement that influence the job tasks of your employees?

C3F1. What expectations do you have that are reasonable?

C3F2. What expectations do you have that are not reasonable?

C4F1. How can the attitudes of employees be improved?

C4F2. How can you improve your attitude to improve engagement?

C5F1. How do you improve your personal ownership of your work environment?

C6F1. How do you improve trust between you and your employees?

C6F2. How might a decrease in job security affect your engagement?

C7F1. How can your leadership skills improve the likelihood of meeting the expectations of your employees?

C8F1. How does communication affect your relationship with your supervisor?

C8F2. How does a strong interpersonal relationship with your employees affect your desire to meet organizational goals?

Following the completion of the personal interviews, I transcribed the responses of the participants and then coded emerging themes by using the qualitative data analysis software NVivo10. To analyze data, I: (a) organized data and transcribed interviews for clarity, (b) reviewed transcripts, ascertaining general mood, depth, and overall creditability of responses, (c) began data analysis by using a coding process that focuses on organizing themes, (d) used the themes as a foundation for theoretical development (e) demonstrated how themes support the qualitative nature of this study, (f) interpreted data, and (g) developed next steps for research.

Software assisted in the coding of themes, collected ideas, and it allowed comparisons between words and phrases used in the interview sessions. I used NVivo 10 because it is a qualitative based analytic software package. This software provided a single point of entry for data collection. The system is a repository of interview recordings, journal notes, and questionnaire results.

Data coding is an important part of data analysis in qualitative research (Nikookar, 2013). My focus was on comparing and contrasting verbal responses to all of the interview questions in order to analyze responses. The goal of researchers is to find common themes based on experiences of participants (Jennings & Van Horn, 2012). Theme development is the focus of data analysis in qualitative research.

The conceptual framework for this study was Vroom's expectancy theory, which suggested that employees work harder when leaders meet basic employee expectations in the workplace (Lunenburg, 2011). Employee motivation increases when leaders meet personal expectations (Lunenburg, 2011). The interview questions enabled participants to generate responses related to the primary themes of (a) psychological ownership, (b) leadership influence, and (c) expectation management. Questions C2, C3, C6, and C7 focused on leadership and expectations, while questions C1, C4, C5, and C8 pointed to psychological ownership.

Answers to the open-ended, semistructured questions provided greater understanding of how meeting employee expectations influences employee motivation. The final stage of this study includes presentation, interpretation, and explanation of the study findings. Data analysis focuses on answering the main question of this study. Interview questions focus on different themes in an attempt to understand the personal experience of health care employees.

Reliability and Validity

The value of research depends on research design and data collection, analysis, and interpretation (Yu, Jannasch-Pennell, & DiGangi, 2011). Ensuring the reliability and validity of data provides objectivity and creditability (Anderson, 2010). I provided opportunities for participants to review transcribed responses in an effort ensuring accuracy captured through thoughts and themes. I kept detailed notes on how the participants modified their response

RELIABILITY

Reliability is the replication of themes and results by other people in different settings (Yu et al., 2011). Reliability for this study first focused on a snowball-sampling method that would lead to a diverse sample group. The use of NVivo 10 software provided another aspect of reliability by using computer aided coding throughout the entire study, thus removing biases. Reliability rests in the consistent themes of data collection. Reliability results from (a) detailed notes, (b) complete documentation of the interviews, (c) accurate transcripts, and (d) accurate coding system for themes (Yu et al., 2011).

Due to many different types of methodologies, achieving reliability may be difficult in qualitative research because of the complexity of data analysis (Anderson, 2010). I enhanced reliability by including audits, data collection descriptions, theme creation, and the development of conclusions. Structured documentation of the research process adds both consistency and reliability by standardizing data collection, analysis, and storage procedures (Cook, 2012; Patton, 2002).

VALIDITY

The goal of this study was to identify reliable and valid processes and information that mitigates the chance of bias and incorrect interpretations (Bernard, 2013). The objective was to have both internal and external validity while making sure saturation occurs when no new data or themes occur (Lakshmi & Mohideen, 2013). Internal validity refers to how accurately the study findings answer the research question (Anderson, 2010). The four methods of validity are triangulation, contradictory evidence, respondent validation, and constant comparison.

Respondent validation provided an opportunity for participants to complete a transcript review. Participants reviewed transcripts for corrections, authentication, and meaning clarification (Mero-Jaffe, 2011). I completed a member check by reviewing the study findings with the participants. This member check provided an opportunity to validate findings by sharing results with the participants (Miles et al., 2014). I achieved respondent validation by having a closing interview with each participant. I provided a transcript of the first interview and reviewed the results from the study. The participant had time to review answers and formally sign the transcript validating the authenticity of the answers. I kept detailed notes on the comments and concerns of the participants. Contradictory evidence refers to personal biases (Anderson, 2010). I mitigated bias by recognizing personal agendas, views, personal beliefs, and experiences.

External validity is the transferability of accurate representation of study results (Thomson & Thomas, 2012); however, transferability is left up to the reader to decide (Marshall & Rossman, 2011). I established validity by ensuring that I conducted the interviews in a consistent and controlled setting (Moustakas, 1994). I conducted interviews by presenting each question in the same order therefore increasing validity by assuring consistent communication. I allowed adequate time for the participants to answer each question thoroughly. Each interview lasted 1 hour and occurred in the same setting. The timing of the interviews coincided with participant availability.

Transition and Summary

In Section 2, I covered the research method and design. I outlined the reasoning behind the selection of a qualitative phenomenological design to explore the phenomenon of meeting employee expectations. I included a description of the role of the researcher, the participants, and the snowball sampling technique. I also presented the selected data collection method of semistructured interview questions, and emphasized the ethical aspects, the reliability, and validity of the study. Section 3 includes the findings of the study and potential implications for social change. In Section 3, I will provide recommendations for action and further study, as well as a summary of the study.

Section 3: Application to Professional Practice and Implications for Change

In this section I describe themes that emerged from personal interviews with health care leaders targeting leadership strategies that affect employee engagement. Section 3 includes an overview of the study and specific findings. I also provide an opportunity to gain an understanding of how the findings might apply to professional practice, the implications for social change, and recommendations for leadership actions. Lastly, Section 3 concludes with recommendations for further study while providing a final summary.

Overview of Study

The purpose of this qualitative, phenomenological study was to explore the lived experiences of health care leaders in their desire to design strategies to engage employees in order to provide better patient care. A qualitative research design offered the best method to understand the social impact of meeting employee expectations on an organizational level. The participants in this research study answered the main research question: What strategies should health care leaders implement to engage employees and enhance patient care? The objective of this study was to explore the lived experiences of health care leaders influencing employee engagement.

The 23 study participants consisted of a diverse group of directors, managers, and supervisors associated with the delivery of health care services. The selection of participants provided valuable insight into strategies that influence employee engagement. Leaders in health care also represent the point of view of an employee, as these leaders were all employees of their respective health care organizations. All participants had reliable experience and knowledge of strategies that affect employee engagement, which contributed to the validity of the data (Lakshmi & Mohideen, 2013).

All participants in this study expressed the need for employee engagement in the optimization of both personal and professional objectives. Responses from participants indicated that employee engagement begins with individual desire and intention to make a psychological bond with the organization. This bond of psychological ownership is essential to create employee engagement.

Of the participants, 91% recognized that meeting employee expectations is a factor in influencing employee engagement. Expectation realization produces a positive effect on interpersonal relationships and secures the employee-organizational bond. Improved relationships foster improved teamwork, positive social interactions, and emotionally safe work domains.

Leadership played a vital role in influencing employee engagement. Trust developed when leaders met the expectations of employees. In the study 81% of the participants suggested that trust influences the employee-leader relationship. Employees that lack trust in the leadership of an organization will not engage emotionally. Leadership provides the necessary motivation to meet employee expectations and reinforce commitment to an organization.

The findings of this qualitative, phenomenological study underscore the need for leadership strategies on the improvement of employee engagement, which creates positive organizational outcomes. Specific responses from participants supported the results of the theme analysis, with specific conclusions: (a) participants expressed consistent understanding of employee engagement, (b) employee engagement is critical in creating positive organizational results, (c) psychological ownership creates the personal initiative needed for employee engagement, (d) meeting employee expectations is necessary in developing employee engagement, (e) communication between employees and leaders creates opportunities to influence interpersonal relationships, (f) leadership meeting employee expectations creates an environment of trust, and (g) trust influences the employee-leader relationship. The findings suggest there are four leadership strategies that affect employee engagement: (a) improving psychological commitment, (b) expectation realization, (c) trust actualization, and (e) decreasing the emotional distance between senior leadership and employees. Organizations need to create strategies that influence expectation realization, improve communication pathways, and increase the trust in employee-leader relationships. Employee motivation increases when leaders meet employee expectations. Leadership improves opportunities for the development of trust by keeping honest and open communication with employees.

Presentation of the Findings

The primary research question addressed in this study was: What strategies should health care leaders implement to engage employees in order to enhance patient care? I developed the interview questions in order to gain an understanding of strategies that influence employee engagement. Responses to the interview questions provided information that led to the themes located in the data analysis section.

INTERVIEW QUESTIONS

PQ1. What is your name?

PQ2. What is your job title?

PQ3. What is your age?

PQ4. How long have you been in the health care field?

PQ5. What is your educational background?

PQ6. How many jobs in health care have you had in your career?

PQ7. What do you do in your job?

PQ8. What does health care reform mean to you?

The following conceptual and follow-up questions related to the proposed research inquiry and formed part of the discussions.

C1. How do you define employee engagement?

C2. How does employee engagement affect the day-to-day operations of your department?

C3. What expectations do you have as an employee?

C4. How does your attitude affect you meeting employee expectations?

C5. How does your personal ownership of the workplace influence your performance as a leader?

C6. How does trust influence your employees' engagement within the organization?

C7. How does leadership influence engagement in your workplace?

C8. How is your motivation affected by your leader meeting your expectations?

Targeted follow-up questions were as follows:

C1F1. What examples do you have of employee engagement?

C1F2. What are the components of employee engagement that influence your employees?

C2F1. What are your key operational tasks?

C2F2. What are the specific drivers of employee engagement that influence the job tasks of your employees?

C3F1. What expectations do you have that are reasonable?

C3F2. What expectations do you have that are not reasonable?

C4F1. How can the attitudes of employees be improved?

C4F2. How can you improve your attitude to improve engagement?

C5F1. How do you improve your personal ownership of your work environment?

C6F1. How do you improve trust between you and your employees?

C6F2. How might a decrease in job security affect your engagement?

C7F1. How can your leadership skills improve the likelihood of meeting the expectations of your employees?

C8F1. How does communication affect your relationship with your supervisor?

C8F2. How does a strong interpersonal relationship with your employees affect your desire to meet organizational goals?

Concept interview question 1: How do you define employee engagement? The purpose of question 1 was to understand and uncover the perspective of each participant on the basic definition of employee engagement. Questions C1F1 and C1F2 provided opportunities to clarify C1. Employee engagement is the emotional connection between an employee and an organization that creates personal motivation to meet organizational goals (Fu, 2014). The answers and comments of the participants demonstrated a slight variety of definitions of employee engagement. Participant 4 commented that employee engagement was the act of an employee caring about the mission and vision of the organization. Engaged employees demonstrate the will to make the organization better.

Participants 1, 12, and 16 acknowledged that employee engagement is essential for organizational success; however, engagement is a personal commitment by employees not only to the organization but also to each other. Engaged employees work to meet organizational goals while working independently to be good team members. The personal relationship with other employees is equally as important as meeting job performance goals for engaged employees.

Participants 15 and 20 described disengagement in an attempt to define engagement. Employee disengagement is a social disconnect between the employee and the organizational environment. Disengaged employees strive to do the basic minimum to maintain employment. In some cases, actively disengaged employees work against organizational goals and team members in an effort to reduce overall productive outcomes.

Concept interview question 2: How does employee engagement affect the day-to-day operations of your department? Questions C2F1 and C2F2 provided opportunities to clarify C2. The purpose for this question was to explore the impact of employee engagement on operational performance. Employee engagement influences organizational productivity, operational performance, and customer satisfaction (AbuKhalifeh & Som, 2013).

Of the participants, 73% acknowledged that employee engagement has a positive influence on operational performance. Disengagement creates opportunities for dissention, decreased service quality, and customer dissatisfaction. The following quote demonstrates the importance of employee engagement:

> *I think employee engagement affects it every day, every minute of the day. Some days you know you're going to have a good day and some days you know by walking in you're going to have a rough day. And I think that has to do with environment. (Participant 8)*

Employee engagement provides the motivation needed to meet organizational objectives. Participant 10 concluded that employee engagement is instrumental in meeting goals and one person can negatively affect the entire team. Active disengagement creates obstacles that reduce the likelihood of successful outcomes, which increases sustainability issues for organizations.

Concept interview question 3: What expectations do you have as an employee? Questions C3F1 and C3F2 provided opportunities to clarify C3. The intent of this question was to explore the connection between meeting personal expectations and employee engagement. Motivation occurs when leaders meet the expectations of employees (Bembenutty, 2012).

According to expectancy theory, a relationship between meeting employee expectations and personal motivation exists (Bembenutty, 2012). A general agreement between the participants demonstrated that expectation realization is key to fostering an environment of employee engagement. Participants 4, 7, 11, 12, and 19 provided common examples of expectations. These examples are: (a) trust, (b) transparency, (c) fair compensation, (d) fairness, and (e) open communication. However, expectations are particular to the individual and can vary.

Lunenburg (2011) expanded on expectancy theory by suggesting that meeting employee expectations could increase employee morale. Unequal and unfair treatment of employees can create disengagement. Leaders who hold people accountable create an environment of meeting expectations. Participant 20 described how fair and equal treatment influence expectations:

> *Employees expect fair and equal treatment. When employees see others not being held accountable, it creates real disengagement. I*

believe that you have to have clear expectations as a leader and hold
everyone to the same standard. When this occurs people engage even
if they are held accountable because fairness is transparent. Meeting
employee expectations with recognition or discipline must be consistent
throughout the organization. (Participant 20)

Concept interview question 4: How does your attitude affect you meeting employee expectations? Questions C4F1 and C4F2 provided opportunities to clarify C4. The purpose of this question was to explore the influence of leadership on meeting the expectations of employees. Leadership has a role to play in meeting employee expectations while building strong interpersonal relationships (Krishnan, 2012). Many of the participants acknowledged that their attitude has a direct influence on the attitude of their fellow employees. The following participant explored the influence of the attitude of leaders:

I think it's huge. I think that if you have a positive attitude, a realistic
attitude, a down-to-earth attitude, you are going to be able to really
influence how they are in a day. Like if I come in here in my day
and be all mad at the world, feel like my needs aren't being met, you
know it's all about me, I'm negative and I'm looking at everything.
(Participant 4)

Negative attitudes from leaders can create an environment that fosters disengagement and negativity (Mutebi, Kakwezi, & Ntayi, 2012). Participants 15 and 21 suggested that the actions of their supervisor affect their attitude. Their supervisor demonstrates a positive attitude, which inspired their efforts to motivate other employees.

Concept interview question 5: How does your personal ownership of the workplace influence your performance as a leader? Questions C5F1 and C5F2 provided opportunities to clarify C5. The reason for this question was to gain an understanding about the role that psychological ownership plays in increasing employee engagement. Psychological ownership is the ability of an employee to take a personal ownership stake in the organization (Kaur, Sambasivan, & Kumar, 2013). Participants 3, 10, 13, and 18 commented that leadership could not make employees take ownership of their workplace. Psychological ownership and commitment is a personal choice of the employee.

Participant 13 commented that leaders needed to take personal ownership of the workplace. The emotional connection between leadership and the organization influences personal commitment. The following quote expands on this thought:

> *Psychological ownership significantly influences it because I own what I do and how I do it. There are days when it's more difficult to own that because you know that you can't change what's happening or you can't change people's behavior but I think it's very important to own what's ours, good and bad. (Participant 13)*

Participants agreed that psychological ownership is the initial step in the process of employee engagement. The decision to engage creates the ability to build emotional connections with the organization. Psychological ownership develops the environment to build organizational relationships, which increases the ability to create positive employee engagement (Nafei, 2014). To add to this concept another participant replied:

> You cannot make a person commit to an organization. The employee must first make the conscious decision to make an emotional connection to the organization. The leader cannot force that decision. Once the employee psychologically commits, then the leader can influence employee engagement. (Participant 7)

Concept interview question 6: How does trust influence your employees' engagement within the organization? Questions C6F1 and C6F2 provided opportunities to clarify C6. The point of this question was to explore the connection between trust and employee engagement. Trust is an important driver that influences the employee-leader relationship (Tuan, 2012). Participants suggested that trust is the product of the consistency of meeting expectations. The level of trust in the organization directly affects employee engagement and attitude.

The realization of employee expectations is the key to building trust. Participant 15 commented that trust is a vital component for the leader-employee relationship. Trust provides a consistent positive connection between psychological ownership and employee motivation. Lack of trust creates negative reactions and disengagement (Tuan, 2012). "If your employees don't have any trust in you, that could be absolutely disastrous because then the things you say or try to implement, there's no validity. Trust is the glue that keeps everything together" (Participant 11).

Trust is essential to build interpersonal relationships (Tuan, 2012). Participant 17 suggested that lost trust is very difficult to regain. Leaders that lose trust fail to properly motivate and lead employees (Tuan, 2012). Employees lose organizational commitment when leaders fail to meet expectations. The following comment supports the importance of trust:

> *I don't care what you do, if you lose trust, you lose everything. Once employees mistrust the leader, then commitment, you've lost the emotional commitment. Leaders must improve communication and meet employee expectations. People build trust once their expectations come true. Trust, once lost, is very difficult to regain. (Participant 18)*

Concept interview question 7: How does leadership influence engagement in your workplace? Question C7F1 provided opportunities to clarify C6. The purpose of this question was to understand the influence of leadership on employee engagement. Transformational leadership provides a positive influence on interpersonal relationships, trust, and communication (Ghafoor et al., 2011). The responses from the participants suggested that leadership has a direct influence on employee engagement. Commitment from leaders to meet employee expectations provides a structure to foster employee engagement.

Participant 13 explained that leaders influence employee engagement by over communicating openly, meeting employee expectations, and building trust. Open communication creates opportunities to increase trust and transparency. Trust increases as leaders meet expectations and build strong communication pathways. Participant 1 suggested that leadership had an obligation to lead by example. Organization requires leaders to set a positive example in an effort to build organizational commitment and positive employee engagement.

Concept interview question 8: How is your motivation affected by your leader meeting your expectations? Questions C8F1 and C8F2 provided opportunities to clarify C8. The goal of this question was to determine the relationship between expectations and motivation. Employee engagement occurs when organizations meet the expectations of employees (Lowe, 2012). Vroom suggested that motivation is the product of meeting employee expectations (Lunenburg, 2011).

Participant 11 stated that there was a significant importance to leadership meeting expectations focused on respect, perceived organizational value, and managerial support. Participant 15 suggested a major driver of motivation was an expressed feeling of value from leadership. Several other participants further explained that feeling valued is extremely important to build and keep engagement.

Personal motivation begins with individual desire and is inspired by leadership (Ghafoor et al., 2011). Participant 9 explained that indigent leadership, mistrust, and negative attitudes could adversely impact motivation. In addition, the delivery of fair and impartial treatment influenced motivation, because fairness is an important aspect of employee expectation. The following participant discussed aspects of motivation:

> *Motivation is completely affected by it, because I am very loyal to my leader and obviously this is confidential, you have to be able to trust your leadership team and sometimes if that trust is broken that's*

disengaging. I have to be honest, it does affect my engagement and motivation to a point where I become disengaged when I lose faith in my leader." (Participant 6)

THEME DEVELOPMENT

For this study I used descriptive coding, which is a coding technique for social environments and actions (Miles et al., 2014). The data retrieved from the interview transcripts connect to various categories, which then led to the development of the main themes of the study. The themes corresponded to the main research question, conceptual framework, information included in the literature review, and the lived experiences of leaders in health care. The primary research question for this study was: What strategies should health care leaders implement to engage employees in order to enhance patient care? Based on the data analysis from personal interviews, the following themes were found: (a) consistent definition of employee engagement, (b) psychological ownership, (c) drivers of employee engagement, (d) trust, (e) expectation realization, and (f) leadership power distance. Table 3 lists the themes and key words/phrases derived from the 23 interviews. The *Participants'* column indicates the number of participants who mentioned the words/phrases and the *References* column specifies the number of times the participants mentioned the words/phrases.

Table 3

Themes and Key Words/Phrases From Personal Interviews

Themes	Key Words/Phrases	Participants	References
Theme 1: Lack of consistency in defining employee engagement.	Employee are positive	16	19
	Good worker	12	13
	Go the extra mile	10	12
	Positive to work with	3	4
Theme 2: Psychological ownership is the first step in employee engagement.	Do the right thing	14	14
	Hard worker	9	11
	Pride in job	8	9
	It is my business	8	9
	Cannot teach it	6	6
	Not engaged without	6	6
	personal ownership	5	8
	First step	5	8
	Good team members	5	5
	Impact		
Theme 3: Defined drivers of employee engagement	Open communication	20	23
	Transparency	17	17
	Feeling valued	16	17
	Respect	10	10
	Recognition	9	9
	Trust is important	7	9
	Communication	4	7
	Fairness		
Theme 4: Significance of trust.	Absolutely necessary	21	21
	Key to engagement	20	21
	Reason for	19	22
	disengagement	19	21
	Lack of trust is bad	17	17
	Hard to repair	13	13
	Honesty needed	11	11
	Harm relationships	5	5
	Lead by example		

Theme 5: Importance of expectation realization	Trust in leaders	21	21
	Meet my needs	20	22
	Very important	19	19
	Clear expectations	14	15
	Job security	14	15
	Communication needed	10	12
	Listen to me	6	6
Theme 6: Leadership influence.	Trust is necessary	20	21
	Fairness	18	19
	Transparency	17	17
	Clear communication	16	17
	Good attitude	15	16
	Show value	14	16
	Lead by example	9	12
	Honesty needed	9	12
	Distance from employees	9	10

Theme 1: Consistent definition of employee engagement. There was a slight difference in interpretations of the definition of employee engagement throughout the entire pool of participants but it was consistent with the literature review. Nieberding (2014) suggested that employee engagement is the personal relationship of the employee with the work environment. Nasomboon further explained that employee engagement is the motivation of the employee to dedicate emotionally to an organization. The following quote supports this particular view of employee engagement:

> It's defined by that employee that comes in and gives 110%, is willing to do the work and cooperate and collaborate with his coworkers, and buys into the understanding of what the hospital and department want to accomplish. (Participant 9)

Participant 9 suggested that employee engagement is not just an internal process but also a process of collaboration with team members. This would suggest that employee engagement has influence over the dynamics of people working together. Disengagement can negatively influence other employees by creating barriers to relationship building (Hynes, 2012). Participant 6 explained that employee engagement influences the dynamics of teamwork:

> *To me employee engagement is not only participating in patient care, it's participating with coworkers, helping whenever you can, making a tough situation better, being involved with upper management as they make decisions. (Participant 6)*

Participant 6 believed that better outcomes occurred when employees and management worked together in making key decisions. Improving employee engagement may lead to better relationships with coworkers and managers. Positive relationships between employees and leaders may lead to higher employee engagement and better patient care (Lowe, 2012). "Employee engagement to me is accountability, responsibility, ownership. An employee that is accountable and responsible feels part of a team" (Participant 6).

This definition covers personal responsibility and collaboration with the work team. Employee engagement can influence overall team dynamics (Swarnalatha & Prasanna, 2013). Team members need to have a psychological commitment to the objectives of the team in order to firmly support the team vision. "A disengaged employee is someone who really doesn't want to be here. They don't work hard, are not a good team member, in fact makes it very difficult to work here" (Participant 13).

Disengagement has a direct effect on service quality (Atta, 2012). Improved service quality influences customer satisfaction and loyalty (Metha, 2011). Decreasing employee disengagement will result in improvements in service quality. Meeting consumer expectations in service quality may lead to improvements in customer satisfaction.

Theme 2: Psychological ownership. Psychological ownership is the purposeful act of an employee taking emotional ownership in an organization (Pan, Qin, & Gao, 2014). Vroom suggested motivation occurs when leaders meet employee expectations (Lunenburg, 2011). Psychological ownership, motivation, and expectations interconnect within employee engagement (Nafei, 2014). Of the participants, 72% commented on the importance of psychological ownership as the initial step in employee engagement. The following response is an illustration of the significance of this theme:

> If an employee does not want to be engaged you cannot make them. There is no way to make someone want to engage. It is a conscious decision by the person. Leaders can only do so much. Again, you cannot make a person emotionally connect. It is a personal choice. (Participant 17)

Participant 17 explained that engagement cannot occur without the personal choice of the employee. This would suggest that psychological ownership is a personal choice and the first step in employee engagement. The participants acknowledged the will of the individual is critical in facilitating employee engagement. Participant 14 acknowledged that a leader cannot force an employee to engage without that employee having the desire to do so. Another participant commented on the importance of the connection between a positive attitude and psychological ownership:

> *I'm going to go back again to positivity. I don't know how else to put it. I enjoy working here. I think this is a great place to work. Being in business on my own for 25 years I understand that there are trials and tribulations that you can't control and as far as that is concerned there are people in positions higher than me that control that; that's not my forte. So my attitude here is to do what is best for not only my employees but also for the patients that are here as well. It comes down to patient care/employee care. I decide to have a very positive attitude when I come to work. (Participant 9)*

Positive attitude is a subtheme to psychological ownership. Employees who connect emotionally to an organization proceed to develop positive attitudes. Attitude starts at the individual level and can influence job performance. "If I don't have a good attitude then my employees are not going to respect me, they're not going to listen to me. My attitude as a leader reflects on the people in my department" (Participant 14).

Employees with negative attitudes create issues of engagement and personal commitment. Improving the attitude of an employee is difficult and causes significant problems within the work unit. A negative attitude can spread to other employees, transforming positive employees to negative complainers. Participant 21 expressed how the attitude of a leader influences the attitude of employees:

I think it's critical. I think that your actions promote the values that you're talking about. You can't go into a unit meeting and talk about this strategy for 2015 and talk about what direction we're going, but yet what they hear you saying and what they see you doing are two different things. So I think you really have to align your behavior with the goals and with the expectations of the organization. I mean, for teamwork. They expect a smile. If a manager comes in and doesn't smile, if I say hello to one employee but there's four other ones that see me say hello to that employee, what does that imply? (Participant 21)

Employees who decide to emotionally connect to an organization create a sense of personal ownership. This connection strengthens the sense of personal involvement, accountability, and responsibility (Han et al., 2010). An employee who connects psychologically feels a sense of ownership and accountability. Sieger et al. (2013) suggested psychological ownership creates a bond that facilitates trust and engagement and creates a collaborative team environment. Participant 9 suggested that psychological ownership is an important part of personal commitment:

I have looked at psychological ownership in each one of my positions. As a director, I have looked at my department as my own little company. I have always felt that way... and in an effort to try to excel, I'm a highly competitive person, so we always want to make sure we're putting the best out there that we can. As a part of that, I guess I'm a business owner of a larger corporation, which is this hospital, so I want to make sure that my business is running as best as it can as well as the people within it being finely tuned. (Participant 9)

In the study, 67% of the participants suggested that employee engagement is not possible without personal investment and leadership support. Dollard and Bakker (2010) explained that leadership has a responsibility to create an environment to foster psychological ownership. Lack of this environment can hamper the fostering of personal commitment and psychological ownership (Dollard & Bakker, 2010). Participant 13 indicated that leadership has influence over the environment, which influences psychological ownership. The following quote supported this view:

> *I've had several bosses over time. I can tell you the good ones made me want to work harder, but I had a few who made me disengaged because of their actions. I really felt out of place with them, no trust, bad leaders. (Participant 16)*

Psychological ownership is the first step in the engagement process. Personal commitment is essential to creating employee engagement (Guerrero & Seguin, 2012). Participant responses supported the importance of psychological ownership and the influence of leadership. Meeting employee expectations may influence the degree of psychological ownership and motivation. The attitude of leadership may ultimately influence the degree of psychological ownership. Participant 20 explored the importance of personal commitment as a driver of engagement:

> *Personal commitment has a huge impact. If I'm not engaged and I am kind of grumbly or when I picture an employee who's not engaged, I'm picturing someone, you know, that kind of attitude and I can't get that, you know, I can't get that way. If I'm steering the ship and I want*

them to be engaged, I have to feel the same way. So it's important that
I maintain a healthy relationship with the Foundation as a company
and that, I feel that my needs are met and that I feel my questions are
answered so that I can build relationships. (Participant 20)

External influences may have an impact on employee engagement (Guerrero & Seguin, 2012). The attitudes of leaders, teamwork environment, and personal issues influence the personal commitment of employees. Psychological ownership and personal commitment create the environment for increased employee engagement. Participant 19 explored how external factors can decrease engagement:

External factors can have a great effect. I'm the type of person who
feels like you know when you walk through these doors you leave
everything else behind, you don't drag your personal issues into work.
You cannot let things that happen at home affect what happens at
work. (Participant 19)

Theme 3: Drivers of employee engagement. Drivers of engagement can be both internal and external to an individual. External drivers of employee engagement represent actions and behaviors that influence the attitude and engagement of an employee that exist in the work environment (Gruyter, 2014). Internal drivers include personal goals, biases, and perceptions that influence employee engagement. External and internal drivers influence employee engagement, which may negatively impact service quality, patient satisfaction, and health care delivery (Lowe, 2012). The participants collectively remarked on several levels of drivers of engagement. These are: (a) communication,

(b) transparency, (c) trust, and (d) feeling valued. In the study, 61% participants believed that these drivers created opportunities to influence employee engagement. However, external drivers cannot influence an employee with the absence of personal commitment because psychological ownership creates the foundation for engagement. Leaders who fail to meet external drivers of engagement can negatively influence personal commitment.

Communication. Communication is a vital component in the employee-leader relationship (Welch, 2011). Open communication allows people to express views and opinions without fear of retribution. Guay (2013) suggested that leaders have a fundamental responsibility to actively listen to employees. Guay remarked that sometimes listening is a bigger driver then using verbal communication. Participant 10 illustrated the importance of communication as an external driver of engagement:

> *Communication has to be a key part; that has to be the number-one thing. With having several different realms of management here it needs to be a collaborative effort again. We need to know kind of like what the left hand needs to know the right hand is doing. (Participant 10)*

Participant 14 further explored the importance of communication in the context of improving patient care:

> *I would say the same as before. If you are able to communicate with them if they're there and they're actually communicating with you, it makes you more engaged to be able to want to try to work together*

and change things rather than them not being receptive to you or not being available when you need them to be. (Participant 14)

Transparency. Improved communication leads to transparency. Transparency is the act of providing open communication in an honest format, which delivers the truth while building creditability (Welch, 2011). Employee engagement increases as transparency increases (Welch, 2011). Increasing transparency improves the interpersonal relationship between employees and leaders. Participant 21 commented that it was very important to have transparency because honest and open communication reduces specialization, gossip, and assumptions. The following response from Participant 21 supports this claim:

Having transparency and open communication with senior leadership is very important. I need to feel good about working here and I want the truth, good or bad. If a leader is dishonest, I lose interest in the organization. Too many times, I've seen leaders hide things only for the truth to come out later. I can handle praise and criticism. I expect to be told the truth in all circumstances. (Participant 21)

Trust. Trust is the foundation for building strong employee-leader relationships (Tuan, 2012). Trust is the byproduct of expectation realization. It is a feeling of understanding that there is an anticipated reaction to an action (Tuan, 2012). Trust builds strong relationships between leaders, employees, team members, and patients, with each link having a unique connection. Lack of trust may affect personal commitment by damaging the employee-leader relationship. Participants emphasized the importance of trust in the ability to engage with the organization. Participant 12 suggested that trust is necessary to foster relationships. Lack of trust is a driver of disengagement. The following comment demonstrates the significance of trust:

> *It's huge. If people don't trust you they don't buy into what you're saying. It is one of the problems that even here not only in our department but also in our organization there's always been this trust is that five letter word. That is the bad word, and we have teased and kidded about that and we've tried to promote a value of trust to each other. I trust that they come to work to do the best job they do. I trust that they are going to do these things. I think we're getting through that. There was a lot of distrust because of the way things were handled in the past. I think we've overcome a lot of it but we still have some work to do. So it has a major impact. (Participant 9)*

The following comments further supported the importance of trust:

> *It is everything and I think you build trust by communication. I don't know that you can make every single person feel that trust, but with enough communication you can build some trust. I think it's not just trust, it's trust with our physicians, it's trust between administration, different departments, it's trust everywhere and communication I think is the bridge to help that. (Participant 3)*

Feeling valued. Employees who feel valued are more satisfied and willing to work harder in meeting the mission of the organization (Sawang, 2012). The feeling of worth improves self-confidence while improving baseline attitudes (Sawang, 2012). Leaders have a duty to ensure that employees have a sense of well-being and feel that their efforts create value to an organization. Participants 11,17, 20, and 21 explained that the feeling of value was important because it provided a sense of a meaning in life. Value becomes important when leaders took the time to appreciate personal effort. In addition to value, a feeling of respect and fairness also influenced engagement. Fair and respectful treatment creates an environment that fosters employee engagement (Fearon et al., 2013). The following comment supported this finding:

I want to feel valued. I want to feel that I make a difference for the organization and my patients. When I feel valued, I feel the leaders respect what I do and how I do it. This makes it all worthwhile in the end. (Participant 5)

Drivers of engagement play an important role influencing employee engagement (Timmerman, 2009). Fearon et al. (2013) suggested that employee engagement begins with a personal commitment but external drivers influence that commitment. Of the participants, 76% commented that external drivers exist and do influence their engagement:

Well, I can tell you that I walked in the doors of this hospital at 18 years old and I've been here now for 25 years. I feel like I do have a stake in ownership in this facility. That is where it all starts. I think we've seen it grow together. You know, it's allowed me to raise a family, be successful. (Participant 16)

Personal commitment is the foundation for the development of employee engagement. External drivers of employee engagement can influence personal commitment, which affects employee engagement. Participant

14 explained that personal commitment is the foundation of employee engagement:

> *Actually I feel like I have ownership in any job that I've ever had. I take great pride in my work. I always put my full effort forward, I'm always willing to do whatever's asked of me. I am always willing to go above and beyond. I have always had great pride in my work and I always try to work at the top of the scale. (Participant 14)*

Theme 4: Trust. Trust is a significant driver of the employee-leader relationship (Kottke & Pelletier, 2013). All of the participants felt that trust was an important aspect of the employee-leader relationship. Trust is the product of expectation realization. Leaders who consistently meet the expectations of employees build a foundation of trust that influences the engagement of their employees (Agarwal, 2013). Improvements in trust may lead to increased employee satisfaction and improved employee retention. Trust was an important topic for all of 92% of the participants. "If your employees don't have any trust in you that could be absolutely disastrous because then the things you say or try to implement there is no validity" (Participant 2).

Trust is an attribute that takes time to acquire (Tuan, 2012). Trust in the employee-leader relationship improves the likelihood for positive employee engagement. Participant 23 suggested that there are current members of the medical staff who have a high level of distrust in the senior leadership team. This mistrust affects the engagement of the medical staff. Participant 23 explained this distrust with the following response:

There are pockets within the medical staff that distrust the senior leadership. This creates all sorts of issues. The physicians will not engage into the strategic objectives of the hospital. This has to affect the operation and efficiency of the hospital. (Participant 23)

The significance of trust between leaders and followers influences the integrity of the employee-leader relationship (Tuan, 2012). Without trust, this relationship succumbs to distrust, conflict, and disconnection. Failure in the development of trust decreases the possibility of personal commitment and expectation realization in the workplace. Meeting expectations increases motivation (Lunenburg, 2011), which is the basis of the conceptual framework for this study. When leaders meet expectations, motivation increases because employees start to trust the intentions of their leaders (Kottke & Pelletier, 2013).

Theme 5: Expectation realization. I chose expectancy theory as the conceptual framework for this doctoral study. This theory made evident the notion that employee motivation increased when employers met the expectations of the employees (Lunenburg, 2011). Communication within the employee-leader relationship may lead to expectation discovery. This discovery is a bidirectional process between employees and leaders. Employees have a desire to understand the expectations from the employer in addition to having their personal expectations met (Mone et al., 2011). In this study, 84% of the participants felt that bidirectional expectations affected engagement. The following comments illustrated this concept:

I expect the organization to treat me fairly, value my services, be honest, and give me the tools to do my job. Actually, what is equally important is I understand my boss's expectations of me. I don't see how you can be engaged if I don't know what the hospital wants me to do. Expectations are important from both sides of the equation. (Participant 11)

Employee expectations are a set of personal desires and needs (Lunenburg, 2011). These needs may differ between employees. Meeting these expectations is an objective of leadership. Common expectations are fairness, equal pay, honest communication, and having the tools to do the job. Participant 21 described how meeting expectation affects performance:

I guess reporting to a vice president here, I expect the organization to develop me as a leader for the organization. I expect clear communication from my vice president on what is expected of me just like my employees would expect the same. I want to know what's expected of me. It is important to feel valued while understanding that my contribution is making a difference. (Participant 21)

Participant 7 explained that trust suffers when the organization fails to meet expectations. Distrust is the result of not meeting employee expectations (Tuan, 2012). Participant 7 further emphasized what happens to engagement when management fails to listen:

Well, the enthusiasm of the techs is down, because you know management does not really care and you know not that you are here for passing is buck. Part of it is like you say the overall employer, the whole hospital, they say you're doing a real great job but they give you a...your cost of living raise is way below the average and you're not even catching up with the cost of living. If you express your opinion to management and you know it's just going in one ear and out the other, then you tend to not engage in them at all. (Participant 7)

Motivation is an important aspect of employee engagement. Personal commitment builds a base for motivation, while expectation realization provides the necessary fuel for motivational endurance (Eisele et al., 2013). Bembenutty (2012) explored the connection between motivation and expectations. Expectations have a direct effect on personal motivation (Bembenutty, 2012). The participants identified several drivers of expectations but focused on job security as a key expectation. Employees expect that their jobs have a certain amount of security (Nasomboon, 2014). This viewpoint underscored the importance of job security:

I think job security is very important. I expect management to make good decisions for the organization. I know for me, I get totally distracted when I hear layoffs are coming. I immediately start to distrust the leaders of the organization. I start to look for other employment opportunities. (Participant 1)

Expectation management is a key function of leadership teams. Organizations must deliver clear expectations to employees while understanding the expectations of the work force (Mone et al., 2011). Expectation realization is a fundamental aspect of employee engagement and the development of trust. Expectation realization fosters employee engagement by meeting the desires of the employees.

The ability of leaders to gain an understanding of employee expectations is important to maintain and improve employee engagement. Meeting expectations develops opportunities to improve trust between employees and leaders while improving the likelihood of increasing employee engagement. Expectation realization generates opportunities to motivate employees by connecting leadership empathy with personal needs of the employees. Participant 16 explained that honesty is important while organizational direction is necessary:

> *I expect for them to be consistent and honest with me. I expect the organization to have a direction. If I'm floating then I have a problem. If I know where I want to go then I usually feel pretty good. It doesn't always have to be perfectly sound or absolutely to the letter, but you have to pick your direction. And that's what I expect from my organization. (Participant 16)*

The responsibility of expectation realization rests with both employees and leaders. Employees must understand and communicate personal expectations. Leaders need to be proactive in the ability to listen and learn about the expectations of the employees. This interaction develops the necessary foundation for the employee-leader relationship. Leaders have the opportunity to influence personal commitment and expectation realization.

Theme 6: Leadership power distance. Leadership has an active role in improving employee engagement. Leaders have the ability to improve communication, respect, and trust (Tims et al., 2011). Simola et al. (2012) suggested leadership influences service quality, profitability, and productivity by influencing employee engagement. Of the participants, 87% felt that leadership plays a significant role in influencing employee engagement. Leaders influence engagement by supporting a positive attitude, reducing the power distance, and influencing drivers of employee engagement. Participant 3 remarked that leaders have a fundamental accountability to have a positive attitude. The attitude of the leader sets the tone for the employees. The following participant reply links to the response of Participant 3:

> *I think it has a probably 100% effect. If I have a bad attitude, if I am constantly complaining, if I am nasty or negative, they notice that easily. You have to portray a positive attitude, we have some stumbling blocks, we've got some problems, we've got some challenges to get over, but you know we've got a smart group of people and we need to get over this together. So I think it has a huge effect on it. (Participant 9)*

Leadership influence depends on the ability of the leader to emotionally connect with employees. The strength of this connection depends on the emotional distance between leaders and employees, otherwise known as the power distance (Loi, Lamar, & Chan, 2012). The power distance is the emotional distance between senior leadership and frontline employees (Loi et al., 2012). This distance can affect employee engagement because length of distance can hinder interpersonal relationships, decrease communication, and create gaps within expectation realization (Loi et al., 2012). The health care industry has lengthy vertical organizational structures with long power distances (Winkler, Busch, Clasen, &

Vowinkel, 2014). Several participants commented on the lack of senior leadership connection to the employee because of the vertical nature of the organizational structure. This senior leadership disconnection creates opportunities to increase disengagement while decreasing the motivation of employees. The following remarks support the importance of the power distance:

> *I feel the management of the organization fails to really understand what happens on a day-to-day basis. They are too far from where things happen. I'm not sure many of them know who I am and surely don't know my employees. I often wonder if they really care what happens in my department. (Participant 18)*

The power distance may prevent feedback from traveling back up through the organization (Loi et al., 2012). An obstruction of communication can lead to unacceptable operational outcomes, decreases in service quality, and customer dissatisfaction. Participant 19 expressed appreciation for the support of senior leadership but expressed concern in the perception of the separation between leadership and employees. The following remarks support the context of this subject:

> *I believe that my vice president does care about what happens in my area, but her bosses seem to be completely disconnected from what happens here. Decisions get made with really no clear connection to what really needs to happen. I often wonder how things can get so mixed up and we make bad decisions. (Participant 21)*

The power distance between employees and senior leadership creates disconnection between expectation realization and leadership influence and understanding. Increasing the power distance decreases the opportunity for leaders to build interpersonal relationships with employees. Building interpersonal relationships creates an environment where leaders gain an understanding of the expectations of employees. This knowledge gives leaders an opportunity to meet expectations, which has a positive influence on employee engagement by increasing communication, active listening, and empathy.

Improved communication leads to transparency between leaders and employees (Tims et al., 2011). Transparency builds leadership creditability, which improves trust (Tims et al., 2011). Participants in this study commented on the importance of transparency. Many felt that transparency was necessary in the evolution of trust and the employee-leader relationship. Participants were more interested in the truth than in hearing about positive data. The following remarks illustrate the importance of transparency:

> *I don't care what the message is I just want to know the truth. I think there are things that management cannot tell us, but I would at least like to know what's going on. Maybe we can all come together in tough situations and find solutions. I get angry when our management team doesn't tell us what really is going on. (Participant 11)*

Communication and transparency provide leaders with a chance to improve the flow of information. Improvements in communication channels make decision making easier. Another participant supported this premise:

Communication is huge for engagement. I think constant communication is also important. You are kind of assessing and reassessing as you go along within a process or whatever change or whatever you want to do or have a vision for your organization or for your department, and then to be able to get that feedback and that two-way communication where you know explaining why this is important or why it is working or not working is important. (Participant 4)

Leaders have the ability to encourage communication as a driver of employee engagement (Tims et al., 2011). Opening communication pathways creates dialogue between employees and leaders. Employee-leader dialogue generates information transfers and supports emotional connectivity and personal bonding. Leaders have the responsibility to build relationships that influence personal commitment, expectation realization, and employee engagement.

Enhanced leadership skills develop interpersonal relationships (Krishnan, 2012). These interpersonal relationships build the foundation for trust by understanding the importance of expectation realization. Ultimately, leaders cannot force an employee to engage, but ineffective leaders can definitely discourage personal commitment and effectively make employees disengage from the organization.

CONCLUSIONS FROM THEMES

The conclusions of the theme analysis create an opportunity to build a model to influence employee engagement. Specific responses from participants supported the results of the theme analysis, with specific conclusions: (a) participants expressed consistent understanding of employee engagement, (b) psychological ownership creates personal initiative for employee engagement, (c) meeting employee expectations is necessary in developing employee engagement, (d) communication between employees and leaders influences interpersonal relationships, (e) leaders who meet employee expectations created an environment of trust, and (f) leadership power distance influences the employee-leader relationship.

The purpose of this qualitative, phenomenological study was to explore the lived experiences of health care leaders in their desire to design strategies to engage employees in order to provide better patient care. Based on the theme analysis, I suggest there are four leadership strategies that influence employee engagement: (a) improving psychological commitment, (b) expectation realization, (c) trust actualization, and (d) reduction in the power distance of leadership. Leadership strategies focused on these strategies provide the best opportunity to influence employee engagement.

Psychological commitment. Psychological ownership and commitment begins with the desire of an individual to emotionally connect with an organization (Zhang, Nie, & Yan, 2014). Psychological commitment is the foundation for employee engagement. Improved personal commitment increases productivity, innovation, and customer satisfaction. Without psychological ownership, employee engagement cannot occur.

Expectation realization. Vroom described expectancy theory as a link between employee expectations and motivation (Bembenutty, 2012). Employees commit with a set of personal expectations. Leadership can influence expectations with improved communication, active listening, and improving the employee-leader relationship. Meeting expectations creates an environment to foster employee engagement and improve business outcomes.

Trust actualization. Trust is an individual's reliance on actions of another person to meet personal expectations (Tuan, 2012). Trust is the product of consistently meeting expectations. The establishment of trust improves teamwork, interpersonal relationships, and the ability to meet the goals of the organization. Distrust creates opportunities for damaged relationships, decreased employee engagement, and loss of institutional commitment.

Reduction in the power distance of leadership. Health care organizations have a vertically integrated health leadership structure, which creates a high power distance (Winkler et al., 2014). Increased power distance between employees and senior leaders can hinder expectation realization and trust, resulting in a decrease in employee engagement. Leadership has the responsibility and authority to reduce this distance, which creates an opportunity to gain an understanding of the employee expectations. Reducing emotional distance provides a better chance at improving employee engagement, patient satisfaction, and increasing sustainability in a changing workplace environment.

Application to Professional Practice

The culture of consumerism is starting to change the customer-supplier relationship in health care because of health care reform (Baird &

Gonzalez, 2011). Educated consumers now focus on quality, cost, and perception of health care services. The new age in health care is the convergence of health care and hospitality. New demands from health care customers create challenges for health care organizations in service quality, improved patient satisfaction, and meeting new customer expectations (Lowe, 2012). Service quality in health care historically has focused on meeting quality outcomes from medical services (Baird & Gonzalez, 2011). New demands on service quality focus on hospitality items such as (a) cleanliness, (b) food taste, (c) quietness of environment, (d) empathy of staff, (e) caregiver communication, (f) dignity, and (g) respect (Kompaso & Sridevi, 2010).

Changes in health care consumer requirements create a demand for changes in the employee-patient relationship. Based on the six main themes of this study, the four leadership strategies are: (a) improving psychological commitment, (b) expectation realization, (c) trust actualization, and (d) reduction in the power distance of leadership. These findings provide the best chance to influence employee engagement in order to meet the new requirements of health care consumers. Improving employee engagement in health care provides an opportunity to strengthen the connection between employees and patients. This study has application to professional practice by focusing on practical solutions that will influence the main findings of the study: (a) improving the hiring process, (b) developing leadership, (c) building trust, and (d) reducing the power distance of leadership.

Improving the hiring process. Psychological ownership begins with self-actualization and the desire of an individual to emotionally connect with an organization (Rothmann & Welsh 2013). From the research findings, 72% of participants believed that personal commitment was important in developing positive attitudes and employee engagement. Leaders in organizations must identify those candidates who fit the culture of the organization. Leaders need to initiate mentoring to improve employee engagement and performance while removing disengaged employees from the organization. Increasing the number of engaged employees provides an opportunity to improve profitability, productivity, and sustainability (Nasomboon, 2014).

Developing leadership. Vroom described expectancy theory, which suggested that leaders influence employee motivation by meeting employee expectations (Bembenutty, 2012). Leaders have a responsibility to develop interpersonal relationships with followers. Of the participants, 84% suggested that understanding and meeting expectations leads to improved employee engagement and the development of trust. Leaders should take time to gain an understanding of the expectations of their employees. Once leaders understand the expectations they can develop system-wide strategies to improve expectation realization. Consistently meeting expectations will lead to improved motivation and employee engagement.

Building trust. Trust influences the employee-leader relationship (Goh & Low, 2014). From the research findings, 92% of participants mentioned that the development of trust influenced the strength of the employee-leader relationship. Leaders in health care must gain an understanding of trust issues within the organization. Improvement in trust develops the ability to strengthen interpersonal relationships while improving employee engagement.

Reducing the power distance of leadership. Health care has a vertical power distance. Eighty-four percent of leader participants believed the emotional distance from leaders to employees influenced employee engagement and trust. Implementation of a more horizontal hierarchy provides an opportunity to reduce the distance between senior leaders and employees (Zwingmann et al., 2014). This can be accomplished by reducing the number of management layers (Winkler et al., 2014). This reduction may improve communication, understanding of employee expectations, and may increase the likelihood of trust actualization by placing leaders emotionally closer to employees (Loi et al., 2012).

Implications for Social Change

The findings of (a) improving psychological commitment, (b) expectation realization, (c) trust actualization, and (d) reduction in the power distance of leadership indicates a connection between personal commitment, leadership, and trust, which influence employee engagement. Seventy-two percent of the participants mentioned that personal commitment is the first step in influencing employee engagement. While 67% of the participants believed that employee engagement was not possible without leadership support. Improved employee engagement has an influence on patient care and satisfaction (Lowe, 2012). All the participants believed that employee engagement had a positive influence on the organization. Employee engagement increases service quality, which leads to better medical outcomes (Ramez, 2012). Improved patient satisfaction provides an opportunity for patients to concentrate on healing (Ramez, 2012). Improved personal health may increase the ability of people to interact socially. A healthier society creates a stronger social network and community.

I made a business case for reducing the management layers in health care administration to decease the power distance between senior leaders and frontline employees. Of the participants, 83% suggested a reduction in the power distance of leadership increases the likelihood of improving the employee-leadership relationship and increased employee engagement. High employee engagement increases productivity, profitability, and service quality of health care organizations (Lowe, 2012). Improving operational results influences organizational sustainability. Improving the sustainability of health care organizations provides a stable framework for social interaction and improves the health of the community as the population ages.

The Baby Boomer generation is the largest population segment in the history of the United States moving to the retirement phase in a social setting (Chiesl, 2012). This segmentation may change the fundamental culture of consumerism in health care by demanding that hospitality merge with health care creating a new social platform for caring for the emotional and physical needs of patients (Wu & Robson, 2013). Sections 1 and 2 and the results in Section 3 focused on the social, corporate, ethical, medical, and business need for better strategies to encourage the likelihood of increasing personal commitment, meeting employee expectations, and developing trust in an effort to improve employee engagement. From the research findings, 72% of the participants suggested that personal commitment was necessary in developing employee engagement. While 84% of the participants believed that employee engagement was important in developing employee engagement. Improving personal commitment, expectation realization, trust actualization, and reducing the leadership power distance may increase employee engagement. Eighty-seven percent of the leader participants agreed that reducing the power distance would influence employee engagement. Increasing employee engagement influences consumer satisfaction, which may improve the overall health of the patient. Improved personal health may create social change in health care.

Recommendations for Action

Employee engagement supports the mission of health care organizations by increasing patient satisfaction, service quality, and patient loyalty (Lowe, 2012). All the participants suggested that employee engagement had a positive influence on meeting organizational goals and consumer expectations. Health care organizations would benefit from improving personal commitment, expectation realization, trust actualization, and reducing the leadership power distance as strategic objectives. Sixty-seven percent of the participants mentioned the need for leadership focus and support to improve employee engagement. Strategic objectives provide health care organizations an opportunity to develop action plans for improvement and implementation. I would recommend several steps in a process to access, diagnose, and improve employee engagement. The steps are: (a) complete an employee engagement survey, (b) complete an expectation audit for employees and the organization, (c) create an action team composed of senior leaders and front-line employees to develop a strategy to decrease the power distance, (d) develop action plans focused on improving trust within the organization, (e) develop hiring strategies to improve the selection process, (f) remove employees who are disengaged from the organization, and (g) hold senior leadership accountable to improve employee engagement, trust, and expectation realization.

The board of directors has the responsibility for the direction of health care organizations (Guerrero & Seguin, 2012). Leadership strategies for employee engagement begin with the engagement of the board of directors. Directors should provide motivation for the senior leadership team to increase the engagement of the workforce. Improvements in employee engagement should be the ultimate goal of the organization in an effort to increase patient satisfaction and influence the patient care delivery system.

I will disseminate the results of this study by presenting my findings at national professional meetings. These meetings provide an opportunity to present insights into this study while creating interactive sessions by meeting with participants. I could provide consulting services to health care organizations in regards to training leaders and employees on aspects of this study.

Recommendations for Further Study

Following the findings of this study, future researchers should investigate the connection between employee engagement and corporate compliance. As I conducted the research study, I found many of the participants connected employee engagement to personal choice rather than organizational need. Corporate compliance is the process of ensuring that organizations operate within lawful guidelines (Habisch, 2012). Employee engagement may influence compliance. Federal, state and local agencies require a proactive approach to corporate compliance (Habisch, 2012). This compliance is focused on (a) sexual harassment, (b) patient confidentiality, (c) JACHO accreditation, (d) fraud and abuse, and (e) general corporate compliance (Habisch, 2012). Corporate compliance tasks are very important to the success of health care organizations (Kane et al., 2012). Employee engagement may have a material effect on meeting corporate compliance requirements and reducing financial risk.

A major limitation of this study was the absence of secondary stakeholders in health care in the participant pool. For example, medical supply vendors, commercial payers, and equipment vendors have significant relationships with health care organizations (Aslin, 2011). From the research findings, 72% of participants suggested that personal commitment was important in meeting organizational goals. Further study may be necessary to understand the correlations between secondary stakeholder personal commitment and employee engagement in health care. Engagement with secondary stakeholders may influence health care employees by negatively affecting supply product delivery, quality, and functionality.

Researchers may benefit from gaining an understanding of the impact of employee engagement on the decrease of medical malpractice lawsuits. All the participants agreed that employee engagement is important to the goals of an organization. Reducing medical malpractice lawsuits may increase the profitability of health care organizations (Kane et al., 2012). Further study may lead to understanding how employee engagement may influence patient satisfaction and reduce medical malpractice risk.

Reflections

The research process was challenging and emotionally draining. The diversity of the participants provided both an ease and difficulty in the interview process. The different mix of positions provided a unique perspective from various points of view from leadership roles within the organizational structures of health care organizations. However, this same diversity made some of the interviews difficult because of some participants' lack of strategic understanding of current health care issues and strategies. A major unseen benefit of the leadership pool was that the participants were both leaders and employees of their perspective organizations. This combination allowed participants to answer questions from both leadership and employee viewpoints.

I had little trouble finding adequate participants through an effective snowballing sampling technique. I interviewed 23 participants until no new information was gathered and saturation occurred (Walker, 2012).

I maintained a good relationship with all the participants throughout both interview sessions. The data gathered from the interview sessions validated the choice of qualitative phenomenological study as the optimum research methodology and design in answering the main research question in this study. I felt overwhelmed by the dedication of the participants to serve patients. Regardless of position and title, many participants had a goal of helping patients.

My personal view of leadership changed throughout this study. I attempted to remove all biases, but some of my own views on leadership caused me to judge the participants based on the answers to their interview questions. At the beginning of the interviews, I perceived those participants who gave brief or obscure answers as inferior to my own experience and expectations. Leadership is neither standardized nor stagnant and people experience things differently. Just because I did not experience the same lived experiences does not mean their perspectives were wrong. Finally, this entire study was a life-changing journey because the data collection and analysis provided insight into the aspects of employee-leader relationships in health care. This knowledge will provide an opportunity to make a difference for employees, leaders, and ultimately improved patient care.

Summary and Study Conclusions

The focus of this study was to explore the lived experiences of health care leaders in an effort to understand leadership strategies that could affect employee engagement. Responses from personal interviews provided insight into the aspects of psychological ownership, leadership, and employee engagement. An analysis of the responses produced six major themes. These themes produced a set of specific findings that consolidated the results into four leadership strategies for influencing employee engagement: (a) improving psychosocial commitment, (b) expectation realization, (c) trust actualization, and (d) reduction in the power distance of leadership.

The main takeaway from this doctoral study is that employee engagement starts with the individual and leads to expectation realization while influenced by leadership performance. The study also revealed the importance of trust in the employee-leader relationship. Trust is the foundation for improved interpersonal relationships. The participants in this study provided a diverse mix of health care leaders who were also employees of health care organizations. Participants used their lived experiences as health care leaders as a resource to provide valuable information for this doctoral study

Employee Engagement: Health Care is Critically ill

"Reform is changing the landscape in health care" Vizzuso

Today, health care represents 20% of the GNP. The increasing growth in expense over the last 20 years is not a sustainable economic model. Regardless if you agree or disagree with the affordable care act, change was needed to rebalance the economic situation in health care. The ACA creates systematic changes in the management, delivery, and remuneration of national healthcare services. These changes cover a multitude of facets within health care:

1. The federal government mandates all individuals over the age of 18 to obtain insurance coverage through existing insurance pathways, federal mandated insurance exchanges, and traditional federal programs.

2. Insurance companies can no longer exclude people based on pre-existing conditions.

3. In order to lower costs, health care consumers are purchasing high deductible plans, which increases out-of-pocket expenses.

4. The federal government plans on continued decreases in reimbursement to both physicians and hospital organizations.

5. Accountable care organizations provide a capitated environment of reimbursement for population health management services. Improvements in cost management are collectively shared within the accountable care model.

In the past, health care organizations could function in an environment where common business drivers had little effect. Health care consumers had little ability to understand the dynamics of medical care, economics of the delivery of care, and the meaning of true quality in health care. The dynamics of employee engagement are more important today than any other day in the history of business. Health care organizations must gain acute awareness of changing healthcare consumers, economic pressures, and a keen understanding of the moral obligation to deliver high quality healthcare at the lowest cost.

HEALTH CARE CONSUMERS 2020

Health care consumers are completely different than those consumers of goods and services outside of the health care arena. Interestingly, health care consumers have changed over the decades. Years ago, if I had a pain in my left side I would set up an appointment with my primary care physician. This appointment might take weeks to occur due to limited physician access. Once seen, the use of high-end diagnostic procedures was limited and in most cases a diagnosis was given based on low and diagnostic procedures such as lab tests and diagnostic x-rays.

Today, if I experience left side pain, my first step is to go onto the Internet and find conditions that have symptoms of left side pain. Once my curiosity is satisfied, I have three choices to seek care: primary care physician, urgent care, and emergency care. This choice ultimately determines the need to use high-end diagnostic procedures to provide the final diagnosis. The practice of defensive medicine is widely adopted throughout the United States because of the increase of medical liability.

Health care consumers have different attributes then the normal consumer of goods and services. These drivers create gaps that are very difficult to fill. Health care organizations fail to realize the distinct difference between patients and customers:

- Health care consumers do not want to be health care consumers. In fact, they would rather be any place else other than seeking care from a health care provider.
- There is an overarching fear of a positive diagnosis. The fear creates emotional distress, despair, and decreased confidence.
- The consumer of health care services has no ability to estimate the economical consequence of health care services.
- The outcome of the purchase of health care services can result in painful outcomes.
- Health cares not only affect the consumer but the consumer's family.

The distinct difference today versus years ago is that health care consumers are becoming more knowledgeable and are paying more for out-of-pocket expenses. This creates a shopper mentality where one never existed. Health care consumers are poised to change the landscape and force hospitals to deliver high quality at a low cost or loss market share.

CURRENT STATE OF CUSTOMER SERVICE IN HEALTH CARE

The government use HSCAPS questions to ascertain patient satisfaction in health care. The main question on satisfaction asks the following question:

"Would you recommend this hospital to a friend or family member?"

I don't care what hospital leaders say, this question relates directly to the satisfaction of the consumer. Outside of health care, doing what this question asks influences consumer perspectives. The scale is 1-10 with only 9 or 10 being recorded responses. Nationally health care has 9 or 10 answered 72% of the time or what some would say is a C- on the normal grading scale.

Health care organizations fail on many levels when it comes to patient satisfaction. The political climate and general ability to not except responsibility for poor employee engagement, bad operational practice, poor and inexperienced leadership, and general incompetence is wide spread in this industry.

My time in business, I've seen senior leadership not truly understand employee engagement. During this time I witnessed things that would boggle anyone's mind. Several years into my stent at the hospital home, senior leadership decided to do an employee engagement survey. This was the really first attempt to gauge the engagement for the organization.

The first major flaw was the employee had to give their employee Id in order to take the survey. Unfortunately, this created an enormous hurdle because trust between employees and leadership was at an all time low. The survey went on and only 43% of the employees took the survey. In the world of employee surveys this is a devastating result because it automatically places 57% of the employees in the disengaged category. In fact, I would say that really places them in the actively disengaged because they would not take the time or risk to fill it out. Out of the 43% that filled it out 40% were engaged, 43% were somewhat engaged, and 17% were disengaged.

The organizations took a different view of these results. The senior leadership viewed that 83% of the people who took the survey were engaged and they felt that it was a healthy number for the first survey. I have to be honest when I heard this rumor I was sure it was just a rumor. However, I sat in the once a month management meeting and listened to the person say these words.

Was I dreaming? Could an educated person really feel positive about this outcome? A truly unbiased person would not. So I'm sure you're asking yourself how could this happen. Let me take you a tour of how hospital home operates:

1. The director of performance management was a nice lady but more of a mice then a lion. She reported to a very dominant

personality that would not stand to have bad results. Thus, she was forced to walk the party line.

2. There was a new senior leader in the building. He had an open persona and worked hard to endear himself to the masses. He, too bought into this, but why? He was a physician and now living in the business world. How could he not see this? It's easy; I call it "spinning". He wants to spin the issue so it doesn't look bad since it is now on his watch.

3. The remaining senior leadership does not have the courage to go against this strategy. Many health care leaders shy away from confrontation with the new leader's views. In most cases, it is a one-way ticket to the unemployment line.

For all those reasons the view of the results becomes then a positive view from the administration of the hospital. However, behind the scenes physicians, employees, and mid level leaders knew the truth. The truth is that senior leadership was drastically disconnected from the employees, which had created a significant gap in trust and confidence. The act of spinning and denial only increases the disengagement of the organization, which is the exact opposite of the initial desired affect.

Employee engagement has to be a strategic objective for health care organizations. The literature review clearly supports the influence of employee engagement on organizational performance and customer satisfaction. Health care organizations have a moral obligation to provide quality and empathic services. Health care employees must create an emotional bridge with health care consumers. This bridge provides a stable conduit to address the special needs of patients.

EngageME is a methodology that addresses the inherit weakness in employee engagement while creating an environment fostering trust, compassion, integrity, and emotional connectivity. The model focuses on influencing the four steps of engagement:

1. Psychological Ownership
2. Expectation Realization
3. Trust Actualization
4. Power Distance

If you are reading this and you are a leader make your decision now. If you don't believe employee engagement is necessary or you don't think you have issue, you can stop reading this book and give it to a friend or family member. However, if you believe in the emotional connectivity of people and want positive change, please continue on this journey with me, I don't think you'll be disappointed.

John,

I wanted to thank you for taking the time out of your busy schedule to discuss the opportunities at your company. Equally as important, I appreciate your willingness to be open and honest regarding the political issues surrounding the move. Although I was unable to commit at this juncture, I am hopeful that we will have the opportunity to work together in the near future. Your ability to understand my dilemma and take interest in me personally is greatly appreciated. It is no wonder that our administration, your staff respect your abilities and level of professionalism. Again, thank you.

Dave

EngageME: The Engagement Gap

"Disengagement is a social disease." Vizzuso

Health care organizations plan, strategize, and attack the disease processes of the human body. Leaders, physicians, nurses, and other employees develop systems and techniques to develop plans of care for cancers, viruses, and infections. The ultimate objective is to extend life as we know it. In the summer of 2014 my oldest son, Zach (24) became seriously ill. I received a call that he had a constant fever and was not able to walk or communicate. For my wife and I this was horrific news. In my first book, I talked about the loss of our two-month-older daughter in 1993. We survived that ordeal. We would not survive another kid gone. I drove to the hospital tears falling on the steering wheel asking to give my life for his.

I walked into the emergency room and saw him sitting in the waiting room not being able to speak or walk. He was placed in an ER room as the medical professional started to ask questions and find out what really happened. The disease process had started 2 weeks early with a bad headache and flu like systems. He made 2 attempts to seek help at an urgent care only to be sent home thinking it was the flu. He could not speak and he didn't know where he was and he was hot to the touch.

After many tests the diagnosis game back: viral meningitis with encephalitis. This disease was the original disease that took the life of my daughter Laken. Can you say *Déjà Vu?* He was hospitalized for three days left the hospital and the disease came back hard in seven days. There were some minor symptoms that could have turned the diagnosis over to lymphoma. After three months of headaches, fevers, and fear they felt the original diagnosis was correct and he made a full recovery.

I was curious on what was the actual definition of disease, so I went to my dear old friend Wikipedia:

> A **disease** is a particular abnormal, pathological condition that affects part or all of an organism. It is often construed as a medical condition associated with specific symptoms and signs.[1] It may be caused by factors originally from an external source, such as infectious disease, or it may be caused by internal dysfunctions, such as autoimmune diseases. In humans, "disease" is often used more broadly to refer to any condition that causes pain, dysfunction, distress, social problems, or death to the person afflicted, or similar problems for those in contact with the person. In this broader sense, it sometimes includes injuries, disabilities, disorders, syndromes, infections, isolated symptoms, deviant behaviors, and atypical variations of structure and function, while in other contexts and for other purposes these may be considered distinguishable categories. Diseases usually affect people not only physically, but also emotionally, as contracting and living with a disease can alter one's perspective on life, and one's personality.

Death due to disease is called death by natural causes. There are four main types of disease: pathogenic disease, deficiency disease, hereditary disease, and physiological disease. Diseases can also be classified as communicable and non-communicable. The deadliest disease in humans is ischemic heart disease (blood flow obstruction), followed by cerebrovascular disease and lower respiratory infections respectively (Wikipedia, 2014)

Disengagement has become a social disease within the United States. Gallup estimated that 70% of the workers in the United States are disengaged (Gallup, 2013). Disengagement has many of the same attributes of a medical disease process:

- **Process.** Medical disease has a specific process and origin. Patients do not wake up in the morning wanting to be sick. The disease process begins at the cellular level. Most employees join an organization thankful for a job opportunity. Disengagement develops over time through a specific disease process.

- **Diagnosable.** Physicians spend their entire career diagnosing all kinds of disease. I don't care who you are, when you say disengagement visions pop up in your head of leaders and coworkers that are the definition of disengagement.

- **Contagious.** Many diseases can be transferred between people. This transfer of disease can create epidemics within major populations. Disengagement can move through a workforce. It just takes one actively disengaged employee to sicken the entire team.

- **Treatable.** Most disease processes are treatable. Medical professionals create medical plans that use medicine, therapy, and procedures. Disengagement is also treatable. Employee engagement can be repaired and enhanced by focusing strategies found in my research.

- **Removal.** In some disease processes an operation may be needed to remove the disease process from the body. Personal commitment is the fundamental first step in employee engagement. Disengaged employees lose the personal commitment to an organization. The removal of these employees provides immediate relief.

- **Dangerous.** Disease in the real world can be deadly. Mortality is the realization that life is vulnerable. Disengagement can create an environment where organizations fail. The disease of disengagement has the ability to silence the life of a company.

- **Debilitating.** Disease processes have the ability to leave a patient without basic functionality. It can make a fundamental negative difference for the life of the patient. Disengagement has the ability to prevent an organization of realizing true business potential.

THE ENGAGEMENT GAP

All organizations have some form of hierarchical structure. This structure can be horizontal, vertical, or matrix in nature. All structures have the opportunity to suffer from the Engagement Gap. The Engagement Gap is the distance between senior leadership and frontline employees in the day-to-day management of the organization. The larger the gap the more chance the social disease of disengagement will flourish.

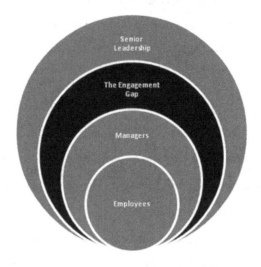

The size of the gap depends on the emotional connectivity between senior leadership in the workings of the organization. The more vertical organizational structure the more likelihood of having a large engagement gap. Unfortunately, in health care most structures are very vertical in nature. The Engagement Gap in health care creates large pockets of disengagement.

BOTTOM UP

The size of the engagement gap also decreases the likelihood of implementing employee engagement initiatives, cultural changes, and systematic improvement because ultimately employee engagement is a bottom-up phenomenon. New strategies starting at the top fail to breach into the departments of the organization because of the size of the Engagement Gap. Many leaders will disagree with me that employee engagement it is not a bottom-up phenomena. I would also say these leaders really don't understand the aspects of employee engagement. The reason that 70% of employees in the United States are disengaged is because leaders think it is a top-down strategy. So why bottom-up?

1. **Personal commitment.** Personal commitment starts from the bottom up.
2. **Culture.** Employees believe in the vision, mission, and culture of the organization. I will agree that leadership has a responsibility to convey vision, mission, and culture but ultimately the decision of the belief rest with the employee.
3. **Customer contact.** Most customer contact occurs at the bottom of the organization.
4. **Interaction.** Most employee-to-employee interactions happen and occur with front-line employees because of the sheer number difference between leaders and organization.

NAVIGATING THE GAP

Navigating the gap is not as simple as one would think. The larger the gap the more pitfalls reside between senior leadership and employees. The most important piece to the navigating the gap is the ability of middle management to effectively mitigate the relationship between senior leadership in front-line employees. Those individuals who on one hand can please senior leaders with good performance and on the other hand can articulate the vision and mission of the organization to the front-line employees creates a link between senior leadership and employee engagement. However, this process can be both tedious and dangerous. In many cases, middle managers are not skilled enough to be able to mitigate both sides to a successful conclusion.

In many cases, senior leaders have gigantic egos that prevent them from gaining an understanding of the front-line employees. This ego also prevents the managers from having the ability to navigate the gap. Employee engagement is not a priority for these types of leaders. Right now as you're reading this, you can visualize the gap in your organization and you understand why the gap exists. The real question is how do you reduce the gap and improve employee engagement?

Well guess what, Engage**ME** is the answer you're looking for.

John,

I hope this e-mail finds you doing well. I still can't believe you are hearing more. You were one of the few senior leaders that actually listened to us frontline employees. Your guidance and support will not be forgotten. I learned a lot from you and I could trust you to do things for the right reason. I only hope that one now that the opportunity to work with you again and we could continue to produce good outcomes of health care in hospitals.

Ann

EngageME: Psychological Ownership Strategies

"Nobody can make me personally commit." Vizzuso

STRATEGY 1: PERSONAL CHOICE

There is no doubt that personal commitment creates the foundation for improved engagement. I don't care what type of leader I reported to, they cannot make me committed. Psychological ownership is a personal commitment, a choice not a demand. My time at the hospital home really taught me the importance of personal commitment. When I started I was very guarded to emotionally connect with my physicians and employees because I was totally committed with the catholic organization and really got psychologically injured. The fact was I knew that the job had to come to an end but I didn't realize they would have treated me with such disrespect.

At the hospital home I soon became very personally committed to living the mission and vision. I can across a person that personified personal commitment. Lee Ann worked very close to me. She had been with the organization for over 23 years when I first met her. As anyone, Lee Ann had her strengths and weaknesses but she was personally committed to providing services to our patients. She witnessed significant leaders using fear and deception as normal operating procedure. Yet she was completely commitment to providing good service. But even as committed as she was she still had her days.

Does Commitment Change?

I recall one day her commitment suffered. On this day she was having a particularly bad day with a physician that had a history of driving her crazy. In this particular case he forwarded an email that had some sensitive information to Lee Ann's direct reports. It wasn't long before she came stomping into my office. I want you to picture a lovely lady walking into your office and her head split apart as her anger boiled over. She said a couple of words and flew out of the office to attack the head of the physicians. My assistant walked into my office and said "John, she isn't breathing. She really wasn't breathing". It wasn't long before I got the call from Tom, Chairman of Radiology to save him from the attacks of an out of control manager of operations.

Listen, personal commitment to an organization or for anything is not unchanging. We cannot be naive enough to think external factors cannot affect how we feel about any topic in our life. Personal commitment operates in an environment that changes, turns, and is unfriendly. Simply, life has highs and lows and these swings can influence commitment.

First of all let me get this topic of my chest:

Personal commitment is the choice of the individual!

Those of you that think that personal commitment is not related to your choice, please put this books down and look in the mirror. Personal commitment is your choice alone. Over the past 27 years I've heard it all:

- The reason my marriage broke up was because of my wife, not me.
- I drink too much because that was how I was raised.
- I embezzled money because they didn't pay me a fair wage.
- I hate my job and my boss.
- I got an F on the test because the teacher doesn't know how to teach.
- I want to get my degree but I just can't find the time.

I could go on and on. *Excuse* is the enemy of personal commitment. For any situation you can find many reasons to stop commitment. In life, we all have choices. Those choices define who we were, are, and will be.

> *The solution to strategy 1 is the hardest and most simplest answer: those of you that are not committed to the mission and vision for whatever reason go find a new job. Many will say, "I have too many years in and can't leave". Well, I say to reengage and personally commit because your distraction is harming those around you.*

STRATEGY 2: FIND GOOD LEADERS

Organizations have the right to demand that paid employees be committed to the mission and vision to the organization. This right is not absolute. This right only holds up as long as the leaders of the organization hold their end of the bargain. Commitment has an internal dependency on trust. Employees must trust that the leadership is fair, honest, ethical, and has integrity.

The hospital home was the poster child for this dilemma: commitment versus trust. I've been in the health care field for over 27 years. In four years at the hospital home I witnessed several different transitions in leadership both at the top and in the middle. The trust level between leadership and employees was not positive, in fact I would say it was a negative number on a numerical scale. This significant lack of trust erased personal commitment to the organization. How does something like this happen?

Well, I think there was moment before I started that started the ball rolling. A new senior leader started at a time when the organization was having financial issues. The first error was the hiring of this individual, not because of who he was but because he had no health care experience. He was now in charge of a billion dollar health care business. His first message in a meeting of all the managers and lead physicians: "Many of you will not be here in the future." Now just think about that. He just told his leaders, **fuck you** I'm going to get rid of you. This combined with no health care experience, egocentric personality, and visible distain for physicians created the environment they have today.

Many of you are saying, *"hey wait a minute, how does someone get a job like that with no experience."* I have seen these so many times that I myself wonder why and how. Ultimately, it is the charge of the board of directors to hire leaders with the proper background, education, and experience to do the job. In my time I've seen it all:

- Cardiology manager with no clinical experience
- Vice president of marketing in health care with banking experience
- CFO with a bachelor degree
- Vice Presidents with bachelor degrees and no health care experience
- COO with little to know experience running hospital operations
- Countless promotions of people with ethical or moral issues

For any one reading this that, and is a director on a board, it is **your responsibility** to find good leaders. Leaders at the VP and C-suite must posse the skills and knowledge that will move the organization forward:

1. **Knowledge:** Leaders must have knowledge of the industry they manage. They need to speak the language and understand the demands and stressors on the employees. Lack of knowledge creates a gap from day one.

2. **Relationship Building:** Leaders need to have the ability to build teams and improve relationships. I know right now your thinking of a vice president that does the opposite, creating dissention and turmoil.

3. **Empathy:** A leader must care for more than themselves. How many bosses have you had that could only love themselves?

4. **Integrity:** As a leader, integrity is critical. You only have your word and name. Nobody can take your integrity away, it can only be given away.

The answer to this strategy is very easy: board of directors fire, reduce, and remove leaders that can't lead.

STRATEGY 3: HIRE THE RIGHT PEOPLE

I'm now hitting close to 27 years in leading and managing people. In that time, I've hired some really excellent people and I've hired people that could be categorized as completely amazing failures. Finding talent is an art, not a science. I realize now that human resource managers and top leaders are smirking at that statement. Science has developed all kinds of techniques and process to find the right person for the right job. They are screaming, "John you're all wrong, we hire the top people based on our practices!" Let me first describe some of these methods:

- **Personality Tests.** Personally tests use scientific questions or words to pigeon hold an applicant into a personality type. My research experience now tells me that without understanding the validity and reliability testing used in the process is critical to understanding the accuracy of such reports. In other words, unless proven validity the report is worthless.

- **Reference Check Process.** Organizations feel confident that the reference process will definitely weed out the bad seeds.

Really? Ok right now I want to you to list the top ten references you would use in a job application. I'm sure on your list is everyone, when called, will say you're the best person in the whole world.

- **Interview Process.** Many organizations claim that the interview process is geared to remove bad applicants. This may have some truth but I think interview processes also eliminate good people because the interview process fails to uncover emotional intelligence.

- **Requirements.** I am totally in favor for positions having requirements, but unfortunately many organizations don't follow their own rules. Stop hiring people that haven't achieved the educational requirements.

HIRE THE HERO NOT THE ZERO

I worked with a lady for several years. Kathryn was a fabulous marketing person. She had flair, style, intelligence, and energy. She had the intangibles of devotion, integrity, and desire. Several months before I left the organization Kathryn got a new boss, Evelyn. Evelyn seemed, to me a person lacking the ability to emotionally connect with her employees. I never saw this first hand but the perception and reality was in the eyes of her people.

Several months later I called Kathryn out of the blue to see how she was doing. In a voice mail she said that she was busy, but would call me later in the evening. That night she called me and I said, "how is the best marketing person doing?" She said three words that shocked me, Kathryn said, "former marketing person?" I was surprised by her words. Evelyn eliminated her job that day. Now, based on my experience, on one hand I realized the pain and frustration she was feeling that day and for the days to come but on the other hand I wanted to hire her on the phone. Why do you say? I realized Kathryn was a winner from the first time I met her and this is why:

1. **Drive.** Kathryn has drive. You can see it in her eyes. No words are needed. I call it **Flaring**. Flaring is when both eyes come together as a smile occurs. Kathryn has drive to succeed and achieve personal and professional goals.

2. **Passion.** Good leaders listen with their eyes closed. Kathryn has passion in her voice. She demands perfection while having the ability to emotionally connect. This passion was probably the main reason Evelyn wanted her gone. Leaders like Evelyn fear people who have emotional intelligence because she has none.

3. **Sensibility.** Kathryn is sensible. You can tell by how she answers questions. People with emotional intelligence will ask more questions then they answer.

4. **Confidence**. Kathryn has confidence. She knows herself and you can tell by the way she sits in a chair. Her back straight, legs folded, and she sits tall. There is no task too tall for her.

5. **Loyalty.** Even though Kathryn dropped suddenly she was still loyal to the people at the organization. Her integrity is strong and her personal relationships enduring.

6. **Family.** Kathryn's view and stance is family first. She has an unwavering devotion to her family.

The answer to this strategy is stop interviewing people. I would rather look, listen, and hire the person that meets the requirements of the job but also have drive, passion sensibility, confidence, loyalty and family devotion because these attributes define personal commitment.

STRATEGY 4: MOTIVATION VS. IRRITATION

All organizations have methodologies to rate and motivate employees to meet professional and personal goals. Leaders have the responsibility through the year to inspire performance and give real time feedback. Leaders please pay attention to this section: feedback should be continuous not just when an employee has a performance appraisal. The Feedback Loop is a communication channel that is in the body of the employee-leader relationship. This communication channel needs to funnel positive and negative perceptions in a bidirectional function. The problem is many managers and leaders fail to use this loop and fail to properly motivate employees.

This lack of motivation creates issue for personal commitment by:

- Decreasing morale
- Negatively influencing the employee-leader relationship
- Curbs innovation and creativity
- Reduces trust which leads to disengagement

CALIBRATION

Now regardless of the performance of leaders with the Feedback Loop, organizations build and plan performance review systems. Generally these systems use forms with categories connected to job expectations. I worked at an organization that used a performance improvement system for leaders called Calibration. Calibration is a system of performance improvement developed by General Electric. This system's ultimate goal was to place leaders and managers into several categories:

- **Top Talent.** Top Talent leaders are those individuals performed at the highest level within the organization. These people are highly valued with exceptional accomplishments

- **Highly Valued.** Highly motivated leaders are those leader that live the core values of the organization and met performance goals. These people get rated from high performers to needs performance improvement.

- **Less Effective.** Less effective leaders were those leaders that did not meet expectations. Typically these people represent the bottom 10% in performance.

THE PROCESS

The process for this style of appraisal motivation is a lengthily one. It consists of several steps:

1. The leader completes a self-evaluation on values and accomplishments for the previous year.

2. The self-evaluation is given to the supervisor and the supervisor does an evaluation. Both evaluations are in one document and given to the performance department.
3. Sessions are then held between peers. For example, all the peer managers meeting with the director of human resources to review all their direct reports that are in this process.
4. At the meeting the individuals name and picture are projected on the wall. The manager begins to go over the accomplishments and values. As the manager presents this employee other managers provide positive feedback or criticism.
5. The employee is then rated and placed on what is called a 9 Block Chart. This places them in the categories I already described.

RESULTS

I've been leading people a long time. I've done appraisals and motivation from every type of style and stance. Calibration was the worst abomination of human cruelty I've seen in my time. This process was dreaded from the first email announcing the start of the process. This process was used to harm and tarnish the good name of hard working people. I want you to imagine you have a direct report that does a great job but in that job she has had to be firm with people in other departments. Her picture goes up and as you read her strengths people start taking negative pot shots at her. These people do not have clue one about her performance or her character. In addition, the director of the process had a personal ax to grind with her for years and she manipulates the conversation.

I cannot tell you how many people I saw get their character assassinated by poor process and manipulation. As part of the leadership team I was horrified and ashamed to be part of the process. There are many things wrong with the process:

- **Poor Management.** The management of the process is critical. Manipulation and bogus reviews place people in top talent who were never there. Friends of high-level senior leaders seem to always be in the top talent category.
- **Conflicts of Interest.** You cannot have conflict of interest with the director of the process and the leadership team. Manipulation was disguised as honest, wholesome, collaborative tension.
- **Confidentiality.** There absolutely was no confidentiality for the employees.
- **Confidence.** There was absolutely no confidence from the mid level managers that the process was fair and balanced.
- **Demotivation.** The process was clearly developed to demotivated and demoralized the people it served.

The answer to this strategy focuses on leaders. Leaders please emotionally connect with your followers. Learn about their likes and dislikes. Give them goals to meet and inspire them to go beyond their wildest dreams.

Lastly, personal commitment is important. It is the glue that cements emotional intelligence to organizational commitment. Without it, organizations really stand no chance to succeed. With it, organizations and employees have an opportunity to meet and exceed shareholder expectations while realizing professional and personal goals.

Dear John,

Hopefully you still remember me because I certainly remember you. This <u>thank you</u> note is long overdue. I am sorry so much time has passed. I just wanted to let you know that even though I only worked with you for a short time I learned so much and you made a lasting impression on me. Because of you, I went back to school after waiting way too long and actually finished last October with a Bachelor in Business Management. I could not be happier to cross this achievement off my list. I could not have done this without your inspiration and encouragement. Thank you so much for your support and guidance. Hope you, Jennifer and family are all doing well. Please send Jennifer my best.

PS Hope you continue with school as well and please let me know when you finish your next book. Can't wait to read another Vizzuso book.

Chris

EngageME: Expectation Realization

"Do you know the expectations of your employees?" Vizzuso

P ersonal commitment and expectations intersect and create the basis for employee engagement. The following true-life event provides a great example of this powerful union. I worked with Gail, one of my office assistants. Gail had been in the same job for many years. Gail had a strong moral code combined with a real stubborn streak.

Gail fluttered between engagement and anger at the challenges at the job. One day she pulled me aside and complained that her job title was lower than other people in the department. This upset her because her expectation was she should be at a higher title with a higher salary. She explained it was not a money issue just a respect issue. Now most of you know when someone tells you its not money, the issue is really about money, however not so with Gail. Her growing up in a suborn home develop strong an ethical and moral attitude. It was purely about respect.

There was a situation that arose that provided me an opportunity to move Gail into that job title. I was excited because I knew meeting this expectation would improve her personnel commitment. New process rules required Gail to take a typing test as a requirement of the new title. I met with Gail and told her she would need to take the typing test. I witnessed the change in her posture as her anger grew. "Do you mean I have to prove I can type? Are you kidding me?" She was completely offended by this requirement. I tried everything to get it waived with no success. She had to take the test.

I got a call from the human resource person several hours after Gail took the test. She told me Gail had failed the test. Was I shocked yes but not for the reason you may think. There is no way she just failed that test. Gail was a master with the keyboard with excellent typing skills. She failed it on purpose to prove a point. When I confronted her about this she denied failing it on purpose and just smiled and walked away.

This story illustrates the bond between expectations and personal commitment. I could not meet her expectations and she held back her personal commitment. Expectation realization is the age-old story of the rat in the maze. The rat has 2 buttons to hit: red and green. When the rat hits the green it gets a slight shock, but when it hits the red food is given. As the rat hits the red button it expects the reward of food. It is now engaged to hit the red button. On the reverse it hits the green and gets shocked and then hits the red to get food. The next time it hits the red and gets shocked and hits the green and gets food. It won't be long before the rat stops hitting any button and is disengaged.

STRATEGY 1: COMMUNICATION

I think in my last three books I write about the importance of communication. Communication is critical to reaching expectation realization. Leaders listen: Employees have expectations! They have needs, desires, and requirements. I honestly believe that a common language divides leaders and employees. In the hierarchy of organizations communication is lost between the top and the bottom. This communication break can be caused by many factors:

1. **Title.** In many cases the title of an individual can create communication barriers. It really fascinates me that an individual can build such an ego that prevents from talking to employees but I've seen this be more the norm then the occasional issue. I found this as a common practice through my research. On participant went as far as to describe the issue of title: "Our CEO does not even know who I am. The previous one new my name, how many kids I had, and really cared about me as a person. If I see the current CEO in the hallway he barely takes the time to say hi. Title Creep is the process of a title-inflating ego creating a barrier to communication.

2. **Leadership Empathy.** I realize this is simple but many leaders really don't care to communicate and really couldn't give one minute to understand expectations. Come on think right now, some leader that fits this bill. My career has been littered with these types of people.

3. **Employee Indifference.** There are those employees who are actively disengaged. The true disgruntled will not

accept communication from anyone. Acceptance of positive communication serves to prove the negatively is a fabrication, something that will affect their negative impression on their co-workers.

4. **Retribution.** How many times in your career did you see the messenger shot for delivering the message? Open discipline of employees who try to communicate absolutely kills communication absolutely. I witnessed at the hospital home time after time. In some cases, you could actually predict when someone was going to be fired for professionally disagreeing with senior leadership.

5. **Downsizing.** I've had the pleasure of being on both sides of the table in downsizing. In fact, I believe there was downsizing in every organization I've work for over the past 30 years. Downsizing creates communication barriers for those who survive.

Communication combined with empathy creates a stable environment for sharing dialogue. Both leaders and employees need to take initiative to communicate and emotionally connect. Communication is a bidirectional commitment.

Easy communication is the answer to this strategy. Leaders must engage the employees by simply taking the time to communicate and curb the fear of emotional connectivity.

STRATEGY 2: LISTEN WITH YOUR EYES CLOSED

Ok I realize that listening is part of communication but it deserves a section devoted to understand the need and use of your ears. All humans have objects on either side of the head. These objects are called ears. Ears hold very delicate pieces and parts that turn sounds into understandable messages. Simple right? Unfortunately, not so simple. Ears without intention, objectivity, and emotions are simply mounds of flesh and parts.

There was a particular senior leader at the hospital home that could not listen. It was like this person was living in a different world. Meeting after meeting going over the same issues, yet to have another meeting where we were at step one again. It was like the movie Groundhog Day. Was it that this person could not listen or understand situations? I kid you not, it got to a point where I would say things 2 or 3 times until this leader would nod the head confirming receipt of the message. True listening and observation is an art not a science:

- **Listen without Judgment.** Can you listen to someone without judging the person. Many years ago my boss announced to me that he was having an affair with one of his subordinates. I sat there listening to his complaints about his wife and that he was in love again. To be honest I'm sure I judged him at that moment. True listening occurs when judgment is left out.

- **Listen with Objectivity.** Keep personal biases out of the listening chamber. Too many times hidden agendas affect what you hear. Objectivity creates an environment where listening and understanding flourishes.

- **Stop Texting.** Please for the love of God stop using texting as the primary communication tool. Please put all phones down and listen to your employees.

- **Turn Up Your Hearing Aid.** Leaders and employees can listen to each other but do they really hear each other? Gaining an understanding of expectations depends on actual understanding of the communication data. Listen, understand, and learn.

The key to listening as a strategy is keeping your ego in check and taking the time to really listen to the employees. Disengagement spreads when leaders don't listen.

STRATEGY 2: COMPLETE AN EXPECTATION AUDIT

Organizations use accounting and consulting firms to audit financial results, process improvement, and compliance issues. Yet, leaders of organizations fail to understand the expectations of the employees. This failure in communication and listening creates the opportunity for disengagement, low morale, and dysfunction. How hard is it really to have an open letter communication with employees to gain an understanding of what they expect from the organization?

Well it must be pretty hard because 70% of the workers in the United States are disengaged. For me, I find expectation understanding a fundamental part of my job as a leader of an organization. It is imperative that not only do I communicate my expectations of the employee I take the time to understand their expectations of the organization and me. When a leader takes the time to understand the expectations of employees great things happened:

- **Foundation of trust.** I will be talking about trust in the next chapter of this book. The beginning of trust germinates at the level of expectation relation. Trust is an essential part of the employee-leader relationship.

- **Value of listening.** Do you remember the value of listening? Listening without judgment provides an opportunity to improve the understanding of human behavior.

- **Discovery of motivational triggers.** Is it important to motivate your employees? Well the only way to do this is understand what motivates them. As seen in my doctoral study, meeting employee's expectations increases the opportunity for improved motivation.

- **Unrealistic expectations and calibration.** We cannot be naïve to think that people don't have unrealistic expectations. Doing an expectation audit provides an opportunity for the leader to understand which expectations are realistic. In the context of an audit, the leader can articulate reasons why the expectation is unrealistic. This reach calibrates the expectations of the employee.

- **Two-way communication.** An expectation audit provides an opportunity for bidirectional communication between the leader and the employee. This process provides an opportunity to set the stage for performance-based goals.

Is expectation realization a fantasy? It is a fantasy for those leaders, managers, and supervisors that really do not care or have empathy for the people that work for them. Good leaders really want to know what their employees think, feel, and need. It is vitally important to understand and meet the expectations the employees. Organizations that fail meeting the expectations of employees will not achieve employee engagement levels to impact operational performance.

During my time at the hospital home I had an occasion that I needed to seek medical care. The physician that I went to was a specialist. I knew her name and she knew my name but we really never met during my time at the hospital home. My appointment lasted 60 minutes. Out of the 60 minutes, 10 minutes was spent actually looking at the medical condition that I had. The other 50 minutes was spent with her telling me how much she didn't want to work with the organization. She described a situation where the leadership of the organization was clearly not engaged with understanding her expectations as an employee. She was stuck working for the organization because of the lucrative retirement plan, but other than that she was miserable. She gave up on talking to any leadership person because her perception was that the leaders were not listening to her concerns and needs. She mentioned that she received a $25 bonus for the last quarter and said that she worked $25 too hard for this miserable organization. She was actively disengaged from the hospital home. Her expectations have been dismissed and her morale destroyed. So, has expectation realization failed?

The answer to this strategy is understanding the expectations of your employees and personal goals. Understanding the employee's expectations is a direct path to capturing the heart.

John,

I just wanted to say thank you for your support and guidance during a very difficult situation. Last week was like an emotional roller coaster for all of us involved. I'm looking forward to a new beginning and feel confident that we have a strong leader behind us to help us when we fall down. Thank you also for your positive reinforcement. It means a lot to me knowing that I have someone willing to listen and be proactive in my successes and failures.

Thanks again for everything.

Kim

EngageME: Trust Actualization

"Trust can be as strong as steel or as weak as straw." Vizzuso

In any relationship, trust is a necessary component, yet is sometimes forgotten or overlooked in importance. I will dare to say that relationships without trust are not true relationships but false ties to another. In my career, I've experienced the power of strong trustful relationships and the weakness of when trust fades. One of my strongest feelings of trust came at the hospital home. I've talked about Tom several times in this book. Tom was a very interesting person. He was a physician that spent his time moving medical coils into the vascular nature of the brain in attempt repair stroke affects. Tom had some very unique qualities of integrity, respect, morality, and breathe of intelligence. In addition, Tom also had an aggressive personality. He did not and would not fear any position, person, and situation. He tackled life but he tackled a brain aneurysm, balls to the wall, 100 mph.

Tom and I immediately connected within our personal relationship. The trust and respect was a tangible force between us. In many cases our relationship was bound by both our integrity and respect for each other. It was as though we were in each other's head as we manage and lead the operations of the radiology department. There was either a time or a situation that I ever felt mistrusted by Tom's intentions. We both believe in the value of our relationship and the trust we built. This trust created opportunities for collaboration, improve operations, and facilitation strategic objectives and goals. The foundation of our relationship was built on the ability to trust each other and listen without judgment.

STRATEGY 1: TRUST LONGEVITY

The ability to sustain trust over long periods of time is the key to providing connection to the world environment. **Trust Longevity** is essential to building successful outcomes.

How does one build trust? I believe trust has several key attributes that must be fundamentally sound to begin the maturation period for trust:

- **Visibility.** A person must be visible within a relationship. This has to be true to the heart. In my own life I am absolutely visible to my family but sometimes fail because I may be physically in the house but my mind is in another place.

- **Consistency.** The consistency of demeanor is critical to trustful relationships. Organizations that are trusted deliver quality goods and services to customers every time.

- **Dependability.** Any level of trust has a dependability factor. In any trust situation there is a delivery and an acceptance perspective. The message that goes between the two factors has to be dependable in the actual meaning. For example, Kevin was a Chief Nursing Officer I worked with. Kevin delivered communication of improvements in operations yet the turnover rate for the nursing department was staggering. The trust level in his assessment was low from my viewpoint because his perception was in the reality of the numbers.

- **Deliverability.** Trust has to have the ability to easily transfer from person to person. The grape vine is the main highway of deliverability. A trust level moves from person to person in the common society platform. Unfortunately, mistrust perceptions can follow the say path and usually at a faster pace.

- **Respect.** Trust and respect go hand in hand. People, organizations and entities that do not deliver respect to all, will not be trusted. The thought of disrespect is disgusting and deplorable. I've seen completely disgusting disrespect too much in my career. Recently I was part of a management meeting in a hospital system. This system had decided to lay off 10 employees. The head CEO of a large healthcare organization claimed this number of people was really no big deal and nothing more than a rounding error. This struck me as cruel, inhuman and very disrespectful for these people and their families. This type of verbal diarrhea sickens me. Later on in the year I read an article with this gentleman's picture bragging about how the healthcare system was adding 500 jobs and the healthcare organization was doing great. However, many people in the community didn't hear about the fifty employees that were just laid off the prior week. He again was masterful with his rounding math. I would be willing to bet that most of the people in the organization have little trust for this individual.

- **Judgment.** A strong trust bond is enhanced by using good judgment. The use of bad judgment usually destroys trust bonds.

Can you be trusted? Once you can answer that then you can build trust.

STRATEGY 2: SELF EXPRESSION

The art of self expression (SE) has been lost in the dust of the ages. SE is the idea that a person can openly express the inner being called self. This process is difficult, critical and impossible all wrapped up in a blanket of self-doubt. Trust is more accessible when a person can openly express their true self.

Personally, I've finally been able to shed the cloak of forgiveness and darkness to be able to truly express myself to others around me. It has taken me over 20 years to be able to do this, through a process I call, **The Self Awareness Jeopardy**.

What does it really mean to express yourself openly and honestly? It is the ability to strip away falsehoods, arrogance, and pride to express the true self to others around you. It is very easy for people to display fake, exterior facades to create safe hideaways from reality. Most people do this and let me describe some people who do this well:

- **Jill.** Jill is a tough-minded nurse I worked with for several years. Jill was rugged, aggressive and to all around her a hardnosed person. Yet I had the opportunity to understand Jill and see beyond this front. Jill was a very sensitive person. Her past relationships and family issues created this hard exterior. She is fearful of expressing herself truthfully for the fear of hurt she had experienced in her personal life.

- **Greg.** Greg is a friend of mine and a person at times I look up to. Greg is a good leader and self-starting person. Greg however works for a faith based organization and interesting slipped on the faith cloak. This cloak is something someone slips on to pretend his or her devotion. Greg's heart is centered on successful outcomes and what his superiors think of him. He used this cloak to secretly enter the world of faith dealers to fit in.

- **Janice.** Janice displayed weak attributes. She was scarred from a life of lies from her husband and mirrored only by a career that was unraveling before her eyes. Janice doesn't realize that she is tougher than most people who are around her.

The answer to this strategy is understand yourself before your try to understand others.

STRATEGY 3: JEOPARDY LINE

This journey will take a person and put everything they now on the **Jeopardy Line**. This line is the thin line between knowledge and self-doubt. A person can truly express oneself but may not like what they see. This line either displays the knowledge of pride or the disappointment of self-doubt. A person must be ready to accept the truth. The model has several key levels of self-actualization that are discovered and maintained as a person:

Desire Level. A person must want to discover their true self. This desire is strong and vibrant. It compels a person to start a search that may or may not lead positive outcomes. The desire to know the truth outweighs the urge to hide the lies.

Discovery Level. The Discovery Level is centered on the truth that surrounds a person. The truth will enlighten the conscious and deliver the soul the true you. At this moment a person can embrace the word or run and hide. It is important to always embrace the truth even though it may be negative. The ability to embrace yourself does not mean you cannot change.

Design Level. The Design Level is the stage where fakers become real. It is the ability to look deep inside the soul and make changes that better the person. This level is very difficult because change itself can seem impossible. It is with this level a person can secure an improvement or deny the truth and stay the same.

Delivery Level. The Delivery Level is the level that a person can then display the true self and expression to others around them. This level is a level of no return for when you can express yourself honestly, there is no turning back. You finally realize it doesn't matter what people think about you only that you express yourself truthfully.

The jeopardy line is real and it takes respect and trust to move past it. Leaders dare to walk the line.

Strategy 4: Don't get a Trustectomy

Trustectomy

I realize that trustectomy is not an actual word. It is a word and phenomenon that documents when trust either fades away or is ripped in a violent transaction. This happens both in our professional and personal lives. The hospital home was by far the worst organization that I've seen where trust had eroded from the fabric of the culture of the organization. I would even go as far to say that there simply was not one ounce of trust between the administration and the positions of the organization. Two point where both sides were working actively against each other for the common good and mission of the organization.

I cannot tell you how many times I sat in meetings at the hospital home with physicians or senior leadership with each side actively diminishing the role of the other. This dysfunction just didn't happen overnight. It started with a transition to a new senior leader that absolutely had no experience in health care. This person had contempt for medical physicians. The start of the trustectomy started with that leadership and vision. As the senior leader started to attempt a changing culture, trust started to fade gradually throughout the organization. I had hoped when the leader left that trust and respect could start to revitalize the morale of the organization. However, loss trust isn't like a disease that can be cured even when it changes. Unfortunately, once a full trustectomy has occurred it is very difficult to return but ultimately possible.

Loss of trust creates significant issues both in our professional and personal lives. It creates a sense of personal loss while imposing questions on future endeavors. Without trust, expectations are not realized and the employee-leader relationship is damaged beyond repair.

The answer to this strategy is do not give your integrity away. People can only give it away and lose trust along the way.

John,

What can I say. We'll miss you and your thoughtfulness and kindness you gave our center. We are thankful for you. Please keep us posted on your whereabouts. We miss you more and more.

Ellen

John,

Thank you for your time and consideration of our clinic. I am so sorry to see you leave, it is such a loss for us all. I wish you the best.

Mariellen

John,

Thank you so much for mentoring and guiding us during these challenging times. We appreciated your time and support. We wish you only the very best. We'll miss you.

Laurie

EngageME: Reduce the Power Distance

"The closer you get the more you know." Vizzuso

A t many of my previous employers the senior leaders were housed in an area called "Mahogany Row". I believe all organizations have this area that houses the senior team of the organization or at least that's what the leaders think. I cannot tell you how many times with my employees and my peers that we would joke about walking and going to Mahogany Row. In one particular case, the hospital home was between CEOs. There was a part of Mahogany Row that was a little outdated. The senior leaders of this area decided to do a remodeling before the new CEO started. But please remember this is a hospital home for health care so dollars are at a premium. I believe this senior leadership team spent over $200,000 updating offices that really didn't need it.

The power distance of leadership is not just where senior leadership sits but is the emotional distance between senior leaders and front-line employees. This distance holds the key for inspiration, motivation, and employee engagement. The further emotionally away the leaders are the less likelihood of influence on employee engagement. Think about it, think about where you work today, do you have a senior leader that barely knows your name, won't say hi to you in the hallway, and completely doesn't listen to your expectations. The power distance of leadership is purely a function of ego, power, and empathy.

Signs of a Large Power Distance of Leadership

- Senior leaders spend more than 90% of the day in their offices.
- During hallway walk-throughs the eyes of the senior leaders are focused on the floor not the people that walked by.
- All feedback from frontline employees are stuffed in the suggestion box.
- The only names known to senior leaders are the senior leaders.
- Mahogany Row is a place where front-line employees never want to go.
- When you walk down a hall and you see a senior leader and you decide to go the other direction so you don't have to pass the person.
- When you received threats from a senior leader but that leader doesn't know your name.

STRATEGY 1: HORIZONTALLY

Vertical organizational structures tend to have a more vertical and longer power distance. These types of structures create artificial silos and barriers to create a departmental illusion. The simple fix for the vertical integrated organization is simply to reduce the layers to the senior leadership. Closer the senior leadership, the more chance to positively influence employee engagement. In some cases, this may transplant middle management or change middle managements role. The main problem is once you reach the senior leadership level; working closer to the front lines is a difficult choice. *Title Displacement* is a serious issue for senior leaders. Once a person gets a title they think that title earns them the right not worry about the little things. It almost creates a barrier between the leader and the followers because the title

Why a horizontal organization:

1. Quicker decision making.
2. Creates expectation realization.
3. Improves trust.
4. Builds emotional connection between employees and leaders.
5. Positive influence on the employee-leader relationship.

The answer is stop vertical integration and flatten the organization.
Flatter is better.

STRATEGY 2 LEADERS: GET OUT OF YOUR OFFICE

But John, you really don't understand how hard my job is, meetings, calls, problems, planning, plotting, building, and so on. I've heard every excuse in the book and all the excuses in the world cannot convince me of this one simple rule:

There is nothing more important then being close to where your employees meet your customers.

CHAIR SYNDROME

The Chair Syndrome is the disease of the butt. Leaders, managers, supervisors of all ages, and creeds can develop this issue over time. The development of digital phones, company email, skype, and text messaging create opportunities to keep the butt of a leader firmly planted in the chair. You know I'm right, you are picturing that one leader that just sits in the office all day to survey the kingdom. This issue is more common than you think. It is not long before the leader and chair form one piece of unmotivated human blob.

GET TO YOUR FEET

The power of travel as a leader in an organization is refreshing. One step closer to the action is where the true difference is made. Please, walk and meet the people that are fighting for you every day. Help them, get into the job, and see how their life is and not just on day shift, how about the other shifts. At the hospital home I enjoyed working 6 P.M. to 3 A.M. in the radiology department. I helped the staff with moving patients around, talked about hospital issues and general challenges of the job. This was some of the most enjoyable time I spent at the hospital home. Being present with your employees provides benefits in so many areas:

- Improves listening
- Improves job understanding
- Building emotional connections
- Creates an atmosphere of empathy
- Proves leadership commitment

Do I really need to tell you the answer here? Get off you ass and be present with your team! Be close to where the action is.

STRATEGY 3: LEADERS: BURN DOWN MAHOGANY ROW

The barrier everyone knows about must come down. In health care, if you are the Vice President of Cardiovascular Services, why isn't your office in Cardiology? Organizations must break down the walls between leaders and employees. These sections of the organization create departments of distrust and dysfunction.

MEETING LOCATIONS

If you're not going to tear down the walls at least don't have meetings in your office. At the hospital home I made it a point to have meetings with my direct reports in their offices. Was I too big and powerful to meet them in their location? I found that meeting in their location created a sense of security for them and that relationship building was so much easier. I hate to be the odd duck here but the world does not rotate about my special corner office. In an organization, the world wraps around the connection between product and customers, employee and customers, and the relationship between employee and leaders.

The real answer is placing your leaders where the action is not in some corner office that they never leave.

STRATEGY 4: LEADERS: USE YOUR TITLE FOR THE RIGHT REASON

I hope there was some reason a leader got a title of authority, however my experience tells me that this is not always case. Throughout my career I've seen people get leadership roles that had no business leading people. The placement of title is important but really the use of that title is the key to decreasing the power distance.

The title of the job in itself creates a barrier between leaders and employees. In many cases egotistical leaders enjoy the barrier the title gives because the power feeds the gigantic ego. At the hospital home I had the pleasure of working with several leaders combined I call the Antichrist. These two leaders would use fear and intimation in their leadership styles. They loved their titles and would walk through the halls of the hospital home head held high refusing the look at the small employees.

In my world, title is only used as a way to show and share respect. I've had all titles over the last 30 years: supervisor, manager, director, senior director, vice president, COO, CEO, and President. My view of these titles is that they are all the same. I would rather have employee look at me as their co-worker then their director.

Title is clearly the enemy of reducing the power distance but there are ways we can reverse the affects of title:

1. Have lunch with different employees everyday.
2. Take down signs that display titles.

3. Stop doing the leadership job and go work in the frontline.
4. Leave your title at the door when improving relationship building.

The answer to this strategy is, leaders stop placing title before duty. Trust me, reduce the power distance of leadership and engagement will flourish.

John,

Thanks for the way you've led the troops. I've learned much from working and watching you. Thanks for all the support you've given me. You've been my light when I've been lost in the fog.

Evelyn

EngageME: The Diagnosis

"What really affects me from engaging?" Vizzuso

PC+ER=TA-PD

D iagnosis is an important process in the treatment of any disease. As I demonstrated earlier, disengagement is a social disease that affects organizations of all types and sizes. Yet in any disease, the patient always wants to know the type, size, location, duration, and prognosis. Disengagement is no different. However, organizations deal with employee satisfaction, employee engagement, and shareholder satisfaction differently. Many leaders think the first step in diagnosis today is doing in employee engagement survey. Unfortunately, the survey does not actually diagnose disengagement in an organization. *Leaders please listen, do not use employee survey as the tool to diagnose disengagement!* True diagnostic services take an in-depth review of both shareholder and stakeholder views and perceptions of the organization by the use of a controlled interview process.

ENGAGEME FORMULA

Through my research study and years of experience I've developed a formula to effectively diagnose employee engagement and organizations. That formula is:

$$PC+ER=TA-PD$$

PC: Personal Commitment

The first area of review in the EngageME Formula is personal commitment. In depth interviews with front-line employees, middle management, senior leadership, and key shareholders unlock the potential of personal commitment. High levels of personal commitment are rated on a scale 1 to 10 with 10 being the highest commitment available. Each interview answers a series of open-ended questions and attempt to ascertain personal commitment levels. This subset group creates the perception for the rest of the organization.

ER: Expectation Realization

The second measure of disengagement is the measurement of expectation realization. A focused review is completed on expectation realization between the following groups:

- Employees – leaders
- Leaders – employees
- Shareholders – leaders
- Leaders – shareholders
- Employees – shareholders

- Shareholders – employees

Higher the understanding of expectations translates to a better chance of having less disengagement. High levels of expectation realization are rated on a 1 to 10 scale with 10 being the highest realization available.

TA: Trust actualization

Trust actualization is the sum of personal commitment rating plus expectation realization.

PD: Power distance

Trust the power distance of leadership influences actualization. The further away leadership is the less impact the leader has on employee engagement. High levels of power distance array on a 1 to 10 scale with 10 having the furthest distance.

<u>Example</u>

An organization has the following numerical statistics:

PC 7 + ER 9 = TA 16 – PD 4 (EE of 12)

Range Table

Engagement	Range	Range
Highly Engaged	20	18
Moderately Engaged	17	12
Average	11	8
Mild Disengagement	7	4
Moderate Disengagement	3	0
Severe Disengagement	0	-3
Active Disengagement	-3	lower

INTEGRATED DIAGNOSIS

Diagnosis of disengagement isn't as easy as you would think. It is not as simple where you plot on this range table. The main problem is organizations use surveys to do the diagnosis workup. The consultant or what I would call physician of engagement has to be more of a detective to the doctor. True diagnosis occurs when the detective integrates into the fabric of the organization. The integrated diagnosis process has several layers of discovery tools for each component of the formula. These tools consist of:

- **Perceptive reasoning tool.** A tool that allows for a valuation of respondent answers to basic questions.
- **Expectation matrix tool.** The expectoration matrix tool allows the engagement doctor to gain understanding of expectation realization, integration, and denigration.
- **Personal commitment evaluation tool.** This tool creates an opportunity to develop a personal snapshot of a sampling pool of employees and stakeholders.

- **Leadership review analysis tool.** The leadership review and analysis tool creates the foundation to measure the leadership power distance.

Diagnosis and detection is generally difficult because the ego of leadership teams creates significant barriers between diagnosis and leadership confessions of poor behavior, lack of empathy, and bad leadership. Let me be frank and honest, bad leaders really don't care about employee engagement and any improvement to employee engagement is indicative of poor leadership, which then puts the blame on bad leaders.

Judgment is a difficult thing to take. As a leader, I have the responsibility to look at my actions, decision-making, people management, and attributes as a leader. My responsibility to the organization is to provide an environment that promotes employee engagement, stakeholder involvement, and creates an environment for innovation and prosperity for the organization. True leaders are not afraid of the results of the diagnosis, but are afraid to do nothing to improve the organization and their leadership abilities.

Dear John,

We would like to thank you for helping us out with the touch of Nathan foundation. Your talk was insightful and inspiring. I know that you helped us win, and you gave me some of the things I've been looking for with Kenny. Thank you for being a friend can have the foundation, but most of all, thank you for your love and support and your willingness to share your experience with us.

Wishing you continued peace.
Jackie

EngageME: The Intervention

"It takes hard work to fix engagement." Vizzuso

Most organizations fail in this step of the EngageME process. An intervention is a process where someone actually does something to either improve disease process, remove the disease process, and the development of action plans to keep the organism healthy. Medical interventions such as surgery, interventional radiology, cardiovascular imaging, and biopsy services provide interventional access to treat, remove, and repair disease processes of the body. Completing an intervention is not a simple process for the human body or an organization. In fact, many organizations lack institutional motivation and true leadership to actually fix and repair employee engagement. This is mainly due to leaders dismissing the importance of employee engagement while being part of the problem.

I briefly mentioned how the hospital home handled dealing with employee engagement issues. The senior leadership team was completely inept and understanding employee engagement, measuring survey results, diagnosis of issues, and a complete failure of any intervention. The results of the worst I've seen in my career. However, the organizational development department took survey data and excluded the 57% of people that would not even take the survey. Yes I didn't miss type, 57% of the employees at the hospital home would not take the test because they didn't trust the leadership of the organization.

Even for multimillion dollar consulting organizations, survey results and suggestive practices seem to be the only interventions created. This is really troubling for me. How frustrating it is for the employees of an organization that a diagnosis of disengagement is completely ignored until make a matter worse the organization hired to improve employee engagement doesn't really have any intervention the community better.

BUILD AN INTERVENTION TEAM

The first step in designing and implementing the intervention you first have to develop an interventional team. In all health care organizations, good surgical teams create opportunities to heal the sick. This is no different in dealing with a social disease of disengagement. The real key to developing interventional team is the makeup of the team members. There are several traits that you want on this team:

- **Leaders.** You need to have leaders of the organization that are willing to not only deal with very difficult situations but are willing to look in the mirror and take responsibility for their inadequacies.
- **Heroes.** You know the heroes at your job right now. Heroes are those people that give all everyday. They don't ask for a thank you, they only want the opportunity to serve the people around them.

- **Informal Leaders.** In any organization there are those people that are the informal leaders of the front-line employees. Due to many years of service, and informal leaders have the respect of their peers and their supervisors.
- **Naysayers.** Now I'm not crazy, in order to fix engagement you need to have some disengagement.

The interventional team organizational structure must report to either chief executive officer of the organization or the Board of Directors. This team must have the ability to make recommendations that start with simple educational processes to completely removing disengaged employees from the organization. Unfortunately, the removal of employees, which many may have many years of service, is a very difficult task for an organization. However, employees and leaders of the organization have an obligation to the shareholders of the organization to create products, profitability, and pride.

DEVELOP A PLAN

Once the diagnosis is done of disengagement, an organization has an opportunity to develop a treatment plan. You cannot treat something you don't know what it is. In any hospital or health care organization, the treatment plan is a process where medical professionals develop a plan to treat a disease process. An *Engagement Plan* is a detailed action plan aimed to treat the areas of disengagement. These areas of disengagement are focused on the four influences global engagement:

1. Psychological Ownership
2. Expectation Realization
3. Trust Actualization
4. Power Distance

The engagement plan must address the issues from the diagnosis. This plan can include a variety of measures and steps depending on the situation, audience, and desired results. You may see these types of measures:

- Segmentation of disengaged employees.
- Reeducation
- Termination
- Employee repurposing
- Mentoring
- Reorganization
- Improved human resource fun
- Timelines for implementation

Planning is a very important part of the interventional process. Lack of planning creates holes in the interventional treatment of disengagement. The plan must have the support of the shareholders of the organization, leadership, and frontline employees. Why front-line employees you ask? Remember that engagement is a bottom up phenomena that starts with front-line employees and his influence on the leaders of the organization.

GET INTO THE WEEDS

This is the most important part of the interventional process. Leaders, employees, managers, shareholders, and Board of Directors you have to be willing to get your hands dirty in the surgical intervention of employee disengagement. This process cannot be implemented or engineered from the top down. It has to start from the bottom up and the only way to do this is by joining the front-line employees in their journey to provide services and products to the end consumers. Simply, get out of your office and get to work!

Through the years, I've seen leaders and organizations try to take the easy way around and buy some ridiculous planner program from a company and attempt to implement new processes and theories from the top down. The problem is the Engagement Gap. New attitudes and theories cannot penetrate the distance in the Engagement Gap. Thus, money poorly spent, no new strategies or improvements ever get to the front-line employees and disengagement continues to breed affect the health of the organization.

Why not try interventions where the employees meet the customer? Are we afraid as leaders of what we will find? Disengagement, poor attitudes, and low morale will flourish until leaders realize that their title and ego really isn't too big to work in the trenches with the front-line employees.

STOP THE EXCUSES

I've heard all, I'm too busy, too many meetings, there is no support, the human resource department will not help me, my boss doesn't understand, I can go on and on and on. Please stop the excuses of why as a leader you will not deal with disengagement at your organization. I witnessed a lot of this at the hospital home. My peers would suffer from depression, frustration, and translation and find ways why we can't do something. I'm would go to director meetings, and be amazed at how people sat in a meeting month after month talking about the same issues with no clue on how to make it better. In these meetings, a senior leader would threaten people's jobs in front of an audience. What was even more amazing was that this senior leader really could not talk well in front of others. It wasn't because this leader wasn't intelligent, you just couldn't understand the words. The leader would usually end the meeting by saying the fatal words "I'm watching all of you, don't think I'm not watching, you better do the job." Really inspirational words uh?

Remember the first influence of employee engagement, personal commitment? As a leader, you have to have a personal commitment to improve employee engagement to really make a difference.

Dear John,

You've made my heart smile and managed to remove one of the monkeys off my back. I wanted to than you for your caring and kindness.

Carolyn

John,

Congratulations on a successful year. Your hard word has paid off and your operations have blossomed. Congrats VP of Operations and QIT chairman. I appreciate your leadership and I believe in you!

Jen

EngageME: Monitoring

"You cannot manage what you do not measure." Vizzuso

Surveying the monitoring very important steps in the ability of an organization to make sure that the surgical interventions are working. The main problem is, most organizations start with doing surveys an attempt to diagnose the problem. Using third-party surveys should be the last step in the process of improving employee disengagement.

So really what makes a good survey tool? Just type in the Google search box employee engagement surveys and see how many responses you get. I think picking the right cerebral is very important for several reasons:

1. **Does it ask the right questions?** Again, organizations by survey tools without really diagnosing the problem. If you actually diagnose the problem before you pick a survey tool, this may give your opportunity to pick questions that are associated with the diagnosis.

2. **Anonymous.** Employees will not answer survey questions without the knowledge that the answers are anonymous.

3. **Web-based.** Using the Internet is an easy way to have people fill out surveys. However, you still need to have paper copies for those people that do not use computers.

4. **Emotional intelligence questions.** I think it is important that some questions address emotional connectivity in the employee-leadership relationship.

THE DASHBOARD

Measuring and monitoring employee engagement is no different the drive your car. As you drive your car there is a set of instruments that tells you speed, how much fuel you have, tire pressure, battery charge, mileage per hour, time, and even cameras to see outside the car. Viewing these instruments provides human ability to safely drive your car to the destination.

Developing the *Engagement Dashboard* is an important piece, monitoring the success of the engagement plan. This dashboard should have key measurements that pertain to the engagement plan, interventional process, and leadership commitment. It can have metrics that focus on a multitude attributes:

- Employee retention rate, leadership participation rate
- Leadership participation rate versus work hours
- Disengagement personas by department
- Customer service scores
- Job performance metrics
- Leadership rounding schedule completion percentage

MEASUREME: WORDS FROM EMPLOYEE ENGAGEMENT

Leaders are afraid of measuring employee engagement. A poor measurement is a direct reflection on the ability of the leader to lead. Disengagement can be a sign of leadership gone wrong. Guess what leaders, it's time to step up and fulfill your duty as a leader, engage employees and measure the success or failure. As an employee, please measure me. Ask me how I feel, what I think, get to know me, stop ignoring me. Why is my boss afraid of really understanding what I think? Are we all afraid of what might be said?

It doesn't matter which side of the fence you sit on, Measure**ME**. Leaders put ego aside and employees leave fear at the door. I can make your organization better or I make it very sick, which would you prefer? Why not Measure**ME**? What are you afraid of?

I really only wish to be a positive influence but so many people ignore me and that is when the troubles start. Unmeasured I can get out of control pretty quickly. That is when both leaders and employees miss me when I go away. Don't you think it is important to see how I am doing? Decide not to measure me and see what will happen.

Vizzuso Annual Review 10/28/1998

John,

John has spent a great deal of time traveling to the KMC imaging centers over the past 12 months. Additional, John has traveled to Buffalo, Salt Lake City, and Texas supporting the Billing and Collection Project. In spite of demanding travel schedule, John is very productive and gets everything accomplished on time. I would like to see John spend more time in the office supporting the imaging, and less time on the road fighting fires. This should be accomplished in 1999 since a billing manager was hired.

John's vital few objectives in 1998 including making the imaging centers profitable and fixing the billing and collection issues. John has been tenacious in both of these areas. He has educated his managers on how to read income statements and reinforced the fact that they are responsible for their budget. John has done really well in digging into the billing problems dating back six years. His efforts have resulted in implementing the first in-house billing in Buffalo.

Like in many businesses, relationships are a key to success. John understands this key concept very well and has responded equally well. He has been successful in creating trust with key stakeholders in the imaging centers. He has been able to turn negative relationships into positive relationships. John has done an excellent job of developing projections, working with vendors and contractors.

EngageME: Home Sweet Home

"When you look in the mirror, you find the answer." Vizzuso

At the beginning of this book, I was at a crossroads with the hospital home. I was completely disengaged from the organization. I secretly wanted the senior leadership to fail. I couldn't look into their eyes without some form of disgust. I would get up in the morning and dread the length of the day. When I looked in the mirror, I saw a 43-year-old man finishing his doctorate degree in business administration, going nowhere from a professional point of view. Yet I loved the people I worked with. They were so very special in my heart. I felt guilty feeling disengaged while leading the team. I had a hard time looking them in the eyes and projecting a positive front.

One night I sat at the computer and logged onto a recruitment website. I saw a job opportunity for a chief executive officer for a large radiology group in Canton, Ohio. Was this the group I worked with back at the beginning of my career? The job ad had some very interesting aspects that really appealed to me. Should I reply to the ad? I loved my co-workers but hated my job. Could I leave them?

I responded to the ad and went on an interview schedule. This was the group I had worked with early in my career. My first interview was very interesting. I sat in front of the board of directors and was peppered with questions developed by a consultant. Around the table sat a very intriguing physician group:

The Elder Statesman. The Elder Statesman had been with the group for many years. His knowledge of radiology and the political playing field was very noticeable. He had seen the group in all kinds of situations and was asking great, probing questions.

The Wise Old Owl. The Wise Old Owl had a rich and interesting history with the group. He was wise in the way he talked and in his comments. He had personal relationships with people that ranged over the past 30 years and amazing political skill combined with undying energy.

The Kid. The Kid was short on stature but large on integrity. He gave me the impression of conservatism combined with a keen eye for detail.

The Horse Farmer. The Horse Farmer shone with honesty and valor. His questions were pointed, yet soft. His empathy toward his partners and practice was placed on his sleeve.

The Young Leader. The Young Leader sat directly in front of me. His presence was tangible. You could see leadership in his eyes. My first impression was that this was a young Tom. I had a feeling he and I would work well together.

Mr. Practical. Mr. Practical looked easygoing but was practical in his questions. He made me feel comfortable by joking through questions.

I received a call from the recruiter about two weeks later. He asked me how I thought the interview went. I was honest—I felt very comfortable with the interview and felt there was an instant emotional connection. He agreed. When the second interview occurred, it solidified my thought that this would be a great opportunity for me.

So, opportunity in hand, I had a decision to make. Could I leave my friends behind? Could I tell Tom I was leaving? Tom was my mentor, provided me substance, and supported me unconditionally. As my mind went through the pros and cons, it finally hit me. The social disease of disengagement was running through my veins. My disdain for unethical behavior, poor leadership, and missed opportunities clouded my vision every day. I started to recall those leaders over the years who amazed me:

Admin 1. Admin 1 was by far the biggest fraud of a generation. Admin 1 had very little talent, a large salary and no real substance. Rumors of affairs, sexting, and bad behavior floated around this person like a cloud.

Admin 2. Admin 2 seemed to rise to opportunities with no real experience. Admin 2 could survive any change in leadership and rise to amazing heights. Admin 2 was amazing in developing the art of doing nothing yet doing something.

Admin 3. The Admin 3 came in and projected a persona while hiding true evil intentions. This person reminded me of the wolf in sheep's clothing. Admin 3 can be truly disastrous because, before you know it, you've lost it all.

Admin 4. The Admin 4 was obsessed with control and would try to push that control by bullying people into doing the things the Admin 4 wanted. What people didn't know was that the Admin 4 tried to use force because there was really no talent.

Admin 5. Admin 5 was one of those people who grew up as a street fighter and lost their moral GPS along the way. Admin 5 lied, intimated, threatened, and treated people like dirt.

Admin 6. The Admin 6 was a fierce competitor who had no problem with manipulation, deception, disrespect, and treating people poorly. The Admin 6 was someone who had no moral compass and would do anything to support an agenda.

Admin 7. Admin 7 was just plain nasty and awful. Admin 7 would have anger fits, fire people on the spot, and just had questionable business practices.

My problem was personal commitment. The organization stole it from me. A series of actions ripped it from my heart. My focus was on what happened, and I couldn't let it go. I had a choice—stay and die or leave and live.

I left the hospital home. The day I told Tom was very hard. I apologized but told him I had to leave. The hospital home was not good for me and I was not good for the hospital home. He was disappointed but realized

I had to move on. It was very hard telling my friends, but the news traveled fast. I did enjoy telling my direct supervisor. Once the words left my mouth and I handed him my letter, my freedom started. I felt like a free man who had been wrongly put in jail for over 30 years. The liberation was overwhelming. As the weeks went by I said my goodbyes.

I started my new role transforming from the mentee to the mentor. I finished my doctorate program and gained a functional understanding of employee engagement and how to fix it. I reached my goal and I have a brand-new landscape on which to paint my future. Employee engagement is a fundamental aspect of the success of an organization. The possibility for personal commitment, expectation realization, trust actualization, and reducing the power distance has the potential to transform vision into reality.

Finally, it is really up to you. Personally commit to your organization, emotionally invest in your coworkers, and follow your heart. Find ways to understand expectations and build strong employee-leader relationships. Leaders, treat people with respect, build teamwork, and listen to your employees. Don't be afraid of an emotional connection with employees and peers. Lead by example and improve the engagement of your employees. Ask employees their names, get to know their hearts, and inspire them to greatness

Leaders, are you listening?

<u>*Note 1*</u>

I wrote in three books about people who had influence on me over the years, both positively and negatively. In my current manuscript, I write about your influence on me as a leader. I do agree with the person who said you had influence on me. Let me take a second and share with you, your influence:

- *Integrity. You demonstrated integrity in everything you did, in some cases, unwavering principle and dedication. You taught me that there are times when standing your ground was not just an action but also a statement.*

- *Details. Your focus on detail with vendors astonished me. I have to be honest, after the first five minutes of bashing a vendor's information, it did get uncomfortable to watch. It taught me the value of substance in products and prices.*

- *Emails. I've never seen anyone dissect an email line by line and respond with such pinpoint words. The precision was surgical in nature.*

- *Business Acumen. You are by far the most business-minded physician I've ever worked with. We developed some really impressive business plans for the hospital.*

- *Compassion. There were several occasions when I saw deep-rooted compassion in your eyes, the type of compassion seen in people who save lives.*

- *Family. Your devotion to your sons and Jenny is evident in the stories you tell. They are lucky to have you in their lives. You taught me that, no matter what happens, you have to support your family.*
- *Education. Without your influence, I would not be on the verge of getting my DBA.*
- *Vision. You have the gift of vision. The importance of vision and strategy is evidenced by your desire for innovation.*
- *Trust. Our trust built a foundation of sustainability for the Department of Radiology. I believe it influenced both of us.*

So I am thankful for this influence. It made me a better person, leader, and friend. I will cherish all the moments, laughs, tears, and cheers. The influence was positive, no matter what some idiot says.

I wish for you and your family happiness and prosperity in everything you do. You're not just the Chairman of Radiology, you're my friend and brother-in-arms.

Note 2

I've been doing this management thing for a long time. Nowhere in my travels have I met a person like you. I know, I've stated that many times in your reviews, but let's really talk about the person that is you. Your devotion to your family is amazing. I envy this trait in you. For me, work has both physically and mentally taken me away from my family. When I look back, those are times that I can never get back.

Your dedication and integrity goes beyond any normal expectation. Your importance to the department is only overshadowed by your dedication to the organization. I apologize for those times I angered you or failed you, for my intent was always pure.

When the day was done, I could always count on you, no matter the issue or circumstance. You are one I will never forget.

Note 3

I should really call you the best damn operations director I've ever worked with. Your dedication to the hospital is outstanding, even in the face of ignorance, stupidity, and incompetence. I remember meeting you through the interview process. My first impression was that here was a bright person focused on a tough job.

There are not enough words to express my appreciation for you as a manager and a person. You get stuck with making tough decisions in impossible situations. The sign of a leader is a person who makes the right decision, no matter how hard it may be. You are a leader.

I wanted to also thank you for your treatment of Zach. He is young and needed a steady place to live and you provided that for him.

Lastly, I wanted to say that I witnessed true compassion as you stayed side by side with your sister through the divorce. You were her rock, as you've been my rock over the past three years.

The decision to leave has been difficult, to say the least, but one I had to make. I apologize for any time I've failed you in my time at MH. Please know my intentions were always true. I wish you and your family all the happiness and prosperity a life can deliver.

Note 4

I'm sorry that I couldn't catch up with you earlier this week. It was due to the fact that you, once again, placed patient care before personal issues. That is what makes you a very special person. You have a unique skill of making a difference look easy.

Your willingness to work fulltime, go to school fulltime, and take care of your family is amazing. I know there were days that our nurses had you wondering if you worked in a mental institution. I saw the frustration in your eyes, frustration that I shared with you.

I'm so excited for you to finish school, get your license and move into a new phase in your career. You will make an excellent NP! The radiology department will really miss your dedication and skill.

My leaving is bittersweet. I know the opportunity is right for me professionally, but the people at the hospital were right for me personally. We all get faced with decisions in life and sometimes those decisions mold our destiny and fate.

I wish you and your family all the happiness and health one can have. I appreciate all your efforts and your leadership.

Note 5

I remember sitting with you as Pedro was leaving. You were visibly upset and felt there was no way you could ever fit into Pedro's shoes. All I can tell you is that you were wrong and you proved me right. My dear, you succeeded in building an IS function and making everything happen while taking on more responsibility.

I appreciate all your efforts and leadership in making radiology a great place to work. I enjoyed watching you grow, struggle, and thrive in the role. I have to admit there were many times you lost me on some technical speech that had my head spinning, but that was my Mary at her best.

Your love and devotion to your family is impressive to watch. I realize that the passing of your father was difficult. You and I have a special bond with losing a child. It is important to realize it is not how we die that matters, but how we live in the hearts of family is the true blessing.

Mary, I wish you and your family happiness and prosperity. You are a wonderful mother, daughter, leader, and friend.

John

Prologue

It is my honor to be asked to write the prologue for "Engage**ME**, *Will Leaders Listen*". I have known and worked with John Vizzuso for only a little over a year but became quickly impressed with his vision, determination, and integrity. This book well encapsulates his personal experiences in the field on engagement in health care and beyond. Health care has much need for this kind of work. There is a significant lack of engagement in health care as detailed by John in this book. As a practicing radiologist and being in leadership positions in both our physician group and at our hospitals, I see this first hand. There is much arrogance amongst health care leaders, which seems to rise the higher up one goes in the chain of command. This breeds a top-down mentality and a culture of fear amongst subordinates. There is a lack of transparency, and information does not flow up from front lines to higher levels. There are numerous silos, and silos within silos. There is unnecessary competition between hospital departments rather than mutual cooperation for the greater good of the patient. There is a restraint of communication rather than an open safe environment for communication.

This kind of hierarchical leadership leads to a high Power-Distance Index (PDI). The concept of PDI came out of research from Hofstede in the 1970's and has since been applied to numerous industries. The concept is a measure of the gap between the more powerful and the less powerful and the acceptance of that power gap by society. Countries with a low PDI are more consultative and democratic, such as the US, Austria, Denmark, Sweden, UK. Countries with high PDI are more authoritarian and paternalistic such as China, Iraq, Saudi Arabia, Ghana, India, Mexico, Malaysia. These are countries where there is much feudalism still being practiced and the institutions are not democratic.

In my experience, there is a high PDI in health care. While this has not been specifically measured, the significant hierarchical leadership and lack of transparency breeds the high PDI environment. Nurses often don't feel comfortable speaking up to physicians. Front line employees don't feel comfortable speaking up to senior administrators. Sometimes there are silos and colliding high PDI attitudes between administrators and physicians as a result, which leads to interesting dynamics and outcomes to say the least.

What are the results of this kind of hierarchical leadership and high PDI? Because not all the right knowledge flows up, and there isn't transparency, there is poor communication and engagement. Studies have shown that intimidation and lack of communication are responsible for half of medication errors. Poor collaboration between caregivers leads to increased mortality and length of stay. Poor communication in the operating room jeopardizes patient safety. The culture of fear causes these errors to multiply and become entrenched. Because the workforce is not engaged, this culture is difficult to change and eradicate. There are initiatives rolled out from the top leadership, which filter down with reduced engagement at each level, and therefore lead to poor adoption and results.

The utility of communication in breaking down silos and having a diverse social network has been studied by business for decades. Now when we talk about one's "social network" we're not talking about how many friends you have on Facebook or the movie made with the same title. We are talking about simply who do you know and what is the relationship. An early study of this is from the American Revolution about the "Midnight Ride of Paul Revere". That's the story about the British navy invading Boston Harbor and the commonly held belief that Paul Revere rode around on his own to warn the community and raise an army to defend itself. Well, what most people don't know is that there was another rider that night as well named William Dawes. He also rode to warn people about the British Navy. But people don't remember him. The reason? Because Paul Revere knew more different kinds of people and had a much more diverse social network that cut across all segments of society without being confined to the typical silos of income, class, career and other social standards. He was a super connector that connected the different silos that existed in Boston at that time. So when he rode to warn people, his impact magnified exponentially as all the different silos woke up and were energized to respond. Meanwhile Dawes' social network was an echo chamber where people did not know too many others outside their network and so the information did not reach many people. Having a diverse social network allows for greater engagement around the mission of the organization. A more modern business example is that of Halliburton which studied their social network in their global organization. They found that there were too many silos in their knowledge workers, which were restricted geographically, which caused lack of knowledge, and human capital being put to the greater good. Once they connected the silos across borders and continents by having diverse teams, their success rates on projects increased, they gained productivity and quality while reducing customer dissatisfaction. It's amazing what one can do when there is a culture of collaboration rather than a culture of mistrust.

I believe that health care in America is practiced in an un-American fashion. In America, we are free to speak up to their elected leaders, propose alternative solutions and the free market and society, and then engage around the best solutions. In American health care, there is a feudal mentality where there is little transparency, or safety for disagreement. Unless top-line leadership takes action to change the culture, which may include changing leadership at multiple levels, the hierarchical culture and poor engagement will remain entrenched. In order to solve this problem, and close the gap of engagement in health care, there needs to be diversity in leadership. I'm not talking about ethnic or cultural diversity (although that's part of it), but diversity of ideas, and experiences. We need true merit-based leadership, rather than simple seniority-based leadership. The challenges facing health care today need new leadership and fresh ideas. If America runs on merit-based leadership where anyone can succeed if they have good ideas and can execute on them, then why not run health care that way too? Both physicians and administrators need to let go of their biases, and focus on transparent data and ideas that have true impact. The evidence must lead the way rather than opinions and the typical "I am the boss so in my opinion, we should do X". The leadership must create a safe space for disagreement and invite alternative suggestions to their plans. And if the alternatives are better, then they should embrace them rather than be threatened by them. This way, the Power-Distance Index gets reduced. Actionable information flows up to the top. The silos get broken down and communication and collaboration happens spontaneously without the leadership pulling teeth. The individual departments collaborate to bring forth solutions that make sense, improve quality and the bottom line, to their senior management without any long, drawn out, top-down change initiative that takes years to implement and fails to get results. By engaging with front line employees and mid-level leadership to include them in strategic planning, the hospital CEO builds loyalty and trust in his organization. This pays dividends over time when there are external challenges such as the difficult health care landscape today. When there are tough decisions to be made, and the path is not clear, the lower PDI organizations with deep trust and loyalty will be able to succeed while others will fail.

How do I know that this can happen and work? How do I know that senior leadership can make a difference by leading the engagement efforts and efforts to reduce PDI? Because I've seen it work. The current CEO of Aultman Hospital, Chris Remark, is such a leader who has managed to make these changes by both talking the talk, and walking the walk.

As a result, the level of cooperation between physicians, and the hospital, and the level of engagement of the staff at the hospital is more than I've seen at the multiple hospitals I've worked at in my career. The teamwork mentality and transparency that has been built up under the leadership of Chris is already strengthening Aultman and will continue to serve it well in the future changing and challenging landscape.

In the end, delivering excellent clinical care reliably is the best business model for health care organizations. Delivering that care reliably means engaging the workforce in care pathways and quality initiatives. Defining "excellence" in quality has to be done in a transparent meaningful manner to patients. It means that mediocrity in health care (as in any other industry) needs to be challenged, that leadership must be challenged to produce results, that changes need to be made if the solutions are not working in a realistic time frame. It means that if the CEO's plan is not perfect and needs to be changed, that he/she should be the one to step forth and do so. It means setting the bar high on quality, such that one would expect the same service that one would want for a family member, to be delivered to all patients. And working towards that goal diligently despite the entrenched feudal culture of health care. Only then can health care be transformed into the reliable high quality model that we all want, and become truly American in its spirit and actions.

Syed F. Zaidi, MD
President, Radiology Associates of Canton
CEO, RadHelp, LLC
April 2015

References

Abadi, F., Jalilvand, M., Sharif, M., Ali Salimi, G., & Khanzadeh, S. (2011). A study of influential factors on employee's motivation for participating in the in-service training courses based on modified expectancy theory. *International Business and Management*, 2, 157-169. Retrieved from www.cscanada.net/index.php/ibm/article/view/j.ibm.1923842820110201.011

Abel, M. (2013). The social and financial benefits of developing employee satisfaction. *International Journal of Management & Information Systems*, *17*(2), 83-90. Retrieved from http://www.cluteinstitute.com /journals/international-journal-of-management-information-systems-ijmis/

AbuKhalifeh, A., & Som, A. (2013). The antecedents affecting employee engagement and organizational performance. *Asian Social Science*, *9*(7), 41-45. doi:10.5539/ass.v9n7p41

Adelman, K. (2012). Promoting employee voice and upward communication in healthcare: The CEO influence. *Journal of Healthcare Management*, *57*(2), 133-149. Retrieved from www.ache.org/pubs/jhmsub.cfm

Agarwal, U. A. (2013). Linking justice trust and innovative work behavior to work engagement. *Personnel Review*, *43*(1), 41-73. doi:10.1108/PR-02-2012-0019

Albdour, A., & Altarawneh, I. (2014). Employee engagement and organizational commitment: Evidence from Jordan. *International Journal of Business and Social Science, 19*, 192-212. Retrieved from www.jibs.net

Ali, S. H., & Ndubisi, N. O. (2010). The effects of respect and rapport on relationships quality perception of customers of small healthcare firms. *Asia Pacific Journal of Marketing and Logistics, 2*(1), 135-151. doi:10.1108/13555851111120452

Alrubaiee, L., & Alkaaida, F. (2011). The mediating effect of patient satisfaction in the patients' perceptions of healthcare quality: Patient trust relationship. *International Journal of Marketing Studies, 3*(1), 103-129. Retrieved from http://www.ccsenet.org/journal/index.php/ijms/article/view/9278/8577

Amin, M., & Nasharuddin, Z. (2013). Hospital service quality and its effects on patient satisfaction and behavioural intention. *Clinical Governance: An International Journal, 18*, 238-254. doi:10.1108/CGIJ-05-2012-0016

Ancarani, A., Di Mauro, C., & Giammanco, M. D. (2010). Patient satisfaction managers' climate orientation and organizational climate. *International Journal of Operations & Production Management, 31*, 224-250. doi:10.1108/01443571111111900

Anderson, C. (2010). Presenting and evaluating qualitative research. *American Journal of Pharmaceutical Education, 74*(8), 1-7. doi:10.5688/aj7408141

Andrew, O., & Sofian, S. (2011). Engaging people who drive execution and organizational performance. *American Journal of*

Economics and Business Administrations, 3, 569-575. doi:10.3844/ ajebasp.2011.569.575

Angelova, B., & Zekiri, J. (2011). Measuring customer satisfaction with service quality using American customer satisfaction model. *International Journal of Academic Research in Business and Social Sciences, 1,* 232-258. doi:10.6007/ijarbss.v1i2.35

Antos, J. R. (2014). Health care reform after the ACA. *New England Journal of Medicine, 370,* 2259-2263. doi:10.1056/NEJMp1404194

Anyan, F. (2013). The influence of power shifts in data collection and analysis stages: A focus on qualitative research interview. *The Qualitative Report, 18*(18), 1-9. Retrieved from http://www.nova. edu/sss/QR/index.html

Aslin, P. (2011). Unveiling the unicorn: A leader's guide to ACO preparation. *Journal of Healthcare Management, 56,* 245-253. Retrieved from http://ache.org

Atta, O. (2012). The efficacy of applying the quality measure of health service on the external patient satisfaction. *Management Review: An International Journal, 7*(2), 83-121. Retrieved from http://www. informs.org/Community/KINFORMS/Publication

Avey, J. B., Wernsing, T. S., & Palanski, M. E. (2012). Exploring the process of ethical leadership: The mediating role of employee voice and psychological ownership. *Business Ethics, 107*(1), 21-34. doi:10.1007/s10551-012-1298-2

Baird, C., & Gonzalez-Wertz, C. (2011). How top performers achieve customer focused market leadership. *Strategy & Leadership, 39*(1), 16-23. doi:10.1108/10878571111095385

Bailey, R. (2013). Health care reform 2010: A landmark achievement for the future. *Journal of Health Care for the Poor and Underserved, 24*(1), 1-5. doi:10.1353/hpu.2013.0034

Barnett, J., Vasileiou, K., Djemil, F., Brooks, L., & Young, T. (2011). Understanding innovators experiences of barriers and facilitators in implementation and diffusion of healthcare service innovations: A quality study. *BMC Health Services Research, 1,* 343-355. Retrieved from http://www.biomedcentral.com/1472-6963/11/342

Baumard, N., Andre, J., & Sperber, D. (2013). A mutualistic approach to morality: The evolution of fairness by partner choice. *Behavioral and Brain Sciences, 36*(1), 59-122. doi:10.1017/S0140525X11002202

Beal, A., & Hernandez, S. (2010). Patient reports of the quality of care in community health centers: The importance of having a regular provider. *Journal of Health Care for the Poor and Underserved, 21,* 591-605. doi:10.1353/hpu.0.0305

Bembenutty, H. (2012). An interview with Allan Wigfield: A giant on research on expectancy value motivation and reading achievement. *Journal of Advanced Academics, 23*(2), 185-193. doi:10.1177/1932202X12436610

Bennett, A. R. (2012). Accountable care organizations: Principles and implications for hospital administrators. *Journal of Healthcare Management, 57,* 244-255. Retrieved from Retrieved from http://www.ache.org/Publications/SubscriptionsPurchase.aspx#jhm

Bergin, M. (2011). Nvivo 8 and consistency in data analysis: Reflecting on the use of a qualitative data analysis program. *Nurse Researcher, 18*(3), 6-12. doi:10.7748/nr2011.04.18.3.6.c8457

Bernard, H. R. (2013). *Social research methods: Qualitative and quantitative approaches* (2nd ed.). Thousand Oaks, CA: Sage. Retrieved from http://www.sagepub.com/

Birasnav, M., Rangnekar, S., & Dalpati, A. (2011). Transformational leadership and human capital benefits: The role of knowledge management. *Leadership & Organization Development Journal, 32*(2), 106-126. doi:10.1108/01437731111112962

Birken, S. A., Lee, S., & Weiner, B. J. (2012). Uncovering middle manager's role in healthcare innovation implementation. *Implementation Science, 7*(28), 1-12. Retrieved from http://www.implementationscience.com/content/7/1/28

Blakley, D., Kroth, M., & Greson, J. (2011). The impact of nursing rounding on patient satisfaction in a medical surgical hospital unit. *Medsurg Nursing, 20*, 327-344. Retrieved from http://medsurgnurse.org

Bleicher, J., Paslidis, N., Brewer, J., Dember, B., Peterson, R., Pugh, D., & Crofford, P. (2012). An innovative process for engaging hospital leaders. *The Physician Executive Journal, 1*(1), 49-52. Retrieved from http://www.pej-acpe.org/pej-acpe/20120506/?pg=50

Bonias, D., Leggat, S., & Bartram, T. (2012). Encouraging participation in health system reform: Is clinical engagement a useful concept for policy and management? *Australian Health Review, 36*, 378-383. doi:10.1071/AH11095

Branthwaite, A., & Patterson, S. (2011). The power of qualitative research in the era of social media. *Qualitative Market Research: An International Journal, 14*, 430-440. doi:10.1108/13522751111163245

Bushra, F., Usman, A., & Naveed, A. (2011). Effect of transformational leadership on employees job satisfaction and organizational commitment in banking sector of Lashore Pakistan. *International Journal of Business and Social Science, 2*(18), 261-269. Retrieved from http:// www.ijbssnet.com/

Camgoz-Akdag, H., & Zineldin, M. (2010). Quality of health care and patient satisfaction: An exploratory investigation of the 5qs model in Turkey. *Clinical Governance: An International Journal, 15*(2), 92-101. doi:10.1108/14777271011035031

Cassatly, M. G. (2011). Stakeholder partners: The new landscape in U.S. healthcare. *The Journal of Medical Practice Management, 1*, 199-204. Retrieved from http://www.greenbranch.com/section_47_MPM-Journal.cfm

Chahal, H., & Kumari, N. (2011). Evaluating customer relationship dynamics in healthcare sector through indoor patients judgment. *Management Research Review, 34*, 626-648. doi:10.1108/01409171111136176

Caspi, A., & Blau, I. (2011). Collaboration and psychological ownership: How does tension between the two influences perceived learning? *Social Psychology Education, 14*, 283-298. doi:10.1007/s11218-010-9141-z

Chan, Z., Fung, Y., & Chien, W. (2013). Bracketing in phenomenology: Only undertaken in the data collection and analysis process? *The Qualitative Repot, 18*(59), 1-9. Retrieved from http://www.nova.edu/ssss/QR/QR18/chan59.pdf

Chat-Uthai, M. (2013). Leveraging employee engagement surveys using the turnover stimulator approach: A case study of automotive enterprises in Thailand. *International Journal of Business and Management, 8*(6), 16-23. doi:10.5539/ijbm.v8n6p16

Cheng, Y., Huang, H., Li, P., & Hsu, J. (2011). Employment insecurity workplace justice and employees burnout in Taiwanese employees: A validation study. *International Journal of Behavioral Medicine, 18*, 391-401. doi:10.1007/s12529-011-9152-y

Chiesl, N. (2012). The intended prioritized selling of the nest egg by U.S. baby boomers during retirement. *Business and Economics Journal, 2012*(51), 1-9. Retrieved from http://astonjournals.com/

Chou, S., & Pearson, J. (2012). Organizational citizenship behavior in IT professionals: An expectancy theory approach. *Management Research Review, 35*, 1170-1186. doi:10.1108/01409171211281282

Cliff, B. (2012). Excellence in patient satisfaction within a patient-centered culture. *Journal of Healthcare Management, 57*(3), 157-160. Retrieved from http://www.ache.org/PublicationsSubscriptionPurchase.aspx#jhm

Cliff, B. (2012). The evolution of patient-centered care. *Journal of Healthcare Management, 57*(2), 86-89. Retrieved from Retrieved from http://www.ache.org/PublicationsSubscriptionPurchase.aspx#jhm

Cook, K. E. (2012). Reliability assessments in qualitative health promotion research. *Health Promotion International, 27*(1), 90-101. doi:10.1093/heapro/dar027

Covell, C. L., Sidani, S., & Ritchie, J. A. (2012). Does the sequence of data collection influence participants' responses to closed and open-ended questions? A methodological study. *International Journal of Nursing Studies, 49*, 664-671. doi:10.1016/j.ijnurstu.2011.12.002

Crane, P. W., Yerman, B., & Schneider, S. M. (2012). A lack of effect on patient satisfaction scores in one large urban emergency department. *International Journal of Clinical Medicine, 3,* 740-743. doi:10.4236/ijcm.2012.37A130

Darbi, W. (2012). Of mission and vision statements and their potential impact on employee behavior and attitudes: The case of a public nut profit oriented tertiary institution. *International Journal of Business and Social Science, 3*(14), 95-109. Retrieved from http://www.ijbssnet.com

Den Hartog, D., & Belschak, F. D. (2012). Work engagement and Machiavellianism in the ethical leadership process. *Journal of Business Ethics, 107*(1), 35-47. doi:10.1007/s10551-012-1296-4

Derr, C. L. (2012). Ethics and leadership. *Journal of Leadership Accountability and Ethics, 9*(6), 66-73. Retrieved from www.na-businesspress.com/jlaeopen.html

Detsky, J., & Shaul, R. (2013). Incentives to increase patient satisfaction: Are we doing more harm than good? *Canadian Medical Association Journal, 185,* 1199-1202. doi:10.1503/cmaj.130366

DeVore, S., & Champion, W. (2011). Driving population health through accountable care organizations. *Health Affairs, 30*(1), 41-51. doi:10.1377/hlthaff.2010.0935

Dikkers, S. E., Jansen, G. W., De Lange, A. H., Vinkenburg, C., & Kooij, D. (2010). Proactivity job characteristics and engagement: A longitudinal study. *Career Development International, 15*(1), 59-77. doi:10.1108/13620431011020899

Dollard, M. F., & Bakker, A. B. (2010). Psychological safety climate as a precursor to conductive work environments, psychological health problems, and employee engagement. *Journal of Occupational and Organizational Psychology, 83,* 579-597. doi:10.1348/096317909X470690

Dorval, E., Rey, J., Soufflet, C., Halling, K., & Barthelemy, P. (2011). Perspectives on gastroesophageal reflux disease in primary care: The reflex study of patient physician agreement. *BMS Gastroenterology, 11*(25), 1-8. Retrieved from http://www.biomedcentral. com/1471-230X/11/25

Eberle, T. (2012). Phenomenological life world analysis and ethnomethodology program. *Human Studies, 35,* 279-304. doi:10.1007/s10746-012-9219-z

Eisele, L., Grohnert, T., Beausaert, S., & Segers, M. (2013). Employee motivation for personal development plan effectiveness. *European Journal of Training and Development, 37,* 527-543. doi:10.1108/ EJTD-02-2013-0015

Emmert, M., Eijkenaar, F., Kemter, H., Esslinger, A., & Schoffski, O. (2012). Economic evaluation for pay for performance in health care: A systematic review. *European Journal of Health Economics, 13,* 755-767. doi:10.1007/s10198-011-0329-8

Erkutlu, H., & Chafra, J. (2013). Effects of trust and psychological contract violation on authentic leadership and organizational deviance. *Management Research Review, 36,* 828-848. doi:10.1108/ MRR-06-2012-0136

Faleye, O., & Trahan, E. A. (2011). Labor friendly corporate practices: Is what is good for employees good for shareholders? *Journal of Business Ethics, 101*(1), 1-27. doi:10.1007/s10551-010-0705-9

Farin, E., & Nagl, M. (2013). The patient physician relationship in patients with breast cancer: Influence on changes in quality of life after rehabilitation. *Quality of Life Research, 22,* 283-294. doi:10.1007/s11136-012-0151-5

Fearon, C., McLaughlin, H., & Morris, L. (2013). Conceptualizing work engagement. *European Journal of Training and Development, 37,* 244-256. doi:10.1108/03090591311312723

Ferguson, L. M., Ward, H., Card, S., Sheppard, S., & McMurtry, J. (2013). Putting the patient back into patient centered care: An education perspective. *Nurse Education in Practice, 13,* 283-287. doi:10.1016/j.nepr.2013.03.016

Frels, R. K., & Onwuegbuzie, A. J. (2011). Administering quantitative instruments with qualitative interviews: A mixed research approach. *Journal of Counseling & Development, 91,* 184-195. doi:10.1002/j.1556-6676.2013.00085.x

Freeney, Y., & Fellenz, M. (2013). Work engagement as a key driver of quality of care: A study with midwives. *Journal of Health Organization and Management, 27,* 330-349. doi:10.1108/JHOM-10-2012-0192

Fritz, K., Kaestner, M., & Bergmann, M. (2010). Coca-Cola enterprises invests in on-boarding at the front lines to benefit the bottom line. *Global Business and Organizational Excellence, 29*(4), 15-24. doi:10.1002/joe.20325

Fu, W. (2014). The impact of emotional intelligence organization; commitment and job satisfaction on ethical behavior of Chinese employees. *Journal of Business Ethics, 122*(1), 137-144. doi:10.1007/s10551-013-1763-6

Fujimura, Y., Tanii, H., & Saijoh, K. (2010). Inpatient satisfaction and job satisfaction/stress of medical workers in a hospital with 7:1 nursing care system. *Environmental Health Preventive Medicine*, *16*(1), 113-122. doi:10.1007/s12199-010-0174-x

Garg, P. (2014). Impact of employee engagement on it sector. *International Journal of Management Research and Review*, *4*(1), 62-74. Retrieved from www.ijmrr.com

Gemmel, P., & Verleye, K. (2010). Emotional attachment to a hospital: Bringing employees and customers into the engagement zone. *The Journal of Applied Management and Entrepreneurship*, *15*(3), 78-97. Retrieved from http://www.huizenga.nova.edu/Jame/

Gerst, R. (2013). Understanding employee engagement and trust. *The Journal for Quality and Participation*, *35*(4), 32-37. Retrieved from http://asq.org/pub/jqp/

Ghadi, M., Fernando, M., & Caputi, P. (2013). Transformational leadership and work engagement. *Leadership & Organization Development Journal*, *34*, 532-550. doi:10.1108/LODJ-10-2011-0110

Ghafoor, A., Qureshi, T., Khan, M. A., & Hijazi, S. T. (2011). Transformational leadership employee engagement and performance: Mediating effect of psychological ownership. *African Journal of Business Management*, *5*, 7391-7403. doi:10.5897/AJBM11.126

Goh, S., & Low, B. (2014). The influence of servant leadership towards organizational commitment: The mediating role of trust in leaders. *International Journal of Business and Management*, *9*(1), 17-27. doi:10.5539/ijbm.v9n1p17

Granatino, R., Verkamp, J., & Parker, S. (2013). The use of secret shopping as a method of increasing engagement in the healthcare industry:

A case study. *International Journal of Healthcare Management*, *6*(2), 114-123. doi:10.1179/2047971913Y.0000000039

Gregorio, R., & Cronemyr, P. (2010). From expectations and needs of service customers to control chart specifications limits. *The TQM Journal*, *23*(2), 164-178. doi:10.1108/17542731111110221

Gruyter, D. (2014). Employee engagement in continuous improvement of processes. *Management*, *18*(2), 88-103. doi:10.2478/manment-2014-0044

Guay, R. (2013). The relationship between leader fit and transformational leadership. *Journal of Managerial Psychology*, *28*(1), 55-73. doi:10.1108/02683941311298869

Guerrero, S., & Seguin, M. (2012). Motivational drivers of non-executive directors, cooperation and engagement in board roles. *Journal of Managerial Issues*, *24*(1), 61-77. Retrieved from http://www.pittstate.edu/department/economics/journals-of-managerial-issues/

Haahr, A., Norlyk, A., & Hall, E. (2013). Ethical challenges embedded in qualitative research interviews with close relatives. *Nursing Ethics*, *2*(1), 6-15. doi:10.1177/0969733013486370

Habisch, A. (2012). The broken tables of stone: A Decalogue approach to corporate compliance practice. *Journal of Management Development*, *31*, 912-924. doi:10.1108/02621711211259866

Han, T., Chiang, H., & Chang, A. (2010). Employee participation in decision making psychological ownership and knowledge sharing: mediating role of organizational commitment in Taiwanese high-tech organizations. *The International Journal of Human Resource Management*, *21*, 2218-2233. doi:10.1080/09585192.2010.509625

Handa, M., & Gulati, A. (2014). Employee engagement. *Journal of Management Research, 14*(1), 57-67. Retrieved from http://www.macrothink.org/journal/index.php/jmr/

Hays, R., Berman, L. J., Kanter, M., Hugh, M., Oglseby, R. R., Kim, C., Brown, J. (2014). Evaluating the psychometric properties of the CAHPS patient centered medical home survey. *Clinical Therapeutics, 36*, 689-699. doi:10.1016/j.clinthera.2014.04.004

Hernandez, M. (2012). Toward an understanding of the psychology of stewardship. *Academy of Management Review, 37*, 172-193. doi:10.5465/amr.2010.0363

Hewison, A., Gale, N., Yeats, R., & Shapiro, J. (2013). An evaluation of staff engagement programs in four national health service acute trusts. *Journal of Health Organization and Management, 27*(1), 85-105. doi:10.1108/14777261311311816

Heyvaert, M., Maes, B., & Onghena, P. (2011). Mixed methods research synthesis: Definitions framework and potential. *Qualitative and Quantitative, 47*, 659-676. doi:10.1007/s11135-011-9538-6

Holzel, L. P., Kriston, L., & Harter, M. (2013). Patient preference for involvement experienced involvement decisional conflict and satisfaction with physician: A structural equation model test. *BMC Health Services Research, 13*(231), 1-11. Retrieved from http://www.biomedcentral.com/1472-6963/13/231

Holzer, B. M., & Minder, C. E. (2011). A simple approach to fairer hospital benchmarking using patient experience data. *International Journal for Quality in Health Care, 23*, 524-530. doi:10.1093/intqhc/mzr047

Horwitz, J. R., & Nichols, A. (2011). Rural hospital ownership: Medical service provisions market mix and spillover effects. *Health Services Research, 46,* 1452-1473. doi:10.1111/j.1475-6773.2011.01280.x

Hynes, G. E. (2012). Improving employees interpersonal communication competencies: A qualitative study. *Business Communication Quarterly, 75,* 466-475. doi:10.1177/1080569912458965

Ikkersheim, D. E., & Koolman, X. (2012). Dutch healthcare reform: Did it result in better patient experiences in hospitals? A comparison of the consumer quality index over time. *BMC Health Services Research, 12*(76), 2-6. Retrieved from http:// www.biomedcentral. com/1472-6963/12/76

Irfan, S. M., & Ijaz, A. (2011). Comparison of service quality between private and public hospitals empirical evidences from Pakistan. *Journal of Quality and Technology Management, 7*(1), 1-22. Retrieved from http://111.68.103.26/journals/index.php/jqtm

Jawale, K. V. (2012). Methods of sampling design in the legal research: Advantages and disadvantages. *Online International Interdisciplinary Research Journal, 2*(6), 183-190. Retrieved from http://www.oiirj. org/oiirj/?page_id=924

Jennings, R., & Van Horn, J. D. (2012). Publication bias in neuroimaging research: Implications for meta-analyses. *Neuroinform, 10*(1), 67-80. doi:10.1007/s12021-011-9125-y

Johansen, M. (2014). Conflicting priorities: Emergency nurses perceived disconnect between patient satisfaction and the delivery of quality patient care. *Journal of Emergency Nursing, 40*(1), 13-21. doi:10.1016/j.jen.2012.04.013

Jones, M., & Alony, I. (2011). Guiding the use of grounded theory in doctoral studies: An example from the Australian film industry. *International Journal of Doctoral Studies, 6,* 95-114. Retrieved from http://www.informingscience.us/icarus/journals/ijds/

Jose, G. (2012). Satisfaction with HR practices and employee engagement: A social exchange perspective. *Journal of Economics and Behavioral Studies, 4,* 423-430. Retrieved from http://www.ifrnd.org/JournalDetail.aspx?JournalID=2

Kane, N. M., Singer, S. J., Clark, J. R., Eeckloo, K., & Valentine, M. (2012). Strained local and state government finances among current realities that threaten public hospital profitability. *Health Affairs, 31,* 1680-1689. doi:10.1377/hlthaff.2011.1401

Karkoulian, D., Mukaddam, W., McCarthy, R., & Messarra, L. (2013). Job insecurity: A whirlpool of chronic powerlessness. *Education Business and Society, 6*(1), 55-70. doi:10.1108/17537981311314727

Katz, M. H., & Brigham, T. M. (2011). Transforming a traditional safety net into a coordinated care system: Lessons from healthy San Francisco. *Health Affairs, 30,* 237-246. doi:10.1377/hlthaff.2010.0003

Kaufman, N. (2013). Net revenue per adjusted discharge continues to drive success. *Journal of Healthcare Management, 58*(1), 8-12. Retrieved from http://www.ache.org

Kaur, D., Sambasivan, M., & Kumar, N. (2013). Effect of spiritual intelligence emotional intelligence psychological ownership and burnout on caring behavior of nurses: A cross sectional study. *Journal of Clinical Nursing, 22,* 3192-3202. doi:10.1111/jocn.12386

Kompaso, S., & Sridevi, M. S. (2010). Employee engagement: The key to improving performance. *International Journal of Business and Management, 5*(12), 89-98. doi:10.5539/ijbm.v5n12p89

Kottke, J. L., & Pelletier, K. L. (2013). Measuring and differentiating perceptions of supervisor and top leader ethics. *Journal of Business Ethics, 113*, 415-428. doi:10.1007/s10551-012-1312-8

Krishnan, V. (2012). Transformational leadership and personal outcomes: Empowerment as mediator. *Leadership & Organization Development Journal, 33*, 550-563. doi:10.1108/01437731211253019

Lakshmi, S., & Mohideen, A. (2013). Issue in reliability and validity of research. *International Journal of Management Research and Review, 3*, 2752-2756. Retrieved from www.ijmrr.com

Lampropoulou, S., & Myers, G. (2013). Stance taking in interviews from the Qualidata Archive. *Qualitative Social Research, 14*(1), 1-23. Retrieved from http://www.qualitative-research.net/index.php/fqs/article/view/1813/3468

Lee, S. M., Lee, D., & Kang, C. (2012). The impact of high performance work systems in the healthcare industry: Employee reactions service quality customer satisfaction and customer loyalty. *The Service Industries Journal, 32*(1), 17-36. doi:10.1080/02642069.2010.545397

Leicht, K., Honekamp, W., & Ostermann, H. (2013). Quality management in professional medical practices: Are there effects on patient satisfaction? *Journal of Public Health, 21*, 465-471. doi:10.1007/s10389-013-0575-6

Lis, C. G., Rodeghier, M., & Gupta, D. (2011). The relationship between perceived service quality and patient willingness to recommend at a national oncology hospital network. *BMC Health Services Research*, *11*(46), 1-8. Retrieved from http://www.biomedcentral. com/1472-6963/11/46

Liu, J., Wang, H., Hui, C., & Lee, C. (2012). Psychological ownership: How having control matters. *Journal of Management Studies*, *49*, 869-897. doi:10.1111/j.1467-6486.2011.01028.x

Loi, R., Lamar, L. W., & Chan, K. (2012). Coping with job insecurity: The role of procedural justice ethical leadership and power distance orientation. *Journal of Business Ethics*, *108*, 361-372. doi:10.1007/ s10551-011-1095-3

Lowe, G. (2012). How employee engagement matters for hospital performance. *Healthcare Quarterly*, *15*(2), 29-40. doi:10.12927/ hcq.2012.22915

Lunenburg, F. C. (2011). Expectancy theory of motivation: Motivating by altering expectations. *International Journal of Management, Business, and Administration*, *15*(1), 1-6. Retrieved from http://www. nationalforum.com

Luxford, K., Safran, D. G., & Delbanco, T. (2011). Promoting patient-centers care: A qualitative study of facilitators and barriers in health care organizations with a reputation for improving the patient experience. *International Journal for Quality in Health Care*, *23*, 510-515. doi:10.1093/intqhc/mzr024

Marini, D. (2013). Employee engagement key to health care reform compliance and slower cost inflation. *Workforce Solution Reviews*, *4*(5), 24-26. Retrieved from www.ihrim.org

Marshall, C., & Rossman, G. (2011). *Designing qualitative research* (5th ed.). Thousand Oaks, CA: Sage Publications.

McKnight, L. (2013). Transformational leadership in the context of punctuated change. *Journal of Leadership, Accountability and Ethics*, *10*(2), 103-114. Retrieved from http://www.na-businesspress.com/JLAE/jlaescholar.html

Meng, J., & Berger, B. K. (2011). Measuring return on investment roi of organizations internal communication efforts. *Journal of Communication Management*, *16*, 332-354. doi:10.1108/13632541211278987

Mercer, S. W., Jani, B. D., Maxwell, M., Wong, S., & Watt, G. (2012). Patient enablement requires physician empathy: A cross sectional study of general practice consultations in areas of high and low socioeconomic deprivation in Scotland. *BMC Health Services Research*, *13*(6), 1-10. Retrieved from http://www.biomedcentral.com/1471-2296/13/6

Mero-Jaffe, I. (2011). 'Is that what I said?' Interview transcript approval by participants: An aspect of ethics in qualitative research. *International Journal of Qualitative Methods*, *10*, 231-247. Retrieved from https://ejournals.library.ualberta.ca/index.php/IJQM/article/view/8449

Mesu, J., Riemsdijk, M., & Sanders, K. (2013). Labor flexibility in SME: The impact of leadership. *Employee Relations*, *35*(2), 120-138. doi:10.1108/01425451311287835

Metha, S. (2011). Service quality as a predicator of patient satisfaction: A study of the health care sector. *Journal of Health Management*, *13*(211), 1-20. doi:10.1177/097206341101300206

Miles, M., Huberman, M., & Saldana, J. (2014). *Qualitative data analysis*. (3rd ed.). Thousands Oaks, California: Sage Publications, Inc. Retrieved from http://www.sagepub.com

Mone, E., Eisinger, C., Guggenheim, K., Price, B., & Stine, C. (2011). Performance management at the wheel: Driving employee engagement in organizations. *Journal of Business and Psychology, 26*(2), 205-212. doi:10.1007/s10869-011-9222-9

Moustakas, C. (1994). *Phenomenological research methods* (1st ed.). London, England: Sage Publications, Inc. Retrieved from http://online.sagepub.com/

Mozes, M., Josman, Z., & Yaniv, E. (2011). Corporate social responsibility organizational identification and motivation. *Social Responsibility Journal, 7*, 310-325. doi:10.1108/17471111111141558

Muchiri, M., Cooksey, R. W., & Walumbwa, F. (2012). Transformational and social processes of leadership as predictors of organizational outcomes. *Leadership & Organizational Development Journal, 33*, 662-683. doi:10.1108/01437731211265241

Mutebi, H., Kakwezi, P., & Ntayi, J. M. (2012). Ethical work climate in Ugandan procuring and deposing entities: Implications for leadership. *International Journal of Business and Social Science, 3*(18), 34-39. Retrieved from www.ijbssnet.com

Nafei, W. A. (2014). Assessing employee attitudes towards organizational commitment and change: The case of the King Faisal Hospital in Al-taif Governorate Kingdom of Saudi Arabia. *Journal of Management and Sustainability, 4*, 204-221. doi:10.5539/jms.v4n1p204

Nasomboon, B. (2014). The relationship among leadership commitment organizational performance and employee engagement. *International Business Research, 7*(9), 77-90. doi:10.5539/ibr.v7n9p77

Ncube, F., & Jerie, S. (2012). Leveraging employee engagement for competitive advantage and the hospitality industry: A comparative study of hotels A and B in Zimbabwe. *Journal of Emerging Trends in Economics and Management Sciences, 3*(4), 380-388. Retrieved from http://jetems.scholarlinkresearch.org/

Needham, B. R. (2012). The truth about patient experience: What we can learn from other industries and how three Ps can improve health outcomes strengthen brands and delight customers. *Journal of Healthcare Management, 57*, 255-265. Retrieved from http://www.ache.org/pubs/jhmtoc.cfm

Nichols, T., & Erakovich, R. (2013). Authentic leadership and implicit theory: A normative form of leadership. *Leadership & Organization Development Journal, 34*, 182-195. doi:10.1108/01437731311321931

Nieberding, A. (2014). Employee engagement and other bonding forces in organizations. *Consulting Psychology Journal: Practice and Research, 66*, 320-323. doi:10.1037/cpb0000022

Nikookar, A. (2013). Heuristic evaluation method: A proposed workflow. *International Journal of Innovation Management and Technology, 4*(1), 80-82. doi:10.7763/IJMT.2013.V4.362

Oliveira, V. C., Refshauge, K. M., Ferreira, M., Pinto, R. Z., Bechenkamp, P. R., Filho, R., & Ferreira, P. H. (2012). Communication that values patient autonomy is associated with satisfaction with care: A systematic review. *Journal of Physiotherapy, 58*, 215-228. doi:10.1016/s1836-9553(12)70123-6

O'Reilly, M., & Parker, N. (2012). Unsatisfactory saturation: A critical exploration of the notion of saturated sample sizes in qualitative research. *Qualitative Research Journal, 13*(2), 190-197. doi:10.1177/1468794112446106

Orszag, P. R., & Emanuel, E. J. (2010). Health care reform and cost control. *The New England Journal of Medicine, 363,* 601-603. doi:10.1056/NEJMp1006571

Otani, K., Waterman, B., & Dunagan, C. (2012). Patient satisfaction: How patient health conditions influence. *Journal of Healthcare Management, 57,* 276-296. Retrieved from http://www.ache.org/ PublicationsSubscriptionPurchase.aspx#jhm

Pan, X., Qin, Q., & Gao, F. (2014). Psychological ownership organizational based self esteem and positive organizational behaviors. *Chinese Management Studies, 8*(1), 127-148. doi:10.1108/ CMS-04-2014-0088

Patton, M. (2002). *Qualitative research & evaluation methods.* (3rd ed.). Thousands Oaks, California: Sage Publications, Inc. Retrieved from http://www.sagepub.com

Pelzang, R. (2010). Time to learn: Understanding patient-centered care. *British Journal of Nursing, 19,* 912-919. Retrieved from http://www. magonlinelibray.com/toc/bjob/current

Pendleton, A., & Robinson, A. (2011). Employee share ownership and human capital development: Complementarity in theory and practice. *Economic and Industrial Democracy, 32,* 439-457. doi:10.1177/0143831X10387650

Petasnick, W. D. (2011). Medicare: Will it last? *Journal of Healthcare Management*, 56(4), 229-233. Retrieved from http://www.ache.org/PUBS/jhm564.cfm

Petrullo, K., Lamar, S., Nwankwo-Otti, O., Alexander-Mills, K., & Viola, D. (2013). The patient satisfaction survey: What does it mean to your bottom line? *Journal of Hospital Administration*, 2(2), 1-8. doi:10.5430/jha.v2n2p1

Poulsen, M. G., Poulsen, A. A., Kahn, A., Poulsen, E. E., & Kahn, S. R. (2011). Work engagement in cancer workers in Queensland: The flip side of burnout. *Journal of Medical Imaging and Radiation Oncology*, 55, 425-432. doi:10.1111/j.1754-9485.2011.02281.x

Purdy, N., Laschinger, H. K., Finegan, J., Kerr, M., & Olivera, F. (2010). Effects of work environments on nurse and patient outcomes. *Journal of Nursing Management*, 18, 901-913. doi:10.1111/j.1365-2834.2010.01172.x

Ramez, W. S. (2012). Patient perception of health care quality satisfaction and behavioral

intention: An empirical study in Bahrain. *International Journal of Business and Social Science*, 3(18), 131-143. Retrieved from http://ijbssnet.com

Rao, N. (2012). American dignity and healthcare reform. *Harvard Journal of Business and Public Policy*, 35(1), 172-187. Retrieved from http://www.harvardjlpp.com/

Rashid, H. A., Asad, A., & Ashraf, M. M. (2011). Factors persuading employee engagement and linkage of ee to personal and organizational performance. *Interdisciplinary Journal of Contemporary Research in Business*, 3(5), 98-108. Retrieved from http://www.ijcrb.com/

Rivera, R. R., Fitzpatrick, J. J., & Boyle, S. M. (2011). Closing the RN engagement gap. *The Journal of Nursing Administration, 41*, 265-272. doi:10.1097/NNA.0b013e31821c476c

Robertson, I. T., Birch, A., & Cooper, C. (2012). Job and work attitudes engagement and employee performance. *Leadership & Organization Development Journal, 33*, 224-232. doi:10.1108/01437731211216443

Robinson, J. (2011). Hospitals respond to Medicare payment shortfalls by both shifting costs and cutting them based on market concentration. *Health Affairs, 30*, 1265-1272. doi:10.1377/hlthaff.2011.0220

Roehrig, C. (2011). Will the health care cost curve be bent? Where we stand at the start of 2011. *Business Economics, 46*(3), 159-161. doi:10.1057/be.2011.14

Rothmann, S. J., & Welsh, C. (2013). Employee engagement: The role of psychological conditions. *Management Dynamics, 22*(1), 14-27. Retrieved from http://references.sabinet.co.za/sa_epublication/mandyn

Sangasubana, N. (2011). How to conduct ethnographic research. *The Qualitative Report, 16*, 567-573. Retrieved from http://www.nova.edu/ssss/QR

Sawang, S. (2011). Is there an inverted u-shaped relationship between job demands and work engagement? *International Journal of Manpower, 33*(2), 178-186. doi:10.1108/01437721211225426

Seppet, E., Paasuke, M., Conte, M., Capri, M., & Franceschi, M. (2011). Ethical aspects of aging research. *Biogerontology, 12*, 491-520. doi:10.1007/s10522-011-9340-9

Shahid, A., & Azhar, S. M. (2013). Gaining employee commitment: Linking to organizational effectiveness. *Journal of Management Research, 5,* 250-270. doi:10.5296/jmr.v5i1.2319

Shannon, D. (2013). Physician well-being: A powerful way to improve the patient experience. *Physician Executive Journal, 1*(1), 1-6. Retrieved from http://www.acpe.org/

Shoemaker, W. (2010). Higher hospital margins distinguished by higher patient satisfaction. *Healthcare Financial Management, 12*(1), 136-140. Retrieved from https://www.hfma.org/Content.aspx?id=2682

Shorbaji, R., Messarra, L., & Karkoulian, S. (2011). Core-self evaluation: Predictor of employee engagement. *The Business Review, Cambridge, 17,* 276-285. Retrieved from http://www.jaabc.com/brcv17n1preview.html

Shuck, M. B., Rocco, T. S., & Albornoz, C. A. (2011). Exploring employee engagement from the employee perspective: Implications for HRD. *Journal of European Industrial Training, 35,* 300-325. doi:10.1108/03090591111128306

Sieger, P., Zellweger, T., & Aquino, K. (2013). Turning agents into psychological principals: Aligning interests of non-owners through psychological ownership. *Journal of Management Studies, 50,* 361-390. doi:10.1111/joms.12017

Simola, S., Barling, J., & Turner, N. (2012). Transformational leadership and leaders mode of care reasoning. *Journal of Business Ethnics, 108*(1), 229-237. doi:10.1007/s10551-011-1080-x

Singh, S., Wheeler, J., & Roden, K. (2012). Hospital financial management: What is the link between revenue cycle management, profitability and non-for profit hospitals ability to grow equity?

Journal of Healthcare Management, 57, 325-342. Retrieved from http://www.ache.org/PublicationsSubscriptionPurchase.aspx#jhm

Slatten, T., & Mehmetogul, M. (2011). Antecedents and effects of engaged frontline employees. *Managing Service Quality, 21*(1), 88-107. doi:10.1108/09604521111100261

Smith, G., Ansett, S., & Erez, L. (2011). How The Gap Inc. engaged with its stakeholders. *MITSLoan Management Review, 52*(4), 69-80. Retrieved from http://sloanreview.mit.edu/article/how-gap-inc-engaged-with-its-stakeholders/

Souba, W. W. (2011). The being of leadership. *Philosophy, Ethics, and Humanities in Medicine, 6*(5), 1-11. Retrieved from http://www.peh-med.com/content/6/1/5

Springer, P., Clark, C. M., Strohfus, P., & Belcheir, M. (2012). Using transformational change to improve organizational culture and climate in a school of nursing. *Journal of Nursing Education, 51*(2), 81-89. doi:10.3928/01484834-20111230-02

Spurgeon, P., Mazelan, P. M., & Barwell, F. (2011). Medical engagement: A crucial underpinning to organizational performance. *Health Services Management Research, 24*(1), 114-120. doi:10.1258/hsmr.2011.011006

Stephens, J. H., & Ledlow, G. R. (2010). Real heath care reform: Focus on primary care access. *Hospital Topics, 88*(8), 98-106. doi:10.1080/00185868.2010.528259

Storch, J., Makaroff, K. S., Pauly, B., & Newton, L. (2013). Take me to my leader: The importance of ethical leadership among formal nurse leaders. *Nurse Ethics, 20*(2), 150-157. doi:10.1177/0969733012474291

Sutharjana, N., Thoyib, A., Taroena, E., & Rahayu, M. (2013). Organizational citizenship effect on patient satisfaction and loyalty through service quality. *International Journal of Scientific & Technology Research*, 2, 288-300. Retrieved from http://www.ijstr.org

Swarnalatha, C., & Prasanna, T. S. (2013). Employee engagement: The concept. *International Journal of Management Research and Review*, 3, 3872-3882. Retrieved from www.ijmrr.com

Thomson, H. J., & Thomas, S. (2012). External validity in health public policy: Application of the re-aim tool to field of housing improvement. *BMC Public Health*, 12(633), 1-6. Retrieved from http://www.biomedcentral.com/1471-2458/12/633

Timmerman, J. C. (2009). A systematic approach for making innovation a core competency. *The Journal for Quality and Participation*, 31(4), 4-11. Retrieved from http://asq.org/pub/jqp/

Timms, C., Brough, P., & Graham, D. (2012). Burnt out but engaged: The coexistence of psychological burnout and engagement. *Journal of Educational Administration*, 50, 327-345. doi:10.1108/09578231211223338

Tims, M., Bakker, A. B., & Xanthopoulou, D. (2011). Do transformational leaders enhance their followers daily work engagement? *The Leadership Quarterly*, 22(1), 121-132. doi:10.1016/j.leaqua.2010.12.011

Tuan, L. M. (2012). The linkages among leadership trust and business ethics. *Social Responsibility Journal*, 8(1), 138-148. doi:10.1108/1747111121196629

Ugah, A. (2011). Expectancy theory Maslow's hierarchy of needs and cataloguing departments. *Library Philosophy and Practice*, 4(1), 1-5. Retrieved from http://unllib.unl.edu/LPP/

Van Rooy, D. L., Whitman, D. S., Hart, D., & Caleo, S. (2011). Measuring employee engagement during a financial downturn: Business imperative or nuisance? *Journal Business Psychology*, 26(1), 147-152. doi:10.1007/s10869-011-9225-6

Vaijayanthi, P., Shreenivasan, K. A., & Prabhakaran, S. (2011). Employee engagement predictors: A study at GE power and water. *International Journal of Global Business*, 4(2), 60-72. Retrieved from http://www.indianjournals.com/ijor.aspx?target=ijor:ijgbc&type=home

Walker, J. L. (2012). The use of saturation in qualitative research. *Canadian Journal of Cardiovascular Nursing*, 22(2), 37-46. Retrieved from http://www.cccn.ca

Warrick, D. (2011). The urgent need for skilled transformational leaders: Integrating transformational leadership and organization development. *Journal of Leadership, Accountability and Ethics*, 8(5), 11-18. Retrieved from http://www.na-businesspress.com/JLAE/jlaescholar.html

Weinberg, D., Avgar, A., Sugrue, N. M., & Cooney-Minor, D. (2013). The importance of a high performance work environment in hospitals. *Health Services Research*, 48, 319-334. doi:10.1111/j.1475-6773.2012.01438.x

Welch, M. (2011). The evolution of the employee engagement concept: Communication implications. *Corporate Communications: An International Journal*, 16, 328-346. doi:10.1108/13563281111186968

Wessel, S. (2012). Impact of unit practices councils on culture and outcomes. *Creative Nursing, 18,* 187-194. doi:10.1891/1078-4535.18.4.187

Westover, J. H., Westover, A. R., & Westover, A. (2010). Enhancing long-term worker productivity and performance: The connection of key work domains to job satisfaction and organizational commitment. *International Journal of Productivity and Performance Management, 59,* 372-387. doi:10.1108/17410401011038919

Winkler, E., Busch, C., Clasen, J. M., & Vowinkel, J. (2014). Leadership behavior as a health promoting resource for workers in low skilled jobs and the moderating role of power distance orientation. *Zeitschrift Fur Personalforschung, 28,* 69-116. doi:10.1688/Zfp-2014-01-Winkler

Woolhandler, S., & Himmelstein, D. (2011). Healthcare reform 2.0. *Social Research, 78,* 719-731. Retrieved from http://pnhp.org

Wu, Z., & Robson, S. (2013). The application of hospitality elements in hospitals. *Journal of Healthcare Management, 58*(1), 47-63. Retrieved from www.ache.org/pubs/jhmsub.cfm

Xu, J., & Thomas, H. C. (2011). How can leaders achieve high employee engagement? *Leadership & Organization Development Journal, 32,* 399-416. doi:10.1108/01437731111134661

Yin, R. K. (2009). *Case study research: Design and methods* (4th ed.). Thousand Oaks, CA: Sage Publications.

Yousapronpaiboon, K., & Johnson, W. C. (2013). Out-patient service quality perceptions in private Thai hospitals. *International Journal of Business and Social Science, 4*(2), 57-68. Retrieved from http://www.ijbssnet.com

Yu, C., Jannasch-Pennell, A., & DiGangi, S. (2011). Compatibility between text mining and qualitative research in the perspectives of grounded theory content analysis, and reliability. *The Qualitative Report, 16,* 730-744. Retrieved from http://www.nova.edu/ssss/QR/QR16-3/yu

Yuan, B., & Lin, M. B. (2012). Transforming employee engagement into long-term customer relationships: Evidence from information technology salespeople in Taiwan. *Social Behavior and Personality, 40,* 1549-1554. doi:10.2224/sbp.2012.40.9.1549

Zhang, J., Nie, M., & Yan, B. (2014). Effect of networking embeddedness on brand related behavior intentions: Mediating effects of psychological ownership. *Social Behavior and Personality, 42,* 721-730. doi:10.2224/sbp.2014.42.5.721

Zhu, H., Chen, C., Li, X., & Zhou, Y. (2013). From personal relationship to psychological ownership: The importance of manager owner relationship closeness in family businesses. *Management and Organization Review, 9,* 295-318. doi:10.1111/more.12001

Zwanziger, J., Khan, N., & Bamezai, N. (2010). The relationship between safety net activities and hospital financial performance. *BMC Health Services Research, 10*(15), 1-12. Retrieved from http://www.biomedcentral.com/1472-6963/10/15

Zwingmann, I., Wegge, J., Wolf, S., Rudolf, M., Schmidt, M., & Richter, P. (2014). Is transformational healthy for employees? a multilevel analysis in 16 nations. *Zeitschrift Fur Personalforschung, 28*(1), 24-51. doi:10.1688/ZfP-2014-01-Zwingmann

About the Author

Dr. Vizzuso offers honest, real, and poignant advice for employees, leaders, and organizations. "Don't be afraid of emotional connection with employees and peers. Lead by example and improve the engagement of your employees. Ask employees their names, get to know their hearts, and inspire them to greatness." In the end, it is up to each individual and  organization to choose whether to be engaged or disengaged.

Dr. Vizzuso recently earned his doctorate in business administration from Walden University. He currently holds the position of Chief Executive Officer for Radiology Associates of Canton and Chief Operating Officer of RadHelp, LLC. Prior to joining the Canton Groups, John held positions as a Senior Director of Radiology, Vice President of Cardiovascular and Imaging Services. Dr. Vizzuso has previous experience as chief executive officer of a large medical practice and medical billing consultation service. He has started and developed over twenty-five businesses locally, nationally, and internationally over a successful twenty-five-year career. Dr. Vizzuso lives in the Cleveland, Ohio, area with his wife and has two sons.

A published author and expert in the field of human relationships, Dr. Vizzuso conducts successful workshops and interventions aimed at transforming organizations by improving employee engagement.

Dr. Vizzuso's other books include, The Leadership Edge (2001), The Difference: Finding the Hero within You (2004), and Shared Sacrifice: Heroes Are Always Remembered Legends Never Die (2009).

Printed in the United States
By Bookmasters